Karen Kissane has been a newspaper and magazine journalist for 30 years. She began as a cadet with *The Age* newspaper in Melbourne, and also reported at *The National Times* and *Time Australia* magazine. She is currently working at *The Age*, where she has been law and justice editor, writing about courts, crime and legal issues.

Silent Death was a finalist for Best Book in the Walkley Awards in 2006 and won two Davitt Awards in 2007 in the categories True Crime and Readers' Choice.

silent death
THE KILLING OF JULIE RAMAGE

KAREN KISSANE

hachette
AUSTRALIA

First published in Australia and New Zealand in 2006
by Hachette Australia
(An imprint of Hachette Australia Pty Limited)
Level 17, 207 Kent Street, Sydney NSW 2000
www.hachette.com.au

This edition first published in 2009

Copyright © Karen Kissane 2006

This book is copyright. Apart from any fair dealing for the purposes of private study, research, criticism or review permitted under the *Copyright Act 1968*, no part may be stored or reproduced by any process without prior written permission. Enquiries should be made to the publisher.

National Library of Australia
Cataloguing-in-Publication data

Kissane, Karen.
  Silent death : the killing of Julie Ramage.

  ISBN 978 0 7336 2175 8.

  1. Ramage, Julie. 2. Ramage, James - Trials, litigation, etc. 3. Murder – Australia – Case studies. 4. Provocation (Criminal law) – Australia – Popular works. 5. Murder victims Australia. 6. Trials (Murder) – Australia. I. Title.

364.1523

Cover image courtesy NewsPix archive/Photographer: Rebecca Michael
Cover design by Luke Causby/Blue Cork
Original cover design by Darian Causby, highway51.com.au
Text design and typesetting by Bookhouse, Sydney
Printed in Australia by Griffin Press, Adelaide

Hachette Australia's policy is to use papers that are natural, renewable and recyclable products and made from wood grown in sustainable forests. The logging and manufacturing processes are expected to conform to the environmental regulations of the country of origin.

'Summertime'
George Gershwin/Du Bose Heyward/Ira Gershwin
© 1935 (Renewed) George Gershwin Music/
Dubose and Dorothy Heyward Memorial Fund Pub/
Ira Gershwin Music
For Australia and New Zealand:
Alfred Publishing (Australia) Pty Ltd
(ABN 15 003 954 247)
PO Box 2355 Taren Point, NSW 2229
International Copyright Secured. All Rights Reserved.
Unauthorised Reproduction Is Illegal.

*With love and thanks to Mary, Maureen, Russell, Ryan and Paddy and, most specially, Will and Alice.
For everything.*

CONTENTS

PART ONE: *Crime*
    The Killing   3

PART TWO: *Julie and Jamie*
    Young Love   11
    Barbie and Ken   16
    Beginnings of an End   27
    Death in the Family   34
    Investigation   43

PART THREE: *Justice?*
    Counsel for the Defence   51
    People Like Us   58
    Trial Without Jury   63
    The Edited Marriage   72
    Final Words   81
    The Judge's Cut   85
    The Case Begins   87
    Family Histories   108
    Obsession   126
    Sex v Death   141
    The Workmates   158
    From the Grave   171

Until Death	176
Leckie: It's Murder	190
Dunn: It's Manslaughter	199
Pietà	212
The Jury Goes Out	216

PART FOUR: *Behind Closed Doors*

What the Jurors Didn't Know	219

PART FIVE: *Court in the Crossfire*

Verdict	241
The Case for Change	248
A Vindication of the Rights of Woman	252
The Case Against Change	256
Julie's Lawyer	262

PART SIX: *Reading the Entrails*

To Have and to Hold	271
Love, Honour – and Obey	281
The Dance of Anger	285
Men's Business	298

PART SEVEN: *The Scales and the Sword*

The Plea	307
The Sentencing	315
The Art of the Advocate	325

PART EIGHT: *Aftermaths*

No Place Like Home	341
The Lover	345
The Friends	348
Julie's Best Friend	358
Julie's Sister	365
Jail	369
Epitaphs	379

Postscript	383
Acknowledgments	387

Part One

CRIME

THE KILLING

JAMIE RAMAGE has a sweet name, an endearing little-boy name, and nice hands: strong, capable, shapely. They are the kind of hands that a woman looks for in a man. This day, though, he must have driven gingerly with the right one; it was swollen, the fingers like sausages. Blunt trauma, the police doctor would later say, causing fluid to leak from the veins into surrounding tissues. But Jamie's hand was the least of his worries.

He said later that he drove in a daze. Perhaps it was true; perhaps he took all the busy city roads and curving country tracks in the vague trance of the preoccupied driver. The last bit of road, the part later videotaped by police, wound on and on. It seemed evidence of how focused he must have been on his task: a journey of about an hour, so many twists and turns, so many chances to think better of what he was about to do. But then Jamie had always been goal-oriented, unable to brook any delay in getting on with whatever aim he had set himself, sweeping in his recruitment of others to his causes. This task, he knew, was his alone. Police would later check out a fuzzy report that someone else had been seen with him in his sleek Jaguar on that trip, but it came to nought. Who would he have asked along, anyway? His teenage son? His dinner-party companions, the lawyers and doctors and businesspeople of middle-class Melbourne? Some of them would be useful at his trial for the murder of his wife, Julie. But not now. Not with Julie's bruised and bleeding body, wrapped in a bed-ruffle, rocking in the boot.

Jamie later said that when his hands were around Julie's throat she fought him a little, but not for long. It was a lunchtime in July, a mid-winter Monday, but one of the neighbours in the quiet street they lived in had her doors and windows open because it was her cleaning day. She heard nothing. Strangulation is like drowning: a silent death. All the talking Jamie had done in the past five weeks, with Julie, friends and a bevy of counsellors – the phone calls, the coffees, the therapy sessions, the obsessive pleading for help – that whole great torrent of words ended in this terrible, bloody silence.

Prince Charles, gazing upon the body of Diana, is said to have asked, 'How did it come to this?' It seems Jamie Ramage did not pause for such reflection. He'd never been inward looking. He'd always marched through life mastering the externals, whether they be work or wife or cocktail-party conversations. He fetched a bucket of water and teatowels to wipe up Julie's blood. She was bleeding because he had punched her and knocked her to the ground before strangling her. He dragged the body of his wife – the body he knew so intimately, the body that had borne his two children – out into the backyard and around the side to the garage. He heaved her into the boot of the Jaguar, which had a finish in soft pistachio green with a metallic sheen, like a gelato ice-cream. He liked pretty things. Julie was pretty. He changed into jeans and a jumper and Blundstone work boots. He packed a shovel, her handbag and the clothes he was wearing when he killed her. Exhibiting a presence of mind that was to last the rest of the day and into the night, he phoned the plumber and told him not to come around that afternoon after all. He took Julie's car, a silver Mini Cooper S, and parked it 800 metres from the house behind the family's favourite Italian restaurant. Then he took off in the loaded Jag. Even if he had been seen driving away from his home in Marock Place, no one would have thought twice about it. Suburban routine is so unremarkable.

Jamie didn't tell police much about how he buried his wife in an isolated piece of bushland off Running Creek Road, Arthurs Creek, near Kinglake National Park. He mumbled something about having chosen a spot near where Julie used to go horse-riding. He didn't mention to the police that they'd always fought over her favourite pastime; he hated her having a hobby of her own and used to call her riding-club friends 'bush pigs'. So it is unclear whether the choice of site was due to a fleeting moment of tenderness – 'Julie would have liked it here' – or a final gesture of contempt. Either way, her body did not go easily into that dark place. The scrapes and bruises of drag marks on her shoulderblades were later found to be deep and wide. Unlike her grave. Police have a name for the sort of hole Jamie dug for Julie. It is 'an accountant's grave' – short, shallow, the kind of digging you get in hard earth by a man with soft hands. Jamie had studied as an accountant. Many who knew him saw him as a chronic account-keeper, someone who assessed the value of every relationship in terms of his social 'bottom line', his personal balance sheet.

The rest of Jamie Ramage's day could provide material for the script of a black, black comedy. Relentlessly methodical, he made several phone calls on the drive home, including to his wife's mobile and to her office number. He stopped at a service station in the outer suburb of Diamond Creek and bought petrol and washed the car. In a continuation of the dark domestic motif that ran through his crime, he phoned Acropolis Marble in the northern suburb of Reservoir to say he would be over to look at the granite for his kitchen bench. The kitchen was in the open-plan family room in which he had just killed Julie. He arrived at Acropolis two and a half hours later, just after 3 pm. The female staff would later tell police that Jamie was calm and pleasant, if a bit fidgety with those hands. At one stage he took off a boot to adjust his sock. He debated a tricky question about how best to join the side panels of the bench-top; Jamie Ramage knew the devil is in the details.

When he finally got home he had a bath and washed his clothes. His son Matthew, then seventeen, noticed nothing unusual when his dad opened the front door to him after school that afternoon. Matthew was in his final year of secondary school and wanted to complete a physics assignment that was due the next morning, but his dad insisted they go out for dinner. Jamie took Matthew to Colombo's, the restaurant where he had dumped Julie's car, for a kindly father-and-son chat about Matthew's goals in life. They decided Matthew's goals revolved around university and career. Jamie's revolved around 'moving on' from Julie's decision, five weeks earlier, to leave him and end their marriage. Jamie warned Matthew that he was almost eighteen years old, almost his own person. And he told Matthew that he had grown up perfectly and was everything he had ever hoped for in a son.

His defence counsel would later paint Jamie as a devoted family man.

To the lawyers and police managing the case, it began as just another domestic homicide, albeit one in a comfortable demographic. Jamie and Julie Ramage were worth $2.6 million between them; they lived in a nice house and moved in the right circles. But the case was to cause unprecedented consternation in the leafy suburbs. It would catch the imagination of middle Melbourne because the victim was not a checkout chick from a working-class area, and the perpetrator could not be dismissed as an alcoholic, or a roughneck, or as being from a culture where the men are known for attitudes that lead to this sort of thing. Julie and Jamie were PLU, 'people like us': successful white Anglo-Saxon Protestants, hard-working, aspirational, family-focused and conservative. They were part of the eastern suburbs private-school set on which Melbourne's defining 'clubbiness' is based.

The people who mixed with the Ramages were people who had faith in the law. They expected it to provide justice. But Jamie Ramage had dominated and abused his wife Julie for more than twenty years, and he did it again at his trial. Julie's voice was strangled out of her a second time by the laws of evidence and the legal defence of provocation. That very silencing, however, turned the case into a much-debated cause célèbre. Julie's story exposed the brittleness of the middle-class veneer and the subtle viciousness of another kind of silent death: the abusive marriage. Jamie's trial for murder exposed the way ideas of 'good' and 'bad' women were still enshrined in the law – and how the notion of 'crimes of passion' favours the passions of men.

Part Two

JULIE AND JAMIE

YOUNG LOVE

THERE IS a wistfulness to childhood happy snaps in a family that has suffered a tragedy. They are reminders of a lost innocence, of a time when this family trusted in life's beneficence in a way they no longer can after a savage twist of fate. Julie's childhood pictures are full of scenes of what the Chinese might call 'double happiness'. She was a twin, five minutes older than her identical sister, Jane. The photographs show two little girls, mirror images of each other, barrelling their way through an active childhood: blonde two-year-olds in pudding-bowl haircuts and identical frocks and ankle-socks, a proprietorial Julie hugging Jane; the two girls at eight, smiling shyly, cheek to chubby cheek, in a photo booth; at eleven, proudly side by side on white ponies at riding school. By fifteen, they had started to carve out more separate identities; they stand side by side at the beach, each with a hand on a hip but in different bikinis and with different hairstyles.

The girls' parents, Patricia and Raymond Garrett, married in England in 1956. Four years later, on 11 September 1960, they went to Barnet Hospital to make their contribution to the post-war baby boom. The Garretts worked in their own corner shop and supermarket businesses for most of the girls' childhood, iconic representatives of the nation of shopkeepers.

The girls had a happy childhood, the remaining Garretts agree. They had spent their early years living in Edmonton in north London. When the twins were eleven, the family moved to Cheshunt in Hertfordshire. 'We didn't have any brothers, so Dad encouraged us to play sport,' says Jane. Julie represented the county in shot-put and discus, and both girls played tennis and netball and joined Young Mariners to learn sailing. They did Girl Guides and had summer holidays in France. They were popular and outgoing and had a wide circle of friends. 'We were very close; we did everything together,' Jane later told police. 'We would think the same, laugh at the same things and share a giggle. We never lost that as we grew older; that bond was always there.'

But there were differences between them. Friends in Australia say that Julie's front teeth were slightly bent in a way that Jane's weren't, and her face was less rounded. Her personality, too, was her own; people who knew them both say Julie was a softer version of the more exuberant Jane. But the truly fateful differences were not so visible to outsiders. Jane remembers noting features of her sister's relationships with others when they were in their late teens. Julie didn't rely on her circle of girlfriends as much as Jane did; when she fell in love, she fell hard; and she was attracted to strong men.

Many teenage girls naturally outgrow Mills-and-Boon syndrome, the romantic fantasy of the strong, laconic, lantern-jawed hero who will protect and cherish them. That was not to happen for Julie Garrett. She would soon foreclose on her future.

JAMIE RAMAGE was named after his father – almost. His father, James Ramage, was Scottish and his mother was English. James Ramage became a business executive in England. He moved to Melbourne to set up an Australian branch of a large insurance company. The family returned to England a few years later. When the first son was born in Melbourne in 1959, he was named Jamie Stuart but

Jamie later came to prefer being called James. When he first met Julie Garrett in 1977, Jamie Ramage was a bit of a dish. He exuded energy and confidence. Physically he was tall and lean, in the way of many gangly teenage boys. Although he was handsome enough, with a long narrow face and curly dark hair, he was not as handsome as Julie was pretty. Her hair had darkened with adulthood and she had deep blue eyes and an open, girl-next-door smile. Jamie was seventeen and she was sixteen.

Patricia Garrett thinks Jamie and Julie might first have met at a party: 'I know that when she met him he impressed her. She thought he was flash; he had the use of a nice car.' Says Jane, 'My first impression of Jamie was that he was very self-assured. He was always boasting about his sporting prowess.'

And Julie, it seems, was looking for an out. She had arrived at adulthood in a family with conservative values at the beginning of an era in which young women could readily leave home on their own, and at the end of one in which their only respectable way out was marriage. The traditional norm had a stronger pull on Julie. Many years later, a few weeks before her death, she would tell a counsellor that she had fallen for Jamie because 'he was charming and good-looking [and] I was a bit oppressed at home. We both liked sport, going out and dancing, we were both Virgos, we always talked a lot'.

Hindsight is a cruel lens. This is a tragedy that involved many characters and many events building one upon the other. The Garretts and others who knew Julie and Jamie now look back and wonder if there was a point at which all this could have been averted; a point at which they might have seen it coming, when they could have said or done something that would have made a difference. Who wonder, *If only . . .*

The first glimpse of trouble was at the Garretts' house during Jamie's courtship of Julie. According to Ray Garrett, 'Jamie and Jane had an argument. It was trivial; they were all going out as a group. Jamie charged upstairs like a madman. He started shouting at Jane. I had to speak to him. I was appalled, really. I told him that if there was any need for my daughter to be chastised, then it was up to me. It was after this incident that I realised that Jamie could be a hot-head. It wasn't normal behaviour for someone to come into the house and start running it that way.'

There is a photograph of Jamie and Julie taken around that time. He is sitting in a cream armchair against a background of 1970s brown floral wallpaper. He is smiling at the camera, his eyes to the lens. Julie sits at his feet and leans into his lap. Her smiling face is turned up towards Jamie; she has eyes only for him. That affection was to cost her dearly. When her father discovered that she and Jamie were sleeping together, he removed her from school. He told her that if she was old enough for sex, she was old enough to earn her own living. Julie Garrett never completed her A-levels. *If only . . .*

She decided she would join Jamie in coming to Australia. One of Jamie's father's contacts, a man based in Melbourne, had offered to teach him about the business world. On Jane and Julie's eighteenth birthday their parents threw them a party at the local community centre. Part-way through the evening, Julie told her parents she knew it was hard for them that she was leaving to live on the other side of the world. Then she showed them her solitaire engagement ring. Recalls her mother, 'She thought that this would make us feel that she was going to be looked after. At the time it broke my heart, but we had brought [the girls] up to be individuals, and if that is what she really wanted, then we would support her in any way we could.'

Jamie left England early in 1979 and Julie followed him to Australia in March. They flew back to Britain at the end of the year and were married in January 1980 at Northaw Church. The negotiations over the wedding reception offered more pointers to the future. The Garretts wanted it small and quaint; Jamie wanted it to go later into the night and to have more guests. This would cost an extra 400 pounds, but Jamie's parents told Pat and Ray that they would pay half of the extra. According to Pat Garrett, 'What really sticks out is when Jamie came to give us the 200 pounds, he just walked in and threw the envelope at us. He didn't thank us . . . I suppose, looking back, it was an indication as to how Jamie was going to treat people.'

Ray's sour memory relates to the end of the evening. 'The wedding went off well; it was lovely. [But] I can recall at the end of the reception, Jamie's family gathered up all the gifts and left. My family was left with the task of cleaning up.' Decades of distant and fractious dealings between Jamie Ramage and his in-laws would follow.

After the wedding, Julie and Jamie returned to Australia to seek their fortune together. At eighteen, Julie Ramage had made her bed.

BARBIE AND KEN

MELBURNIANS HAVE long been trying to live down the famous line of the city's founder, explorer John Batman. In 1835, searching for new pastoral land, he dropped anchor in the Yarra River and declared, 'This is the place for a village.' In many ways, Melbourne is still a small town.

The people who run politics and business and the professions tend to come from shared backgrounds. The most important hub for the formation and maintenance of what passes for an 'Establishment' are the wealthy inner-eastern suburbs such as Hawthorn, Balwyn, Toorak and Kew, and the elite private schools with which they are dotted. The tramlines that run through the area used to be renowned as places where privileged boys would meet potential trophy-wife girls. Perhaps the most telling thing about Jamie and Julie Ramage is that, despite having arrived in Australia as teenagers with little education and nothing behind them, they managed to embed themselves so deeply into the eastern suburbs private-school set. They were determined to crack it.

Julie's first few jobs in Australia were unremarkable. She worked in a factory making can-openers and then for several other businesses before settling for a while in a finance company. Jamie got a taste for the good life early. His patron was a wealthy businessman and took him to places such as the best golf courses and the members stand at the Melbourne Cricket Ground (MCG). Jamie was already mixing with the set to which he aspired. That mentoring relationship fell apart after his boss discovered Jamie was trying to better himself by studying accounting at night. Jamie went on to work for companies such as McDonald's, Country Road and Jardines. He and Julie bought their first home in Prahran and later moved to Percy Street in Balwyn. They had two children, Matthew and Samantha.

They came to prosper. About 1993, Julie answered a newspaper ad for a job as book-keeper with a fashion house, Eco-d. Julie set up the company's accounting systems and computerised its finances. She was also instrumental in setting up the software system that connected all the chain's shops. By 2000, she had turned the role into a four-day-a-week job. She kept Wednesdays free for her horse-riding.

Jamie Ramage and Anthony Brady had met at Jamie's 21st birthday party. Although their relationship later became purely professional, at that time they became friends, recalls Anthony: 'We used to go out socially and went away a couple of times and did the dinner-party thing.' In 1987 they branched out together, starting a confectionery business called Jazzies that expanded to twelve stores. The pair sold Jazzies in 1997 to manage Mr Whippy, an ice-cream van company. Twelve months later, they bought Thermoglaze, which imported a product for resurfacing porcelain baths. Jamie handled the accounting, financial and overseas aspects of the business and Anthony ran it day to day. It seemed Jamie's professional life was going well.

The domestic front was stormier. Although it was not known to many – Anthony Brady had no idea – the Ramages' marriage was often troubled and had what would be referred to in court as 'a history of violence'. Julie and Jamie had separated for several months in 1984 and both had relationships with others. Soon after reconciling they conceived Matthew, and their daughter Samantha was born in 1987. Over the years, Julie tried to leave her husband again at least four or five times; often she would arrive at the home of her sister, Jane. (Jane Ashton, as she had become upon marriage, had come to Australia with her husband Howard several years after Julie. So had the twins' parents, Pat and Ray.) But after every attempt by Julie to leave, Jamie wooed her back with flowers and charm and promises to change. And the choice for Julie was now more complicated: there were two children to consider, as well as the potential loss of considerable financial security. Her sister Jane, interviewed by police after Julie's death, said that after returning to Jamie in 1984, 'Julie told me that she felt helpless as no one likes to admit that they have made a mistake. I believe that at this point she had decided to make the best out of a bad job, and that's how she continued. She liked the nice house and the money.'

It's a question feminists duck in the domestic-violence debate: the role of 'golden handcuffs' in a woman's decision to stay in an abusive relationship. Both Julie and Jamie had worked hard for their lifestyle and she didn't want to lose it. In the end, Julie broke away only when she had a solicitor's assurance that she would be all right financially, and a plan that allowed her to take a six-figure sum of money out of the family business to tide her over and protect her children's places in private schools. Julie liked the gilding on her cage.

ABOUT 1997 the Ramages moved to their final home together, a two-storey, red-brick English-style house with white shutters on a small block in Marock Place, Balwyn. The house was solid, if in need of a makeover, but it was a good real-estate buy because of the position. The Ramages were now living in a small court off Balwyn's Golden Mile, the stretch of Mont Albert Road between Balwyn Road and Burke Road. Balwyn is a comfortable, insular, 'white-bread' suburb. It is politically conservative and upper middle class, with a population dominated by managers and professionals. The area 2 kilometres around the Ramages' home had an average household income 50 per cent higher than the average for the rest of the state of Victoria; less than 7.5 per cent of the neighbouring households held divorced or separated people; and English was the language spoken at home by 84 per cent. While Balwyn was perfectly respectable, it was not top-drawer. The Ramages were sensitive to this and used to tell people their address was Canterbury, a neighbouring suburb a notch higher on the social league table (a distinction that would be lost on anyone from outside this eastern-suburbs set). They needed to make no apologies, though, regarding the site of their next purchase, which qualified as dress-circle real estate. Together with the Bradys, they bought a modest holiday house on one of the best pieces of land at Eastern View on Victoria's most beautiful stretch of coastline, the spectacular Great Ocean Road.

The Ramages' choices about their children's schooling were equally upwardly mobile. First the children went to the local state primary school, Deepdene. The Ramages were active at school functions but not everyone was enamoured of what some saw as their plastic perfection; the more caustic parents privately dubbed them 'Ken and Barbie'. 'They looked like the perfect couple,' says Julie's best friend, Gilda Pekin. 'Everywhere they went they were perfectly groomed. Julie was tall and slim and blonde, the Barbie, and [Jamie was] Ken, the manly strong person. She was the accessory for him.'

At secondary level, Samantha went first to Ruyton and then to Lauriston Girls Grammar School. Matthew won an art scholarship to the highly regarded Trinity Grammar. In a telling move, Jamie and Julie pulled Matthew out of Trinity in Year 10 and sent him to the grander and more prestigious Scotch College. This meant they lost Matthew's scholarship and had to pay full fees. Even in this set, it was a remarkable decision. Julie's friend Christine Howgate says, 'Trinity was full of film-makers and journalists and creative people, and they wanted him to mix with the business world. Julie said he would meet "a better class of people" at Scotch. I said, "Julie, this is so ridiculous. He's happy, he's doing well, he's good at football." And I don't think he wanted to go at that stage. But Jamie wanted him to go.'

Perhaps it was Jamie who wanted to meet a better class of people. The Ramages were serious networkers. They knew Aingers, 'the antiques people'; Doggetts, 'the paper people'; and Dyson Hore-Lacy, SC, a criminal barrister better known as one-time chairman of the Fitzroy Football Club. Jamie played touch rugby on Sunday mornings with a team of middle-aged 'tragics' including the high-flying Dr Rob Moodie, formerly a Geneva-based epidemiologist with the World Health Organization and currently chief executive officer of VicHealth, the Victorian Health Promotion Foundation. The Ramages regularly dinner-partied with property developers, doctors and lawyers. Scotch College offered them another form of entrée.

One of the Ramages' neighbours who was also a Scotch parent, Rhonda McMurtrie, recalls Jamie being open about his networking. 'Once, in conversation, he said, "God, it's not like Julie and I haven't socialised enough. We've put on some of the best dinner parties with the best people." And it was almost like [he was asking], But were they getting the invitations back? They would have, for the sake of Julie, but I don't know too many people who would have lined up to go another round with James.'

Dr Catherine (Kate) Clark is an anaesthetist who had a neighbouring holiday house at Eastern View. She also knew the Ramages as fellow Scotch College parents and became friends with both Julie and Jamie. 'They were always very confident about meeting people,' she says. 'They were on the march, getting image and position right. I never knew how much this was Jamie and how much this was about the both of them, but at the beach house, Julie was always the one making the connections. She was certainly always marking out the calendar for the time they were there. They'd want to be catching up with the so and so's, and the so and so's.'

But there could also be genuine warmth behind the calculated social-climbing. Clark will never forget that when her marriage ended, Julie and Jamie remained her friends. 'They often asked me to dinner. It didn't matter if they had six people to dinner, if they had nobody to dinner. I found it so exceedingly nice; all my more upper-middle-class friends seemed to struggle with single women at their dinner table.' There had to be an element of kindness in it, she says now, 'and it must have come from him, because *every*thing needed to be approved by him'.

THE APPEARANCE of a perfect family was important to both the Ramages. They took great pride in the children's achievements. One of Julie's horse-riding friends, Annette Luckman, recalls that during long talks on rides there was friendly rivalry between herself and Julie 'over our sons and our cooking, and the private versus the public schools thing. She was very proud of Matt's public speaking, and we were in competition about who loved their children more, or who thought more of their children. She was very proud of Sam'.

No one who knew them doubted that Jamie and Julie genuinely loved their children. Julie, in particular, was steady and even-handed in her affections. Says Kate Clark, 'When you were with them and their children it was like they were on show, the perfect family . . . Julie's relationship with her children, which I would see at close quarters quite a bit, seemed to be healthy and happy. And so ordinary, I suppose. There was never ever any tension with her and the children. Ever. She was benign. She was an attentive mother. She was a bit obsessed with what they ate. And I often thought, "No, you've got it wrong, it doesn't matter if Matt has a whole lot of things that are big and greasy and fattening because he's getting so much exercise." And Samantha – I think she was always a bit worried about Samantha's weight and size because beauty was nearly everything [to Julie].'

Rhonda McMurtrie remembers Julie's anxiety about Samantha too, as one that revolved around how the world was a tougher place for women than for men. 'She often talked about her fears for Samantha, being a female, that life would be more difficult; that society would place expectations on Samantha to be a certain way that she felt would not be placed on Matthew.'

Julie also told Rhonda McMurtrie that she was concerned that Jamie was sometimes too hard on Samantha. If this issue between the Ramages had been defused, it might have helped to avert the disaster that was looming. But over this difference between them, as over so many things, Jamie brushed aside Julie's protests and held to his course.

EVEN THOSE who only knew the Ramages socially assessed Jamie Ramage as a difficult man. Kate Clark describes him as abrupt and domineering. Rhonda McMurtrie recalls, 'Dinner parties were pretty much dominated by James, in so much as he always led the conversation. He was like a dog with a bone. He would never let go of anything until he was absolutely satisfied that he got the answer he wanted.' A favourite target for his criticisms was Scotch College; now that he was paying top dollar, he wanted to be sure he was getting value for money.

Jamie and Kate Clark did hit it off on a social level. He was able to argue good-naturedly with her, and they connected over music, often swapping CDs. But she was aware of his limitations. She recalls, 'You just thought of him as a rather bigoted, narrow-minded, right-wing reactionary Englishman, with limited life experiences, not able to have a compassionate view. He was really hard.'

Jamie Ramage could be just as hard on himself when it came to sticking to principles that he valued. He and his partner once subleased business premises from Gilda Pekin's husband. Jamie could not be faulted as a tenant, says Pekin: 'He was always extremely scrupulous about his business relationships. Never generous, but if he cut a deal, he stuck by the deal.'

While many found him abrasive, Jamie Ramage was not a social pariah. There were friends who admired his drive and determination to make something of himself. Rob Moodie did not find Jamie bullying. He says Jamie would have strong views in arguments but he allowed Julie and others to have their say too. 'To me, he was likable. Very ambitious; work-wise, society-wise, he wanted to create space for himself. I think in a sense he was out to prove himself, that he could make it in Victoria. The thing I liked about James was that, with me, he was quite able to laugh at himself. Politically, we were completely different; he was very much the small businessman, and I see the world in quite a different way. We would take the piss out of each other. That was the most endearing feature of Jamie. And I liked the way he seemed committed to the kids. Although I could see the notion that he was gaining reflected glory from them, I genuinely thought he loved them as well. I still think that.' Gilda agrees with Rob Moodie on this: 'Jamie really did love his family. And he was serious about creating security for them, real financial and social security. It was not just about social-climbing.'

ROB MOODIE saw Julie and Jamie as equal partners in their networking, but others thought she might have been a conscript on Jamie's forced march towards success. Julie had a quality whose lack in Jamie was to prove so devastating: empathy. 'Julie was just nice,' says Christine Howgate. 'If she did some baking or something, she'd make a batch of cookies for you. And if you were sick, she'd ring and see how you were feeling. Very generous.' Gilda Pekin remembers the time Julie dropped in to visit after their babies had been vaccinated and Pekin's son was screaming with fever. Julie walked the floor with Gilda's baby for hours. 'I'd only met her a few weeks before, and she was there for me already.'

Julie had what a psychologist would call a sense of 'The Other': she saw other people as separate from herself and understood that they had their own wants and needs. And she knew how to win them over. In a part of her world that was quite separate to her life with Jamie, Julie Ramage was developing into a leader.

Annette Luckman is not part of the eastern-suburbs set. She works as a personal carer and lives in a modest house with a gentle view of green hills in the semi-rural suburb of Hurstbridge. She first met Julie in 2001 when she decided to join the Hurstbridge Adult Riding Club. 'I think I must have met Julie the first day I was down there. I was a bit concerned: adult riders can sometimes have a reputation for being a bit precious. But Julie was warm and welcoming.

'She was the Wednesday rally co-ordinator. She was the person we dealt with making bookings, organising instructors, organising events. At that time I think there were only about seven or eight active members in the club; very small. And by the time Julie died, I think there were 70. So by 2003, the club had blossomed under her. She became the treasurer, and to promote the club she wrote articles in the association newsletter, she organised clinics and events.

'She had brilliant ideas and she'd encourage people to go to events. She actually lent me her daughter's horse and she taught me how to tow a float. She physically took me around the roads and showed me how to do it and next thing you know I was heading off to a top teams competition. There were a lot of us nervous about "floating". We got a bit of a reputation for being welcoming, so anyone would come knocking on the door of the club and if they had any concerns Julie would lend her float. She'd arrange the program around people's kinder sessions and school pick-ups and those sorts of things. She made it accessible to a lot of people.'

And when Julie turned on the charm, says Annette, she was hard to resist. 'I remember one time we went for a ride – and this is just the power of Julie – and we were riding around the roads, and these guys were coming out of their paddock and Julie trotted up to them and, in her beautiful English accent, said, "Do you mind if we go for a gallop in your field?" And they just opened the gate and we went in and bolted up the hill and back down again. I don't know of anyone who would have had the nerve to ask and make it sound so nice and sweet.'

JAMIE RAMAGE was seen as colder and more calculating. It is hard to know, now, how marked these qualities really were in him; the killing of his wife casts a shadow over people's memories, and those closest to Julie have long had trouble seeing him in any other light. Gilda Pekin says, 'For the better part of twenty years, I've observed Jamie Ramage preoccupied with his personal balance sheet of money, possessions and useful connections. Julie wanted friends regardless of their value in terms of his personal balance sheet.' Gilda and

Jamie never got on, partly, Gilda began to suspect, because Jamie feared that Julie confided in her about the marriage.

Christine Howgate and her husband found Jamie boorishly self-aggrandising. Christine and Julie met about 1990 at a master's swimming class. 'We were the only two girls in it because all the men were training for triathlons, and we were the slowest. So we used to do our 40 laps and then get the kickboard and kick up and down and chat. And occasionally we would meet for coffee.

'The whole time we lived out at Research [an outer-suburban area] there was never any invitation [from the Ramages]; never any interest in pursuing the relationship with the boys [their husbands]. After we moved into Balwyn, suddenly there was an interest. Julie told me that Jamie would never socialise with people who lived down in Research because he called them bush pigs. Then we built the big house in Canterbury, and it was suddenly, "When's your next free Saturday night?" because Jamie had chased up what clubs my husband was a member of and thought he might be useful to him.'

Jamie made it clear to Julie that it was her task as a good wife to help with this, Christine says. He told her off one year for having failed to win them an invitation to the Oaks Day races at Flemington. Winning invitations was not always easy, given that Jamie was renowned for being argumentative. He had little sensitivity to the social nuances of the circles to which he aspired. Christine says, 'He was quite bigoted and very right-wing. He used to tell racist jokes and think they were really funny. At one time he said it would be good to throw a free Aboriginal concert at the MCG and then drop a bomb on the place.' At a dinner party one night, he saw his host's daughter about to go out for the evening in revealing clothes. The rest of the gathering made no comment and left it to the girl's parents to take up the issue. Jamie embarrassed them all by barking, 'Anyone can get a root if they go out dressed like that!' He offended Gilda Pekin in this way too. Her husband is often away on overseas trips for work. At one dinner party, Jamie made a snide remark about his absences and what that meant for their sex life. A mortified Julie rang Gilda the next day and apologised profusely.

Jamie Ramage was also renowned for being tight. He once came to a fundraising cocktail party for a Liberal Party candidate at Christine Howgate's house and ate and drank but ducked paying – saving himself all of $10. Asked for donations to the school fete, he refused to give away lollies from Jazzies and instead sold them at cost. In the kindergarten years, he would not go to working bees but would try to get out of the maintenance levy he owed in lieu by arguing that Julie's contribution should suffice.

Julie Ramage, for all her warmth and kindness, had her faults too. She cheated on her husband, and she lied to him and to others to protect her affairs. As one caller to her husband's lawyer would point out acidly after her death, Julie Ramage was no Goody Two-Shoes.

BEGINNINGS OF AN END

A LASTING marriage does not necessarily mean a happy one. It is hard to walk away from a long, shared history. Often a kind of teeth-gritting stasis is reached in which the stability is based not on mutual fulfilment but on a meshing of neuroses: two people stay together because each person's unhappiness fits with the other's. Maybe the form the unhappiness takes – 'I was always bossed around', for example – is familiar from childhood and feels like home. Or perhaps they both feel their joint misery is less anxiety-creating than living alone would be. In such marriages, trouble begins if one partner begins to grow and change, and the other does not.

Julie Ramage was changing. The first time I asked Jane Ashton what had made Julie finally decide to leave Jamie, she chuckled and said, 'She got to 40!' She was reaching midlife, that stage when, Jung argued, an individual pauses to reflect on whether the goals they have achieved are still the ones they want. He believed that most people spend the first half of their adult lives achieving the goals that they have taken as their own from parents and society: marriage, home, children, career, material security. Once these boxes have been ticked, there is a pause, often followed by the question: *Is this all there is?* And Julie, say friends, had started to realise that money didn't buy happiness.

Her riding-club experiences gave her the pride of accomplishment and confidence-building feedback from others. The job at Eco-d gave her another world outside the home, more girlfriends in whom she could confide and a sense that she could earn a living. She was increasingly finding Jamie an embarrassment. He made no effort with people at functions she invited him to that were outside the set, such as riding-club fundraisers or office Christmas parties, and would complain bitterly afterwards. She tried to distance herself when he was laying down the law to others in dinner-party conversations. The more serious marital problems continued, largely hidden from the rest of the world. At the trial, they would be kept hidden from the jury, too.

Early in 2003, Julie acted on the advice of her friend Gilda and saw a family lawyer, Caroline Counsel. Julie discovered that she would not be on the streets if the marriage ended. She planned to stay till the end of that year to see Matthew through the Victorian Certificate of Education (VCE). She knew how important it was and didn't want him derailed. But then, on 6 June, there was yet another fight with Jamie. It began as an argument over Samantha but turned into something much more. Julie changed her plans. Jamie, unaware of his wife's decision, left for a business trip to Japan and Korea. While he was gone, Julie rented a townhouse in Toorak and on 13 June, exactly a week after the row, she left, taking their daughter Samantha. Matthew stayed in the family home. Julie took the precaution of having her beloved horses moved to a concealed paddock. She feared Jamie would hurt or kill them.

What followed would become the stuff of local legend: Jamie's obsessive attempts to win Julie back; Julie's plan to let him down gently; and the fateful entry into her life of Laurence Webb, the man who would become known as The Lover.

THERE IS a reliable air about Laurence Webb. It is partly his build, which is solid, and partly his manner, which is phlegmatic. He is in his early forties, with ungreyed brown hair and a face that is tanned from his weekend life outdoors. He has a slight English accent and the bluff, unremarkable features of a country squire or yeoman farmer. Like the Ramages, he emigrated to Australia from England in early adulthood.

We meet in the foyer of the large Collins Street office block where he works as a sales director for Telstra. He shakes hands like a businessman, pleasant but distant. We go up in the lift to the penthouse suite of meeting rooms: sweeping views of the city, plush décor and absolute privacy. It is rather a grand and formal venue for an interview. Perhaps he is keen for his status to be recognised. A proud man, he is still affronted at the way he was treated during Jamie Ramage's trial, where the defence called him 'the unemployed bush poet'. At the committal, Jamie's lawyer had asked him if he was a cad. There could be no greater insult to a romantic with chivalrous ideals.

Laurence and Julie had first met briefly four years before she left Jamie. Laurence was a recently separated dad taking his anxious ten-year-old daughter to her first competition at pony club. He arrived five minutes before the event; they were supposed to arrive an hour before. 'And there's mums everywhere and they've got plenty of space between the floats; they're about 10 yards apart,' he recalls. 'But when you try and park, they all come out and scream at you because they've got to have room for their horses, which aren't there. So you can imagine, your daughter is very uptight – and this angel comes up and says, "Can I help you?" It was Julie. She calmed us all down, negotiated with someone over the parking and then calmed down the horse.'

Laurence *is* a 'bush poet' – he writes and reads poetry about horses and the bush, Julie's great loves. Four years after his first chance encounter with Julie, Jane Ashton, whom he had met through horse-riding, told him he should meet her now-separated sister. On Sunday 6 July 2003 Jane brought Julie along to one of Laurence's poetry readings. Julie caught up with him at the end of the evening and told him she wanted her riding group to have a poetry night and they exchanged telephone numbers. Neither of them realised they were about to be struck by The Thunderbolt.

Laurence did know that he liked Julie from the start: 'She was very classy. I come from an English background, as did she, and I guess it sounds snobby but you're aware of that. She was open and fun. A lot of English people that are classy are affected. It's very refreshing to see someone who has style but not affectation. And she was not stunning-looking but she was nice-looking.'

The rapport was instant. They got to the Athenaeum Theatre for their first date barely on time and had to climb, laughing, over one row of seats to get to another. They drank champagne during the interval of the play and had supper at a café on level 35 of his office building: French champagne and Caesar salad. 'About half an hour into the show – and it's not a funny or romantic show, it's about a woman who loses her sanity – we started holding hands. To this day I can't remember who started it. And after supper, we were kissing in the lift like teenagers.

'We went back to her place, had a coffee and talked. That night she also told me a lot about the sexual side of her marriage, and I thought, "My goodness, how will I ever make love to this woman who's been treated this way?" But we also talked a lot about pleasant things.' Both of them cancelled other dates they had lined up over the next few days. 'Within a couple of days she was the most wonderful woman in the world, and still is.'

The stories about his time with Julie come pouring out of Laurence Webb as if they are still at the forefront of his mind. They are clearly memories that he has often taken out and gone over, like a mourning mother stroking the clothes of a baby she has lost. On another level, the role of the tragic lover seems one he has adopted with panache. Romanticism was already part of his nature before he met Julie.

Laurence believes that he and Julie were an instant fit. 'I had a very demanding list. She's got to be comfortable in the boardroom, entertaining at the CEO level, and she's got to be comfortable out in the bush with my friends, with quite ordinary people. When she'd seen me with the poetry, like a country gentleman, I said, "That's fine, but that's only one side of it." And then, when she saw the other side of it, me being comfortable in the city . . . If we had to put on a sheet, "What do you both like doing?", we would put ten out of ten the same thing.'

They slept together on the second date and started to meet regularly, one staying at the other's house overnight as long as no children were present. 'There was no question of my sleeping over when Sam was in the house. Julie treasured her children as her highest priority. "The children first, each other next, and then the rest of the world." That was Julie's idea.' They also decided that they would not socialise with each other's friends for at least three months because Julie's separation was so new. But Laurence had decided that Julie was the woman for him, and they began planning a future: more time together, shared between their two houses, and a holiday in separate apartments with their daughters at Noosa in the coming September school break. Laurence thought Julie was well-established in her new single life: she had set herself up in her townhouse and she had already had her first sexual encounter following the break-up. (Julie told him she had slept with a businessman from Sydney, Simon, whom she met at the Botanical Hotel in South Yarra while out with the girls from work.) As far as Laurence was concerned, Julie had clearly left Jamie behind: 'Her actions should speak for themselves.'

In Julie's mind, too, she had started a new life – but she also knew that Jamie had not cut *his* ties to *her*.

THE LAST full day of Julie Ramage's life was Sunday 20 July 2003. She spent it with Laurence. They met at 10.30 am at his house. She arrived wearing a short red jacket, black jodhpurs and a huge smile. Laurence says, 'I can still see the sun shining through her hair.' It seems that for him, the dead angel will always be golden.

He introduced Julie to his daughter and, after they dropped his daughter at her mother's, they went back to Laurence's and had lunch. They made love. They sat by the fire and talked and then put both their horses on her float and drove to Panton Hill for a ride.

It's hilly there; semi-bush, dirt roads. Laurence's horse was skittish. Julie calmed down both horse and rider enough to get them off the path and on to the road. 'Then we had a bit of a canter which turned into a gallop. And it was the first time I'd galloped this young horse. I'm someone who only took up riding to keep my daughter company. I'd had twenty-year-old Clydesdales before, very slow and heavy. Normally I would have been scared but somehow, with her, I was fine going flat out all around this long track. The bush was so much more bright and beautiful than I'd seen it before. We were just experiencing our senses far more than you normally would. Julie was exhilarated.'

On the walk back the tired horses drew together. Laurence says it reminded him of a Henry Lawson poem called 'Reedy River' that he then recited to Julie.

He recites it fully from memory for me, sitting across the board-table in this modern city office tower. He has a practised voice that is confident of how the cadences should rise and fall. It is a startling quality in a 'bloke'.

The poem tells of a young man declaring his love for a Mary Campbell while they are out riding. But Laurence had forgotten, until he reached it, the twist in the tail.

And over all forever go sun and moon and stars
But of the home I built, there are no traces now
And many rains have levelled the furrows of my plough
The brave bright days have vanished
For sombre branches wave their wattle
Above my Mary's grave.

The last line hangs in the air between us. We look at each other in silence. What had made him think of that poem that day – a coincidence? An expression of his unconscious fear that such happiness could not last? Or prescience?

At the time, he shook off his vague disquiet. At the pub in Panton Hill, they had wine and some food. Later he drove Julie to her parents' home, where she had parked her Mini, and they waved goodbye. They had known each other only two weeks. The following morning Julie would tell friends that she had found her great love, and that this Sunday had been the most perfect day of her life.

Those words would be repeated over and over in the defence of her husband.

THE NEXT time Laurence Webb saw Julie Ramage was the following Wednesday morning in a small pink room, the colour of a baby's nursery, at the city mortuary. Julie's family had asked him to identify her. She lay on one side of a partition and he stood on the other, looking in at her through a large pane of glass. Julie was still and white on a trolley, with sheets over her body and cloth carefully arranged to hide her neck. Nothing hid the big lump that swelled on one side of her head, grim and bare under the harsh fluorescents. That kind of lump, he felt, could only have been produced by extreme physical force. He was drained. It had been a gruelling 36 hours. He felt grief for himself and for Julie. But it was taking a while for the truth to sink in – what he felt most keenly was a longing for Julie's eyes to open.

DEATH IN THE FAMILY

HER TWIN sister Jane would later say she had a visionary flash at lunchtime on Monday 21 July 2003, around the time that Julie was killed. Jane was in the stables on her semi-rural property. 'It was really weird,' she recalls, struggling for words. 'I had this amazing . . .' and she makes a sound, *'chhhhhh'*, a shimmery drifting sound, and holds her fisted hands up and flashes them open, trying to describe the sudden, fleeting feeling. 'Oh, it was all about understanding revenge and why people did awful things to each other.' But the feeling was not connected to anyone in particular. A clearer vision of what had happened to Julie would come to her later.

The evening of the day Julie went missing, Samantha was the first person to worry. Julie failed to pick her up from athletics practice at 5.45 pm. Her mother had never forgotten to pick her up from anywhere before. Samantha caught the tram back to the Toorak townhouse. She tried to ring her mother's mobile phone several times but it was turned off. Unknown to Samantha, Julie's workmates had also wondered about her whereabouts when she hadn't returned from lunch. She'd said she was only going out for a quick bite and had left her computer and her heater on. But Julie's hours had been a bit erratic while she was moving house, and they thought she had just got caught up somehow.

No one thinks of death as a first possibility.

At 7.30 pm, an increasingly worried Samantha rang Jamie to see if her mother was having dinner with him. She would later tell police, 'He was absolutely normal. He was absolutely himself. We just spoke normally about the rowing and about school and he even said, "She's probably off with that Laurence bloke or something." He then said, "If she doesn't come home in about an hour, give me a call."'

Jamie was coolly bluffing it out. Not only did he point the finger at an innocent man, he lied to his own daughter about her dead mother. But then, it is hard to imagine how you would tell your child that you have just killed her mother. Are there words for something like that? How would you face the weeping and recrimination? How would you ever 'apologise' – such a limp, pale, inadequate word – for such a thing? Jamie obviously didn't know. The macho man took the coward's way out. Jamie Ramage would leave it to strangers in uniform to break the news.

Others became involved in the growing crisis. Samantha rang Gilda to ask, 'Are you out with my Mum?' Gilda could tell by the skip in her voice that the girl was upset. At 7.35 pm, Laurence rang the townhouse to speak to Julie. He had been about to walk on to a tennis court but was immediately concerned to hear from Samantha that Julie had not arrived home. He rang Jane and suggested she file a missing person's report and told Samantha to call Julie's boss, Felicity Holding. It was on the phone to Felicity that Samantha finally gave in to her tears. Felicity lived only a few doors up the street and raced over to her. She found the girl still crying and shaking with distress. By now Felicity, too, was seriously worried. Felicity rang Jamie, who suggested this time that Julie might have been in an accident.

Meanwhile, Jane was becoming distraught. She recalls, 'I rang the police, and they said "We'll just report her as a missing person."

And I said, "No, she's been in a violent relationship and I think something terrible's happened." I had a committee meeting at my house that night and I got everybody on their mobile phones – I kept the other phone clear – to ring all the hospitals, and then the police arrived. It was a young policewoman.'

By this time an image had solidified in Jane's mind and it would not leave her. 'I said "He's strangled her. She's in the boot of the car." And she said "Don't be ridiculous!" I just knew. I said three or four times, *"He's strangled her, she's in the boot of his car. Get on to him!"*' Her voice is bitter now: 'I was told off for being hysterical.'

Jane did indeed 'just know'. Police later confirmed that she had repeatedly insisted to attending police that this was her sister's fate. A more senior officer would later tell Jane that he had learned never to ignore visions by mothers of small children or by siblings who were twins. But this was a police investigation, a process based on the discovery of hard facts, and that night it was Jane's fate to be dismissed as over-emotional. She became more and more furious as the police followed protocols that did not focus on Jamie. 'Then the policewoman said, "Because you've notified us, we have to search your house." And we live on 10 acres and I said, "Well, unless you've got dogs and torches . . . !" I was very angry. I wanted them to go to his house because at that stage I thought I might be wrong but that she might be kidnapped or tied up somewhere or need help. I really did have this premonition. And then the police left; they'd done everything by the book but missed all meaning.'

Local police called in the detectives assigned to the area, and then both uniformed and detective units became involved in the hunt for Julie. Jane was worried that Samantha's safety might be at risk too. Felicity told her that Jamie had said he was on his way from Marock Place to pick Samantha up. Jane's voice trembles as she tells of it: 'I rang Felicity, who had Samantha with her. And I said, "Whatever you do, *don't let Samantha go with her father*. Make out she's got a headache, make out she's in the bath, *just don't let her go!*"'

LAURENCE WEBB shared the phoning around and tried to search for Julie physically. He says, 'About 10.30–11 o'clock, I was at the factory, the business that [Jamie] ran, with a couple of people from the tennis club. Searching that, or trying to. We couldn't break in but we could see underneath. We were at the point now where we thought he may have killed her or beaten her horribly. We were hoping that she would be alive and okay, or even bashed up and still alive but hiding because she didn't want to show people.'

The phones continued to run hot with Jane as the central exchange. Felicity, although she was worried, did not understand Jane's high panic. She would later tell police that Jane was phoning her every ten minutes. 'Jane kept ringing me. She was hysterical. She told me that she had told the police that Jamie had strangled Julie and he had her in the boot of the car.' Jane was the only adult in the family in Melbourne that night. Her husband Howard was on a trip to England to visit his family and Jane's parents were on holiday in Queensland. The Garretts had been worried about leaving Julie, but Jamie had been so good about the separation up until then that Julie had insisted that they go, telling them she was fine. Jane says, 'The other harrowing thing was the policewoman insisted that I ring my elderly parents at ten o'clock at night in their caravan in Queensland to check that she wasn't there. So they had to sit there, in the middle of a caravan park, waiting for the news.'

Patricia Garrett had taken that first call about Julie being missing. Ray Garrett would later tell police that when she was on the phone, 'I saw the colour drain out of her face.'

Earlier, Felicity Holding had rung Jane back to say that Jamie had not arrived as he had promised. Jane immediately thought that Jamie might be fleeing. 'I rang [Marock Place] and I said, "Matthew, did he take his passport? Did he take any money?" . . . Then I rang Gilda and [asked] could she go round and be with Matthew.'

GILDA WENT cold when she heard from Jane. Now she, too, had a chill sense that something dreadful had happened to Julie. 'I thought, "He's strung her up to a tree in the middle of the never-never." If they'd had a swimming pool, I would have reckoned he drowned her in the pool. I knew he'd done something to her.' Gilda put down the phone and looked at her brother, who was visiting that night, and said, 'Oh, God . . .'

Gilda took her teenage son with her to Marock Place in case Jamie turned up again. She was concerned about her own safety.

She found the Ramage house bitterly cold. The heating wasn't working so she rang her brother and asked him to bring around an oil heater. While the boys played guitar in the lounge room, her son showing Matt some new chords, a shivering Gilda walked quietly around the house looking for signs of trouble. She saw two or three samples of granite sitting in the kitchen. In the new family-room extension she found what she thought to be bloodstains on the floor. 'I just felt sick. I didn't know what to do. It's like time passes by while you're on the outside of it watching in. I didn't want to leave Matt. I didn't say anything to the kids. They kept playing. And the phone kept ringing; Jane rang, other people rang. It was like a military operation.'

An agitated Matthew kept telling Gilda to leave. 'I said "No, Matt, Jane is worried about Julie, she's told me to wait here so I'd better do that." And I sat there in Jamie's seat, watching the television. There was an empty wine glass there, Stuart crystal, and there was a red wine bottle with a cork in it on the dining-room table, half-full. And there was a catalogue beside me on the floor that had some erotic videos in it, sitting beside Jamie's chair.'

Matthew made her a cup of tea. About 10.40 pm the cordless phone lying on the coffee table rang. Gilda picked it up and said hello. It was Jamie. 'Oh, is that you, Gilda?'

Gilda answered, 'Yes, it is, and, Jamie, everybody's worried. Where are you?'

Jamie wouldn't say. 'Is Matt there?'

Matthew took the phone. He later said that Jamie had sounded slightly emotional. 'I asked him where he had been and he stuttered a bit and said, "Look, I'm on my way to the police station."

'I asked what had happened with Mum and he said, "That's why I am going to the police station now." He said to me, "Make sure you tell Sam I am going to the police station and tell her I love her lots. I've got to go, but I love you lots."'

Not long afterwards a team of police arrived at the house. The leader, Sergeant Paul O'Connell, shone a light in Gilda's face as he came in the door and said, 'Who are you?' Outside, Gilda could hear the beating rotor of the police helicopter whumping above the house. 'It was like, "Whoa, what's going on?"' she recalls. O'Connell asked Gilda if she had seen anything unusual. She took him to the bloodstains. Realising the house might be a crime scene, O'Connell asked Matt and Gilda to sit at the dining-room table and not touch anything. He began firing questions at Matthew.

Julie's sister, her lover, her best friend and her boss – all people who knew something of the truth about that marriage – had circled the wagons. Now, they waited. They would not wait long.

AFTER LEAVING Marock Place at about 8.15 pm – 'I love you lots, I'll see you soon,' he told Matthew – Jamie phoned a family friend, criminal barrister Dyson Hore-Lacy, SC, and arranged to meet him at the Harp Hotel in Kew. There Jamie confessed. A shocked Hore-Lacy told Jamie that he could not advise him because he had also been friends with Julie. As a former parent of Deepdene Primary School, Hore-Lacy also knew several people who would turn out to be witnesses. He told Jamie that he needed independent legal advice and called solicitor Steve Pica. They waited some time for Pica to arrive, and then Pica and Jamie consulted.

It was 11.40 pm before Jamie Stuart Ramage and his newly acquired lawyer walked into the small, mustard-walled reception area of Boroondara Police Station, right across the road from the hotel.

This is the point in a crime story at which high drama gives way to humdrum bureaucracy. Jamie sat down on one of the hard plastic seats in the waiting area and Pica went up to the counter and asked to speak to a sergeant. The duty constable, Jimmy Peios, hunted about but couldn't find one. 'I'm the only person left in the station. You're basically stuck with me,' said Peios bluntly. Pica introduced himself and said he was here with a client who wanted to hand himself in for a homicide. Peios snapped to attention: What was the client's name? Where did he live? Who had he killed? Where was the body? Then Peios went off to call in his seniors before returning to caution Jamie about his rights. It would be a long night at Boroondara.

MATTHEW WAS the first family member to hear the truth confirmed. O'Connell had left the room briefly to consult on his police walkie-talkie. He returned and said, 'Matt, I have to tell you that your mother has passed away.'

Gilda remembers, 'Matthew looked at me, and he looked at Paul, and he put his head down and his hands up, and then he put his hands over his eyes and there were a few uncertain sobs. It was as if he didn't know how to react.' She sighs. 'And you don't react. In fact, I didn't cry until some time later. Thursday night was probably the first I'd cried.'

Not that Matthew had much chance to cry. The policeman gave him only a couple of minutes. He knew it was difficult, he told the boy, but he needed to know a few things now. The questioning began in earnest.

Gilda rang Jane and said, 'The police are here. It's Julie.'

Jane knew instantly. 'He's killed her.'

Gilda said, 'Yes.'

'Where is he?' asked Jane.

'He's on his way to the police station.'

Jane's first thought was for Samantha. She asked, 'Ohhh, will you tell Sam, or will I?'

Recalls Gilda, 'I just thought, "Oh God". I got a bit weak at the knees, even though I was sitting down. I said, "I think you should tell her, Jane."'

JANE HAD many hearts to break that night. She says she could feel her father age over the phone when she called him in Queensland to tell him the news. 'Oh no, oh no, our Julie,' he said brokenly. Then Jane phoned Samantha at Felicity Holding's house. Samantha, all of fifteen years old and her mother's darling, was told that her mother was dead, and that her father had killed her.

Laurence was in the car with a friend, driving home after searching for Julie, when the mobile phone rang. 'My world collapsed.'

Jane says she had not needed to hear about Jamie's confession to know that the worst was true. 'Once he turned himself in to police, I knew she was dead. I knew that she'd been very hurt or she was really dead, so later, hearing it wasn't actually a shock. Once I knew she hadn't come home – I knew on and off for years that he was potentially dangerous.'

What Jane hadn't known, and was to bitterly regret not having known, was that the riskiest time for any woman in an abusive relationship is when she tries to leave her partner. That is when she is most likely to be killed or badly beaten. Frightened women who have tiptoed around the anger of controlling men for years know this instinctively. The rest of the world does not. That's why the most common question about such marriages is, *Why doesn't she leave?*

We so rarely ask the real question: *Why does he do it?*

GILDA'S FAMILY doubled overnight. She and Jane had decided that the children should be together. Before Gilda could leave Marock Place, she sat in a police car with Matthew while he was questioned. She felt trapped there. 'It went on and on and on. I tried to open the car door and get out but there was a lock so you couldn't escape. And I didn't like that at all.' She insisted that Matthew needed to find a place to sleep. Gilda took Matthew back to her house, and at 1 am Felicity Holding and her husband arrived to drop off Samantha and the family poodle. Samantha strode in silently and went straight to the bedroom of Gilda's daughter at the back of the house. 'They sat on the bed and cried together for the next two hours.'

A friend of Gilda's arrived and they brought out mattresses for Matthew and Samantha, but there was to be no sleep for anyone that night. At 2.45 am the phone rang again. Police wanted Matthew to come to the station to make a statement. 'Does he really need to?' asked Gilda. Yes, he really needed to.

Gilda had one more question for O'Connell. She had an almost childlike longing to be told it was all a bad dream, or a terrible mistake. 'I said to him, "You're not going to change your mind about this, are you?" He said, "About what?"

'I said, "About Julie being dead? That she will turn up alive?"

'He said, "No. Sorry. We can't change our minds."'

GILDA TOOK Matthew to the station. He was in shock and struggled to answer questions. Gilda asked the sergeant if Matthew could have time to compose himself and Matthew asked Gilda what he should say. 'I said that he should talk about his family and family life. He didn't need to highlight the bad things but he needed to be honest. He could talk about what he knew and felt about his parents and must tell precisely about recent events as he knew them. And I felt compelled to say, "Nothing will bring Julie back."

He seemed to be somewhere distant. 'He couldn't remember his mum's middle name or his dad's middle name. He couldn't remember their birthdays. He couldn't remember his sister's middle name. He couldn't remember her birthday. I had to remind him of all these things. The inside of his head was a jumble.'

Back at Gilda's house, Samantha came out of the bedroom and sat with Gilda's friend. She said that on Saturday night, she had climbed into bed with Jamie and cuddled him because he was upset and crying over the fact that Julie had left him. Jamie had told his daughter that he loved her. Samantha sobbed, 'And this is what he does to me!'

Samantha, says Gilda, 'Cried and cried and cried a river.'

INVESTIGATION

CONSTABLE PEIOS took Jamie Ramage and Steve Pica to an interview room. Jamie removed his keys from his jeans and said, 'These are the keys to the car I used. It's a green Jag.' He told Peios he had driven to the station separately from Pica and that he had parked the car 100 yards away in Harp Road. Peios patted him down to ensure that he was not carrying anything with which he could hurt himself or others. Jamie emptied out of his pockets a Victorian driver's licence and several coins. He accepted Peios's offer of a cup of water.

The first 'on-call crew' for the homicide squad was already out that night. There had been another killing, a gangland shooting of a drug dealer as he sat in his car. The 1 am phone calls to round up detectives for Jamie Ramage therefore went to the second on-call crew. Its most senior member was Detective Senior Sergeant Jeff Maher, a fresh-faced man with an open manner and light brown hair cut youthfully spiky. Detectives on television are always led by gruff autocrats but Melbourne homicide teams are democratic: members take turns at leading investigations, and this night it was the turn of Detective Senior Constable Darren Wiseman, a serious, dark-haired young man with glasses who has a quietly courteous way about him. It was the first time he had led a murder investigation, and he would spend nine months assembling the brief. In the legal process that would follow, Wiseman would be 'the informant' – the person who has gathered the information on which the prosecution, acting for the state, would base its case.

The detectives arrived at Boroondara about 2 am to meet Jamie Ramage. He had offered to take them out to the burial site, which he did not know well enough to direct them to any other way. 'He was very calm,' recalls Wiseman. 'He didn't appear to be ashamed or upset or anything like that. He wasn't shaking; emotionless, I suppose. What struck us most was how businesslike he was. It was like he was engaging in a business deal between us and him. Very quiet; yes and no answers.'

That suited the detectives. They are encouraged not to speak to suspects outside a formal interview for fear anything exchanged then could later damage their case so they, too, kept their remarks to a minimum. Jamie and three detectives went out to the burial site. He travelled handcuffed in the back of the car. Once at the property he took several minutes to find the place; it was 3.45 am, and he was disoriented in the darkness. He quietly pointed out the grave – 'There' – and was immediately led back to the car by Wiseman, who waited with him in silence. The scene had to be protected from 'contamination' by Jamie: he could not be allowed to drop any sign of his presence at this point that could be confused with evidence of his presence earlier, or to meddle with any evidence. The detectives guarded the scene until local police arrived to rope it off. Then they went back to Boroondara and by 5 am Jamie Ramage was in a cell. They suggested he try to get some sleep. He didn't manage it.

The detectives examined his Jaguar and noted fair hair in the boot. They drove to the restaurant and made sure a crime scene was set up around Julie's car, and walked through the house at Marock Place to familiarise themselves with its layout. Wiseman would conduct a videotaped interview with Jamie at police headquarters in St Kilda Road at 11.30 am. The interview itself would run for about 40 minutes but because they took a short break the encounter only finished at 12.55. Again, Wiseman was struck by Jamie's composure. This was only Wiseman's third homicide as a member of the squad but he had attended at many others. Domestic killings usually take little figuring out because the distraught husband confesses instantly. 'A lot of them are remorseful. They will kill their wife, in circumstances similar to what James Ramage told us occurred, but the difference is they won't put her in the boot of the car; they won't take her out in the bush and bury her. They'll ring an ambulance, or they'll ring the police and say, "This has all gone bad. I think my wife's dead. I've killed her."' Jamie, Wiseman concluded, was exceptionally cool and collected.

At first light that day Detective Senior Sergeant Maher returned to the burial site to act as the 'scene controller', working with the forensic science team to gather physical evidence. The police had a confession but they still needed to ensure the process was meticulous; Jamie might retract it, or might be shown to have lied, and corroboration of other kinds would be needed. The team also had to check for any hint that another person had helped Jamie bury his wife. The forensic science team included a photographer and a video-cameraman whose work would later be shown to the jury. They searched the area to check for shoe impressions, tyre impressions, a weapon, anything that might have been dropped. To get to Julie's grave they had to walk 134 metres along a dirt track and then 7 metres to the east of it. All that was visible at first was a pile of bracken, bark, scrub and logs. With closer inspection, they could see that there was broken soil underneath it. A small portion of Julie's navy pants – two dark parallel lines – and part of an arm were exposed. As they dug, they found she was lying in a roundish hole that was half a metre deep and 1.5 metres wide. She had been buried on top of her own black vinyl jacket and a man's navy Ralph Lauren jumper. She was also lying on top of her pale blue jumper, which was twisted around her left hand. There were dark bloodstains in the bottom of the hole.

After being alerted to the existence of a second hole by police at headquarters, where Jamie was being interviewed, the team found it, 8 metres north of the burial site. Underneath dirt and bark at the base of a eucalypt were trousers and a shirt, shoes, a man's watch, a bed-ruffle, two teatowels, a handbag and a piece of blue rope.

The police and scientific squad would put in a long day. They would later work over the house in Marock Place, which had been sealed off as a crime scene at midnight, and would not finish up till 7.30 pm. They found a short-handled shovel with soil on the blade and a further length of blue rope. They found bloodstains on the floor of the garage, near the rear tilt door. Inside, they found small blood droplets on the original polished floorboards in the northwest corner of the family room, and others 2 metres away in front of a wall unit. They collected a red and a green bucket from the laundry and some bloodstained business papers from Jamie's briefcase in the study. They detected smears of blood in both Julie's Mini and Jamie's 1998 Jaguar.

Over the next few days, Wiseman and other police would do three run-throughs of the route between Marock Place and the burial site, including one at the same time of day on a Monday, to confirm that Jamie could have done it all alone in the time. They concluded that he could.

When the scientists at the gravesite were finally ready to let Julie go, her hands were wrapped in brown paper bags to preserve any evidence on her skin or under her nails. A pathologist certified the fact of her death. She was put in a state-contracted undertaker's van and was escorted by police to the city mortuary, where her body was stored in the locked homicide refrigerator to await a post-mortem. Julie Anne Ramage – kind, pretty, busy Julie – was now a piece of evidence.

JULIE'S DEATH had divided her two families: the one that had created her, and the one she created. Matthew and Jane had a legal fight over her funeral, according to a document written by the vicar of

St John's Church in Toorak that was later tendered in court. Matthew wanted it to be at St John's, the Anglican church used by Melbourne's society figures, so that his and his sister's friends could come. Jane had already arranged for the funeral to be held at the picturesque old artists' enclave of Montsalvat in the green-belt outer suburb of Eltham, close to her family and to Julie's horse-riding friends, and had publicised that without consulting Matthew. The outcome was a service at St John's followed by a wake at Montsalvat.

Julie was cremated privately the day after the funeral. Matthew and Gilda were the only ones who chose to view her in an open casket. She looked strangely shrunken, Gilda says, 'like an elf'. Her face looked severe, and the undertakers hadn't quite got her hair right. Julie's hair was not the way Julie would have done it. Matthew, weeping, took a lock of that hair. Gilda snipped one for Samantha.

While arranging the funeral, Matthew had talked to the priest about how he should conduct his future relationship with his father. Wrote Archdeacon Philip Newman, 'He was acutely aware that he had lost not just one parent, but effectively two.'

As for Samantha, in the first few weeks after her mother's death, she had not been able to bring herself to see her father at all. Newman wrote, 'While James understood that, and said he would probably feel the same if he was [her], he was profoundly grateful when she did go to see him.'

THE DAY after the cremation, Gilda arrived home from a trip to the shops to find Matthew and Samantha carting their belongings out of her house. 'Matt said that Dad thought they should go back to the house because they should minimise their living costs. They should be in the house because that's where they lived. That's where they belonged. Samantha didn't say anything.'

Jamie Ramage sent his teenage children back to live alone in the house where he had killed their mother. They would eat their meals in the room stained by her blood. 'Some people don't think there's a problem with that,' Gilda Pekin says, her voice flinty. '"It's just a house; it's a piece of property; life has no emotional content . . ."'

When Gilda called in on them the following day, Samantha was home alone. 'She was once again in that distraught state where it's hard to get a word out.' Gilda draws a great sobbing breath to demonstrate. 'Where the person is overwhelmed. She was like that.'

For Julie's family and friends, the children's return to the house so soon after the killing was yet more proof of Jamie's domineering, unfeeling nature. It could also be that he was moving into some of the psychological defences used by abusive men, who routinely deny or minimise the seriousness of their actions. In Jamie's case, this would be summed up by his catchphrase, 'I just lost it'. Daddy's murderous attack upon Mummy had been a temporary loss of control, not the stuff of his children's nightmares.

The return of the children to the house might also have been Jamie's way of pulling down the blinds to stop friends and neighbours peeking in on the situation. He reportedly told Matthew after the killing: 'Let's try to keep this in the family.'

OVER THE next few months, the homicide team would often talk about what had happened with the Ramages. They had uncovered lots of stories about Jamie's controlling behaviour and some history of violence. Maher recalls, 'It had become apparent to us that he was a fairly dominant sort of personality. He wanted to dominate his wife; she was choked by his control of her.' Says Wiseman, 'A lot of people rang with a lot of information that we didn't take as statements because it was the same theme over and over again. It appeared to us that it was very much a crime of possession. It was teenage immature thinking: "If I can't have you, no one else can."'

The police thought they had a strong case for murder. They had not counted on Philip Dunn, QC.

Part Three

JUSTICE?

COUNSEL FOR THE DEFENCE

IF MELBOURNE has a Horace Rumpole, it is Philip Dunn, Queen's Counsel. He is portly, florid and genial. He wears the kind of rounded spectacles that suit the wig and gown. A lover of fine wine and wicked anecdotes, he has a big personality and a deep, theatrical voice that he projects in court with an actor's confidence. When sympathy is his goal, his voice drops. It becomes gentle, almost caressing, in its persuasiveness. He pauses after each point to allow emotion to well up in the hearts of his listeners. He is as sentimental as a greeting card. He is a different man when his task is to wear down a witness. Then, he thunders to engender outrage in his listeners. He worries at the hapless creature in the witness box like a dog with a rat. Dunn himself uses a different analogy to describe what he does. His is the blokey metaphor of one who sees himself as playing a game, albeit one with serious stakes. He calls an aggressive cross-examination 'giving 'em the hip and shoulder' and swings his upper body hard and sharp to the right to show what that means. A courtroom, he says, is like a soccer field. And he is known as one of the game's hard men. He has taken on many difficult cases where he has been the defender of the nigh-indefensible.

It is Dunn's policy not to get close to his clients. He finds some objectionable: 'Amoral, dishonest or psychotic.' Even when they are not, he likes to keep his distance. 'If you like your client, or you dislike your client, that can impact on how you handle the case. I'm lucky. As a silk, by and large, you get the junior to deal with the client. I deal with the case.' Even so, he is not immune to the anxieties of those for whom he works, and there is a sense that he does rely a little on his sympathy for their troubles to keep himself motivated. 'There's nothing quite as sobering as someone reaching over and saying, "Is my husband going to get off this?" And you say, "Well, I hope so." And she says, "But hang on, we've mortgaged our house to pay your legal fees. And if my husband doesn't get off we're going to lose the house. Where will the children and I live?" And then somebody says, "We're due to go to court in three minutes now . . ."' Whether the sympathy ever extends to discounting those fees is his secret. In all our discussions, over several meetings, the only question Philip Dunn ever ducked was how much a top silk charges. 'Gee, I don't know. I'll ask one,' he chortled. 'I would imagine they'd be quite expensive, wouldn't they?'

Out of hours, Dunn has the expansive bonhomie of a publican. On a short lunchtime walk through the legal quarter of the city he manages to hail with gusto three barristers, two judges and a Crown prosecutor. He greets a couple of colleagues with 'Two such *learn*ed gentlemen!' and responds to polite inquiries about his health in hearty superlatives: 'Mate, I'm unbe*liev*ably well!' Again like Rumpole, he often quotes Shakespeare. His favourite play is *Julius Caesar*, 'Because of the frailty of men, and "There is a tide in the affairs of men which, taken at the flood, leads on to better things,"' he says. It is a perfect line for a defence counsel, encapsulating as it does the two factors on which he often relies to whip up sympathy in court: human weakness, and the role of fate in a client's undoing. And, like old Horace, Dunn has given his wife a soubriquet. It is fonder and sexier than 'She Who Must Be Obeyed' but it still manages, with its hint of flammability, to take a sly dig at the inevitable power games between husband and wife. It is 'The Redhead'.

DUNN'S 'CHAMBERS' – like so much of the law, it is a term stuck in the 19th century – are in Lonsdale Street, a short walk from the Supreme Court. It is a modern airy office lined with law books and his collection of antique clocks. This is where Dunn was briefed on Ramage the day after Jamie's confession.

Solicitor Steve Pica had returned home in the early hours of that morning pondering Jamie's plight. Jamie had won the first battle: he had convinced his solicitor of his sincerity. Pica says, 'He impressed me as a fundamentally decent man who had snapped. It was blatantly apparent that he dearly loved his wife and that the act of taking her life was unpremeditated and, in fact, contrary to everything that he had done in the past six weeks to save his marriage.' Pica concluded that it would be difficult for Jamie to do justice to his case when confronted by police and video cameras and courtrooms: 'I knew that the genuine emotions and remorse that he displayed on that evening when he first disclosed that he had killed his wife would never be replicated.' Pica chose Philip Dunn because he believed this would be a trial in which the final address to the jury would be crucial. He hoped that Dunn would be able to explain to a jury why Jamie Ramage did what he did. 'Phil is known as a jury barrister,' Pica says. 'He has amazing jury appeal. And I thought this case had Phil Dunn written all over it.'

These two men were no strangers to forensic family dysfunction. Pica had worked for Matthew Wales-King, the son who had killed his wealthy mother and stepfather in what would become known to the tabloids as The Society Murders. Dunn had acted for Matthew Wales-King's wife, Maritza, who had first confessed her knowledge of her husband's crimes in a dramatic scene in Dunn's chambers. Dunn has appeared in many of Australia's high-profile criminal trials including those of politician Carmen Lawrence, footballer Gary Ablett and the businessmen Brian Quinn and Alan Bond.

It is not surprising, then, that Dunn initially thought the Ramage case was 'just another domestic murder'. He read the brief quickly because Jamie was offering to plead guilty to manslaughter. Before Dunn made the decision about the plea, he had Jamie examined by senior forensic psychiatrist Dr Lester Walton: 'We didn't want to be offering him up on manslaughter if he was psychiatrically ill.' His second piece of advice to Pica was that they should stay away from the defence of provocation and argue instead 'lack of intent': that Jamie had not meant to kill or to really seriously injure Julie. Dunn dislikes provocation – the defence that the dead person said or did something that triggered the killer to lose control and lash out – because it lets in evidence about the relationship between the killer and the victim. 'You don't want that because it's always shitty. It's always hearsay; it's always "Auntie Nellie says". What the victim of the marriage tells her girlfriends about her relationship with her partner . . . women will always, in my experience – I'm not saying this in a gender-biased way – the women will always leap on board and then they read into it, everything. The husband becomes the worst thing since Genghis Khan, and he probably is, but even so . . .'

In the end, Dunn did offer the Office of Public Prosecutions (OPP) a plea of guilty to the lesser charge of manslaughter. This would have meant no trial and almost no publicity. It would have been a certainty, he thinks, had Jamie not buried Julie, and had Jane Ashton and the Garretts not 'gone so hard'. The Ramage children backed the move. Says Dunn, 'The children wrote to the OPP and said, in the case of Samantha, "I'm doing my Year 11 exams", and Matthew, "I'm doing my university exams, I don't really want to have this trial. Would the Crown consider a plea to manslaughter? Our father will plead guilty to that." The prosecutor would have met with the [Garrett] family; whatever attitude the Crown would take in this, they would always talk to the relatives. But in this case the relatives were opposed very strongly to the plea.'

Jane Ashton and her parents wanted Jamie jailed for murder. Inside and outside this family, the battle lines were drawn.

ASK DUNN what makes a good advocate and he offers the textbook answer: 'He must be fearless and prepared.' Much of his preparation is done at home. Dunn has a study in his inner-city bayside house but rarely uses it. Instead he likes to spread his papers out on his French-farmhouse kitchen table, like a schoolboy doing his homework. Once The Redhead absents herself after dinner, he settles down and thinks. It is here that he develops what he calls his 'RAT' – a Rational Alternative Theory to the one that the prosecution will argue against his client. What other, kinder explanation would cover the facts laid out in the police brief? Dunn had initially studied law only because it was his father's dream for him. He had wanted to teach history, which captured his imagination. In a way he takes the historian's approach: trying to provide a differing perspective, another thesis, on the significance of past events. He is sharply pragmatic. All barristers know that it is their duty – not just their job, but their *duty* – to do the best they can for their clients. As a trial lawyer, Dunn sees it as part of that duty to use the existing law to best advantage. He doesn't tie himself up in knots over whether that law is right or wrong. He leaves critique to the academics.

It did not take him long to work out his theory for Ramage. Dunn decided it would require him to use the defence of provocation after all, as well as the defence of lack of intent. Provocation is a 'partial' defence that can reduce a charge of murder to manslaughter. For a jury to accept a defence of provocation, it must believe that there is strong evidence of provocative conduct by the person who was killed; that the accused must have lost self-control because of that provocative conduct; and that the same provocation would have made an ordinary person lose control and form an intention to cause grievous bodily harm or death. There would be two prongs to Dunn's strategy. Firstly, he would make good use of five counsellors from whom Jamie had sought help after Julie left him. He recalls,

'Because we would never get this opportunity again, where you get five therapists,' – he counts on his fingers with delight – 'one two three four FIVE!'

What's the significance of that?

Dunn smiles at the sweetness of the memory – it had been such a delicious prospect – and recalls what he told Steve Pica: '"They will all," I said confidently, "*all* be bleeding hearts, and we'll get what we want from them."'

Dunn also planned to take the main witnesses for the prosecution, particularly Julie's sister, Jane, and turn their evidence to his advantage. He did not expect that to be difficult either. 'They didn't even see it coming,' he says with satisfaction.

But there was something Dunn had not seen coming: a growing tide of outrage over the killing of Julie Ramage. It was fuelled by her friends and her sister – savvy, articulate women who knew how to work the system and who had no intention of allowing the courts or the media to be in any ignorance of how they saw the justice of the case. The first meeting – a clarion call to women who knew Julie – was held at Christine Howgate's house. They decided to draw up a roster of women to attend the committal hearing. The committal is a preliminary hearing that decides whether there is enough evidence to send the case to the Supreme Court for trial. The 30 or so women decided against a proposal to wear black scarves as a sign of solidarity. 'It's not a football game,' said Kate Clark, who was concerned that due process be respected. But the women would be silent witnesses at the committal of Jamie Ramage, testimony at least to the fact that Julie was loved and that her death deserved redress. Christine had been warned by friends who worked with domestic violence that any legal case would see Julie 'convicted' of provoking Jamie to kill her. Christine says, 'I believed Julie deserved a presence. I really thought that if the jury could look down and see lots of women there who were Julie's age, who wore clothes like Julie, who had jobs like Julie, who were Julie's friends, they would think, "She can't have been that bad."'

It was when he saw the gallery of women at the committal that it hit Dunn: 'This was not "just another case" at all.'

Then, in the months between the committal and the trial, Dunn began to hear more snippets about female anger turning to activism. He says now, 'Other people suddenly become aware that you are doing the case, and they say, "You're doing the Ramage case; my wife has just had a chain email on provocation." I had a few of those. Then suddenly it's in the paper, "Philip Dunn appeared for James Ramage," and a colleague will say, "We've got a daughter at Lauriston, and you should hear this." Next thing, it was somebody I knew vaguely, lives out Hurstbridge way [home to Julie's riding club], saying, "You'd better be careful; they're having meetings up there and organising rosters of people to come to court. And you're not the most popular person." And I said, "I'm only doing my job. I'm irrelevant to all of this." "Oh, I don't think you are, mate. They don't like you." And on and on it went. Melbourne's only a village, in its own way.'

Dunn realised that this would be like the Wales-King case. He would have to develop a strategy to manage the publicity.

PEOPLE LIKE US

IT WAS the 'Melbourne is a village' factor that first drew *The Age* newspaper into the story. One of the women at Christine Howgate's meeting is the wife of an *Age* journalist. The journalist passed on to an *Age* editor a moving account of Julie's life and death that Christine had written.

Christine Howgate is a property consultant who lives in a new mansion with the grace of an old one in the suburb to which the Ramages aspired, Canterbury. She is small, blonde, bright and stubborn in pursuit of a goal. She has the well-muscled schoolgirl figure of one who has always exercised, and she dresses unostentatiously but with care, in clothes that have soft colours and clean cuts. She also has deep blue eyes and a direct gaze that still burns with indignation over the fate of her friend. She lights up with it even now. She will not let it go. Shortly after the trial, she sent Philip Dunn a white ribbon for Say No To Violence Against Women Day and suggested he wear it. Christine says she wrote the piece about Julie the day after she saw huge coverage in Melbourne's newspapers about the assassination of a gangland figure. 'Here's this bad guy, a killer, a drug dealer; he gets shot and it's all over the papers, like anyone cares! And there is no publicity for these other cases.' But Christine's article could not be published at that time because Jamie Ramage had been charged; the newspaper would be guilty of contempt of court if it canvassed opinions on the case before a jury had reached its decision. This is why there is rarely media publicity over domestic killings. Police usually catch and charge the partner quickly and there can be no discussion in the media until the trial is over, which might be months or years away.

There is another, shabbier truth about why these cases are silent deaths. They are too commonplace. For a story to make it into print it must have a 'hook' – a reason to run it. Everyday crimes such as 'domestics' don't have glamour or urgency or wider importance. They are not seen to 'resonate'. The initial hook in the Ramage case was their wealth and social class. That made the killing unexpected and turned it into what journalists call a 'man bites dog' story. Their social position also meant that the story would appeal to readers' baser instincts. After all, the continued good health of so many women's magazines is underpinned by envy and *Schadenfreude*, that malicious pleasure in another's misfortunes.

I CAME to be involved on the periphery of this drama when the story was passed on to me by an *Age* editor who asked me to follow Jamie Ramage's trial and write a large feature story at the end of it. Another reporter would cover the day-to-day news reports on the case; I would do the 'wrap'. I had been a newspaper and magazine journalist for 27 years and was just returning to reporting after eighteen months of editing. I had written often on social issues, particularly ones that involved human rights. I was initially attracted to this story because of its human interest: What could have happened between these two people?

But this story would also become a saga about the many other 'people like us' – lawyers, therapists, family and friends – who had to deal with what went wrong between Jamie and Julie Ramage.

THE WOMEN'S Information and Referral Exchange (WIRE) is in a small, unobtrusive building off Little Collins Street in the city. Climbing the stairs, you become aware that you are in a headquarters of 'the resistance'. The building is home to a flotilla of small organisations that look after society's little guys: young people at risk, tenants, the deaf, Somalians in need of welfare. It has offices for the Movement Against Uranium Mining, the Rainbow Alliance and the Victorian Association for Peace Studies. The place is a haven of the leftie social conscience. This is where Julie's death has led Christine Howgate, property developer. As a result of Julie's death, she now works as a part-time volunteer at WIRE's telephone counselling service for women. She has insisted I talk to her boss as part of the background for the story. WIRE's manager, Samiro Douglas, is a brisk, cheerful woman in her fifties with short blonde hair. She seems to run a happy ship: there is unexpectedly lively chatter and laughter among the women arming the telephones to take distress calls. WIRE gets 12,000 calls a year and domestic violence is the most common single reason for them.

Douglas dissects all its forms with the clinical air of an emergency-room physician. She finds the story of the Ramages no surprise. She has long known that 'people like us' are just as likely to be battered as anyone else. There are two common myths about 'DV', as it is called in the trade: that the women are disadvantaged, and that they are helpless. Not so, she says. 'They see themselves as being in a difficult situation, but they don't see themselves as helpless. A lot of these women are employed. The family might have a business, they might be in a high economic bracket, their husbands might be lawyers, police, business managers.' In some ways, wealth makes it more difficult. 'Money is used as one of the tactics of abuse for women who are in a better financial situation, or whose family is; they have a lot more to lose. That money can be tied up in trusts, in business; they might have no access to money themselves, independently, although they've got the two new cars and an affluent-looking house and kids in private schools.' She cites the case of one man who took his wife's pay every week. He even tried to negotiate with her employer to have her salary deposited in his own bank account.

How do women get into this? How do they let it happen, really, in this day and age? Slowly, slowly, and unsuspectingly, is the answer. Relationships never begin with abuse, says Douglas. 'In the early days, if you got hit or called a bitch, you wouldn't go on with it. Relationships begin with "I love you", and every single woman is vulnerable to "I love you". I don't know how many times I've heard how loving he was, how special she felt, how he made her feel really beautiful. Which one of us isn't going to be seduced by that?'

But the bubble bursts. 'At a certain point, it changes to power and control. "I love you so much I don't want you spending time with your friends; I want you to spend time just with me. I don't want you to dress like that for anybody else; just dress like that for me. I don't want anybody else looking at you." By the time he actually hits her, she's deeply emotionally involved. And then it's hard; we always want to give our partners chances.'

The first physical blow often comes at a turning point in the relationship where he realises he's 'got her': the wedding night, the honeymoon, the first pregnancy. Douglas says, 'I know women who have been hit on their wedding night and told, "Things are different now." Then he might apologise and cry and say he won't do it again. But the memory that he's hit her returns every time tension builds.' That can be enough to keep the woman in line; she becomes biddable because she fears what he might do if angered. 'He might smash things around the house and not lay a hand on her. Or he might be a big bloke who says, "Boy, you're really lucky I don't hit you. I love you, and I don't. But I could!" And that sets up a degree of fear and control. Women who are hit often blame themselves for it because they have become accustomed to being blamed for everything,' she says.

'Reality checks' become hard for such women. A controlling man usually isolates the woman from her family. He might publicly put her down when her relatives come to visit or abuse them to her after they leave. The woman begins to feel that the only way she can protect herself and her family from his aggression is to stay away from them. She feels particularly alone if her husband has any standing in society. Protective of his position, she is reluctant to confide in others about how his behaviour at home is so different to his public face. It is hard for her to hold on to her own sense of reality in the face of his insistence that everything would be all right if only she got on top of her 'job' to be a good wife and mother.

Douglas says the only escape for some women with possessive partners is to change their names and flee the state; even then, they can spend years looking over their shoulders. In extreme cases the man never gets his head around the fact that she has left and spends years pursuing her.

More commonly, deserted men resort to manipulating their children. This can mean trying to recruit them as aides in their campaign to get their wife back. 'I have known of cases where children on access visits to their father are made to call their mother twenty times: "Phone your mother up and see what she's doing." Often, the man will cry and tell them, "I am so sad, I am so lonely, and this is all your mother's fault. Ask your mother to take me back." And then the children become incredibly confused; they love both their parents. And the other way he can use the children is that he can be verbally abusive of the mother, continuing to say that she's stupid and useless and they shouldn't be taking notice of her. And then they start to question their mother and lose respect for her.' He has probably already spent years telling her she's stupid, she's useless, no one else would ever want her. And, of course, abusive behaviour does not stop at the bedroom door.

Traipsing back down the worn vinyl stairs, I found myself thinking about a line from a Bette Midler movie, *The Rose*. Midler, who plays a troubled rock star, leads into the song *When a Man Loves a Woman* with a satiric monologue about how a woman's longing for love gives her nothing but grief. She cries out to the audience, 'Don't you *lerv* to be in lerv?'

TRIAL WITHOUT JURY

Day One
Monday 4 October 2004

VICTORIA'S SUPREME Court building is just what the romantic might wish. From the outside, it is a grand neo-classic building with a dome, its sandstone now aged and stained by traffic fumes. Inside, its echoing passages are lined with bluestone, its doors are large and carved and its ornate ceilings are high and proud, the creations of a generation that believed in the majesty of the law. But those who work in it know its faults – the temperatures swing between hot and cold, the acoustics are tricky, and the courtrooms are too small for the media packs that follow the glitzier cases.

Court Twelve, which has been assigned to the Ramage case, has a soaring ceiling and cream walls with rosettes and curlicues picked out in pastel pink and blue and trimmed with gilt. Its deep-red carpet with ragged seams speaks of rather a faded grandeur but its carved timber structures have survived the encroachments of time. They make clear the standing of all participants: highest is the judge's bench, with its huge timber canopy; at a lower level is the jurors' box, with two rows of seating; and directly opposite the jurors' box is the witness stand, of which the jurors will have the best view in the house. The bar table where the lawyers sit is at ground level in front of the bench. Even when standing, they will have to look up at the judge and the jury. A previous trial in this court had several defendants, so the standard dock – a box like the witness stand – was removed from the back wall of Court Twelve and replaced by a pew. Here, at the same low level as members of the community but set apart from them, is Jamie Ramage.

He sits in the centre of the pew with his legs apart and his hands clasped between them. The ends of his bench are roped off with the kind of red cord used for banking queues and he is flanked by two prison guards who sit either side of the pew in separate chairs, their arms folded. Jamie is wearing a navy suit with a white shirt and a striped tie and has a blue A4 exercise book and a pen ready beside him. He has a face like an Easter Island statue: long, lugubrious, chiselled, frozen. Even his head has a rectangular shape. His mouth pouts. It is hard to know whether this is due to his features or his temperament, or merely to his mood today. He has hazel eyes and his neatly cut brown hair is thick and springy on top. He is lean and tanned from work in the prison garden; small pouches under his eyes are the only sign of age (he is now 45). He stares down at the carpet, closed off from the rest of the room. This is how he will spend most of the trial, his mien remote, as if he were encased in glass. 'In the zone', a newspaper artist who sketched him would call it. He wears no wedding ring.

I study the clasped hands he is staring down at and realise his fairytale doom. For the rest of his life he must carry around the weapons he used to kill his wife. Every time he eats, or drives, or caresses a woman – or hugs one of his children – he will be doing it with the hands that squeezed the life out of Julie. There can be no forgetting.

THE COURTROOM is largely empty except for legal figures. All witnesses are forbidden to attend at this stage, and journalists and other observers rarely turn up to the first days of a Supreme Court case because it consists of legal argument that cannot be reported publicly until after the trial. This is the 'voir dire', where the lawyers debate which evidence should and should not be aired. The argument is dry and difficult for an outsider to follow because it is littered with references to legal precedents, and the lawyers and the judge are working from the police brief, a collection of statements by witnesses that the observer does not have. But this is where you get a glimmer of the story that the jury will possibly *not* be allowed to hear. Jurors are meant to be the deciders of the facts but lawyers and judges decide which facts they are allowed to know. To the layperson, it can look uncomfortably like the way parents decide what their children are capable of understanding. Jurors are not even permitted to hear that there has been protracted argument over the admissibility of evidence. Think of it as a trade secret.

Christine Howgate, who is not going to be a witness, arrives just as proceedings begin and slips on to the bench beside me. The court rises for Justice Robert Osborn. His robes are fire-engine red with a white jabot and a cummerbund-like sash around the waist. He looks to be in his fifties, with large steel-rimmed glasses, a beaky nose and thin lips. He has a habit of rubbing his wig backwards and forwards on his head as if to scratch an itch, or perhaps as an aid to cogitation. He would turn out to be a gentlemanly judge, dry and courtly in his manner, civil in his exchanges with counsel and meticulous in his attention to proceedings. At no point did he raise his voice; if he disapproved of a course of questioning or argument, he would merely make a laconic remark with an air of hauteur that made clear his distaste.

Julian Leckie, Senior Counsel, is the Crown prosecutor, a lean, husky-voiced man who is almost unfailingly earnest when on his feet at the bar table but who has a quiet sense of humour when off-duty. Only two women are a formal part of this process: the judge's associate and Leckie's briefing solicitor. They are both young, dark and pretty. Their work is done behind the scenes. In court, they are silent handmaidens to the middle-aged men who run this show. Steve Pica sits opposite Dunn.

Dunn's RAT gives him two tasks in the voir dire. Firstly, he must try to demolish prospects of the jury hearing stories about Jamie being abusive to Julie. Secondly, he must fight to keep the right to air as much evidence as possible that paints Julie in a bad light. Your grandmother's advice that 'one should never speak ill of the dead' has no place with the defence in a murder trial.

In his black robe and venerably grey wig Dunn rises to his feet – 'Your honour, is it open for me to start the batting?' – and starts swinging. This is the first public airing of evidence about the nature of the Ramages' marriage, but it is fragmentary and disjointed. His arguments assume a detailed knowledge of the police brief. Trying to see the whole from the parts is like trying to make out an unfinished jigsaw puzzle. Slowly, aspects of Julie's relationship with Jamie emerge. Dunn wants 'out' evidence about previous incidents of violence in the marriage. These are a story about Julie having a black eye (spoken of by two women but not corroborated by her workmates or her children); and accounts of Jamie's alleged sexual abuse of Julie (hearsay evidence, he points out). 'There's *no direct witness* of any act of violence between the husband and the wife in the decade that precedes this incident [the killing],' he says.

From a legal point of view, the problem with hearsay evidence – evidence that witnesses heard from others, rather than saw themselves – is that it comes second-hand. In this case, the court would be relying on someone else's memory and interpretation of what Julie had told them, and it might well be unsubstantiated tittle-tattle. The witness could get it wrong, and it is also possible that Julie might have lied or exaggerated. But in this case, the person who originally made the claims is not available to testify and be cross-examined because she is *dead*. She has been killed by the man the hearsay rule is designed to protect: the accused. The hearsay rule is the dead wife's Catch-22. It makes it difficult to lead evidence of abuse in a marriage. How many men hit their wives in front of an audience? Or put their sex lives on display for others to witness?

But, while Dunn wants to exclude evidence of Jamie's violence, he wants to be able to use evidence of Julie's infidelity. She had two affairs before she left Jamie, and Dunn argues that this is important evidence about her state of mind about the marriage. And, as Dunn would point out often, Julie had lied to Jamie and others in order to conduct the affairs. He also wants the jury to see a particular photo of Julie after her death. The issue of the photograph seems of no real importance, and his formal language obscures his full intent well: 'The defence will be seeking to have at least one frontal photo of the deceased to show the post-mortem lividity indicating that the deceased was in a front-down position for a period of time.' Months later, I would discover another purpose for that photograph.

Dunn objects to other photographs that he thinks are unnecessarily gruesome. As he turns the pages of his spiral-bound book of snapshots, I catch glimpses of some of the images. There is one of a bloodied female face, and another of a nude female torso with a strip of dark pubic hair that has been waxed into a narrow mohawk. It is a sad picture. Julie Ramage has been left no privacy, either of her person or her life.

The judge takes issue with Dunn, and they argue back and forth. In some cases Dunn wants only a word to be forbidden; in others, it is whole paragraphs from witnesses' statements. Christine and I hear teasing fragments. Osborn reads out a passage of evidence in which Julie told a counsellor that Jamie was 'very controlling, possessive, potentially violent and wanted to be with her all the time'. Osborn tells Dunn, who objects to the phrase 'potentially violent', that 'to cut out the words after "controlling" is pretty artificial'.

There is much dancing around evidence that Julie told many people she was frightened that Jamie might hurt or kill her. Dunn wants one witness to be permitted to tell the jury that Julie said she was impressed that Jamie had not done anything hurtful after she left. But, points out the judge, that witness then immediately goes on to say Julie 'thought [Jamie] might have hurt her horse and had been fearful that he would punish her'. Says Osborn, 'Now, it all seems to me to be bound up together. And that occurs immediately after [the witness] says, "James had head-butted Julie while Julie was on the floor and hurt her nose. I gathered this incident had happened early in the marriage."'

So, one of the mysterious 'incidents of violence' was a Liverpool kiss to the mother of his two small children. While she was on the floor. I look over at Jamie. His head and eyes are down and he seems the picture of dejection. The man to whom image was everything is being utterly shamed.

Dunn argues that evidence about the head-butt is 'prejudicial' to Jamie – that it would create unfair bias against him in the minds of the jury. Apparently it is not proper to lead 'propensity' evidence that suggests an accused is a nasty or unpleasant man who might have been likely to commit such a crime. Dunn says the head-butt was so long ago (1991) that it cannot have been a factor in Julie's state of mind at the time of her death.

Dunn also argues that the jury should not hear about the many times Julie told other people that she was frightened that Jamie would become violent over her leaving him. Her initial fears were not relevant, Dunn says, because they had disappeared by the time she died, five weeks later. To prove this, he cites examples of Julie showing a lack of fear during the separation: she invited Jamie to her new place, she drove with him in a car, she lunched with him alone. Evidence of the head-butt would be 'just plain misleading', he tells the judge.

Where Dunn interprets her meetings with Jamie as lack of fear, I sense a concerned woman acting like a mother trying to ease an anxious child into a new situation. It sounded like the way you would get a toddler used to crèche or a prep child used to school. Was Julie trying to wean Jamie off her gradually? If so, was she appeasing him because she was frightened of him?

Wondering about this, I almost miss Dunn's next line: '. . . And to lead evidence of the sexual contact . . . *that he treated her like a piece of meat when they were intimate* is not useful to anything, in my submission'. He sails on in his address, oblivious to the effect of his words on his lay audience. Christine and I glance wide-eyed at each other and then over at Jamie. We catch him shooting us a searching look, his eyebrows raised. The three of us know this could be dynamite. What female juror would forgive this?

But it is 'not useful'. The evidence that he treated her like a piece of meat in bed is also hearsay and will be dismissed. What went on at the level of deepest contact between them does not qualify as relationship evidence. Most of his other abuses of her will not qualify as evidence either. I feel like Captain James T. Kirk watching a debate between analytical, unfeeling Vulcans. The law seems alien, its cold logic repugnant.

AFTER THE lunch break, Dunn's objections continue. Reports that Julie discussed whether to take out a restraining order against Jamie 'may be misinterpreted in some way as being that she was toying with the idea that she was concerned as to her own physical safety . . . the real complaint here is that she's concerned he may be going to injure the horse'. Evidence of Jamie's drinking and bad temper could 'paint the accused in an unsympathetic and bad light and deflect the jury from their task'. Stories of black eyes and other injuries from Julie's best friend, Gilda Pekin, are not corroborated by anyone else, he argues.

Dunn objects to other stories Gilda Pekin told the police about Jamie's domineering ways. He reads from Gilda's statement about Julie buying a dress for her thirtieth birthday party: 'She purchased a black dress to wear. Jamie didn't like the dress. He thought it was too revealing. He took the dress back. He would go to the hairdresser and describe what to do with her hair. She wasn't allowed to have her own opinion . . .'

Julie's life was like this in Balwyn? In Australia, in 2005? The petty, all-pervasive control Gilda is describing sounds medieval, the sort of marital regime popularly supposed to be the fate of women wearing chadors, not women with children at Scotch and Lauriston. It sounds like Jamie Ramage felt that he *owned* his wife; he supervised her grooming the way he would keep an eye on the mechanic servicing his Jag.

Julie Ramage cannot speak for herself, but the law that is supposed to offer her justice does not seem to allow for her experience of life. Every woman knows that a best friend is a repository of secrets that are not shared with others. Of course Gilda Pekin would know things that could not be corroborated – especially painful, shameful, private things. Women's talk is like that; female friends are emotionally intimate in a way that men perhaps are not. But it seems that under our law, as under sharia, one woman's word is not enough.

Dunn challenges further evidence in Gilda Pekin's statement to police. He quotes from it: '"[Julie] told me she wasn't interested in sex but he forced her every morning . . . I told her that it was rape. She replied that she knew this."' Says Dunn, 'What it's really saying is the accused man is a rapist, and as such, it's objected to.' Christine Howgate has left. I am the only person in the room who jolts at the words 'rape' and 'rapist'. But then I am the only person in the room – apart from the professionally impassive stenographer – who is hearing this for the first time.

DUNN HAS one more crucial piece of evidence to attack today. It is about the row that broke the camel's back; the fight that led Julie to decide that she would leave in the middle of Matthew's VCE year after all. Julie told Gilda Pekin there was a row over Samantha in which Jamie called Julie a 'slut'. Julie was terribly upset afterwards but Jamie insisted on having sex with her anyway.

As he listens to this, Jamie's jaw is working and his eyes blink furiously. It is his strongest expression of emotion all day. Anger? Humiliation? Grief? Then he regains control, and his face freezes again.

His lawyer is arguing that it would be prejudicial and unnecessary to go into this level of detail. Dunn suggests the jury hears only the bare facts: there was an argument, nasty things were said, and Julie decided to leave.

AT THE end of the day, Justice Osborn points out that he will need time to consider. Dunn has so far made 66 objections. Dunn throws him a 'Sorry, your honour'.

If he gets his way, that strong police brief will be as full of holes as a slice of Swiss. Perhaps he won't get his way. Osborn must rule on it yet.

We stand and bow to the judge. There was such a contrast between the Ramages' outwardly perfect lives and what Julie told her friends about their private world. It reminds me of another grandmotherly saying: 'Be careful who you envy.'

THE EDITED MARRIAGE

Day Two
Tuesday 5 October 2004

JAMIE RAMAGE has been given a jug of water and a cup. He is taking copious notes today. He sounds like the kind of man who would find enforced passivity hard to take, and here his fate is in the hands of strangers. Maybe he writes furiously as his only way to have input into the proceedings. No doubt his lawyers will get to hear the content later. Right now, Dunn launches into a speech about the rules of evidence with regard to relationships.

It is clear from the previous day's argument that the Ramages had a complicated marriage. And that Julie – light-hearted, easygoing, can't-do-enough-for-you Julie – was more complicated than she seemed, too. Dunn is about to use the way she once lied to illustrate why much of the evidence of her friends should be found inadmissible.

This is Dunn's argument. This court case would formally discuss two affairs that Julie had with married men. The first lover, a family friend she met through her children's attendance at Deepdene Primary School, would be named only. The second lover would testify but for legal reasons his real name cannot be published. Let's call him 'Adam'. Now, once, when Julie was in a car with Adam, her mobile phone accidentally got switched on. The stuff of French farce, *n'est-ce pas*? Anxious that Jamie might have heard them talking, she decided that if he asked her about an 'Adam', she would tell him that she had been talking to the boyfriend of one of her workmates. The workmate's boyfriend had the same first name as 'Adam'. Julie then told the workmate that Jamie was paranoid and had developed a suspicion that Julie was having an affair with her boyfriend. The workmate was unaware of Julie's secret agenda and innocently reported this tale of Jamie's 'paranoia' to police after Julie died as evidence of Jamie's suspicious, controlling nature.

'So the danger of the hearsay is this,' says Dunn. 'That it not only cannot be tested, but that Mrs Ramage may say something, as she did in this case to her workmate, which is untrue. That is, "My husband thinks I'm having an affair with your boyfriend [Adam]," so the workmate then says, "Well, hold on, this Ramage he's a very odd bloke, he's spying on his wife and possessive."' It's an example of how hearsay can completely distort the thinking of a witness, Dunn says.

It is a fair point. Were there other times that Julie had made Jamie out to be worse than he was in order to protect herself or to justify her own behaviour?

How did the emotional currents run in this marriage? Maybe Jamie suspected Julie's affairs, and this was part of the reason he was so insistent about sex. Or could it have been the other way around – that robotic sex with a domineering Jamie had driven Julie into the arms of other men? Perhaps her sexual straying was rebellious self-preservation, her way of keeping alive and free one precious part of herself that Jamie would not be allowed to control. Maybe there was also a tinge of vengefulness: 'Cop this, you bastard!' Or maybe she just hungered for reassurance and affection. Everyone wants a little sugar in their bowl, and it sounds like there was little sweetness with Jamie.

But whatever else she might have been, Julie Ramage was not a woman's woman, in this sense: the first affair spoken of was with a family friend whose wife Julie also knew. Julie had meals with this woman, keeping up the façade of friendship while bedding her husband.

Not that any of that warrants a death sentence.

HER WORKMATES had been worried for Julie. Joanne McLean was the national manager of Eco-d. Dunn objects to McLean saying, '[Julie] was frightened to leave. I felt that if she left Jamie she would be in a lot of danger. I would tell her that he would kill her.' Dunn quotes Julie's boss, Eco-d owner Felicity Holding, as saying, 'I told her to be very careful because he's possessive. I knew this because she told me she had to change her nail polish if he didn't like it . . . I asked her if she was going to get an intervention order. I told her to be really careful because he loved her in a really possessive way and he could kill a dog, kill a horse or kill her. I was frightened for her.' Irrelevant, misleading and prejudicial, says Dunn.

Even if it was prophetic.

Dunn also objects to a comment Julie made to Anthony Brady, Jamie's business partner, when he told her he was shocked to hear about the separation. Julie said simply, 'No one knows what went on behind closed doors.'

THE RAMAGES had gone to see a psychiatrist after that head-butt in 1991. He conducted a marriage counselling assessment on 3 May that same year. Dunn quotes from the psychiatrist: '"They had come to see me as a result of the incident of violence in the marriage. Jamie detailed the incident started late at night when they were in bed. They argued that Jamie was too involved in business and wasn't placing enough importance on Julie's needs. Jamie had grabbed her and shook her and James said Julie had become hysterical. Julie said James was like her father and too involved in business," and so on. Apparently in the course of that was when the incident occurred with the head-butting.'

Dunn goes on to say, 'And significantly, your honour, just in passing, of course, 1991 is not terribly long after the recession we had to have and Mr Ramage is in business with Mr Brady in 1991 and there are other references to the business nearly going bankrupt at that time. Not that that is ever an excuse for anything, but it perhaps puts it in context.'

HERE IS some more context. Long after the trial is over, I learn more about that visit to a psychiatrist. At that stage the Ramages had been married for eleven years and one of the children had recently had serious surgery (so Julie, too, would have been under great stress). Julie was deeply frightened by the head-butt incident and it was at her insistence that they sought counselling over it. That decision to use therapy to sort out their problems did not last long. They cancelled subsequent appointments.

Here was another point at which this story could have taken a different turn. Would the marriage have lasted or at least ended differently if they had been able to work on it then? If he had been able to take responsibility for what he had done, and she had been able to forgive him? *If only . . .*

This seems to be the last time Julie found the strength to insist they needed help. She had managed to drag Jamie into therapy but she had not managed to keep him there. Like the mythic Sisyphus, whom the gods condemned forever to a hopeless task, she had pushed the boulder up the hill only to have it roll back down again. Leaving Jamie must have seemed too hard back then. She had two small children. Julie felt stuck with her boulder.

IT IS only part-way through the morning but the courtroom is starting to feel claustrophobic. It's not the air but what is floating in it. These people and their tortured relationship – it's like *Days of Our Lives* or *Oprah*. There is something suffocating about the intensity of their unhappiness and the multiplicity of characters and the labyrinthine plot. The lawyers seem impervious to it. They are operating at a different level, focused on the logic of their legal points.

Dunn is back to Julie's two lovers. He argues that they are important because the fact that she had affairs suggests that she did find her sex life with Jamie 'unsatisfactory'. This, in turn, makes it more likely that she did say what Jamie claims she said just before he killed her: that sex with him repulsed her. Then, Dunn slips in a claim that Jamie did not make in his 'record of interview' when he was interviewed by police: 'My instructions are that she said to him in the course of the conversation, "There have been others. There have been others."'

His honour says, 'Well . . .'

Leckie interjects instantly: 'That's not evidence!'

It goes no further. But Dunn has managed to let the judge know that Julie might have had affairs other than those mentioned in evidence, and that Jamie has claimed she hurled news of them at him in that last, fatal exchange.

WE ARE now at 99 objections and Dunn rests from his labours. Julian Leckie rises to try and claw back some ground. A thoughtful man, he folds his arms with his hands in the sleeves of his robe like a monk; it fits with his ascetic manner. He is quieter in his delivery than Dunn, but Leckie is a tenacious lawyer and a man with a strong sense of fairness. Fairness is also a professional obligation for a prosecutor in a way that it is not for a defence lawyer. The prosecution must ensure that all relevant evidence is put to the court, even if that evidence runs against its own argument. A defence lawyer has no such duty.

Leckie has been liaising with the Garretts and the witnesses for Julie as part of his preparation, so he has a sense of how much grief this death has caused. And he would have known what to expect from a provocation defence. He launches into an attack of Dunn's efforts to have Julie's last two affairs included in evidence. One affair had finished years earlier and the other had ended by the time she died, he points out. He says Dunn is seeking to air that material purely to create prejudice and sympathy: 'prejudice against the deceased – he wants to blacken her name – and sympathy for a man who has been subjected to this sort of behaviour. That is what it is truly about'. Dunn's assertion that Julie's affairs supported the likelihood that she had spoken to Jamie in the way claimed was 'a very tortured piece of logic'.

So it seems to the onlooker too. But I don't know the law, and Osborn does. He asks Leckie, 'But don't I have to look at it from the highest it can be taken from the point of view of the accused?' This is a principle the Court of Appeal regards as important, he points out. It is Osborn's task to ensure the trial is run according to the existing law so that its finding is not overturned on appeal, which would require a new trial. He and Leckie become absorbed in a discussion of legal precedents. Leckie says, 'Your honour, I suspect my learned friend will want to go to the jury on the basis that his client . . . was really the victim in all this.' Leckie would turn out to be absolutely right.

Leckie argues that the jury should be allowed to see a letter Julie had written to Jamie when she left him, and he puts in an impassioned plea for the evidence about previous violence. The head-butt that left Julie requiring surgery 'is a fairly traumatic and violent episode for a woman to bear from her husband'. He cites another, more recent incident in which Jamie pushed Julie out of bed during an argument. 'She describes the hostility that lies beneath the surface of this relationship by saying the intimidation remained and was demonstrated by [Jamie breaking glasses] . . . To properly understand this woman's state of mind . . . about her husband, one must understand the history of violence which she'd sustained, endured and found ways of dealing with over the years.'

Leckie tells Osborn he wants to be able to ask the jury this question: Given that history of violence and her oft-repeated fear of Jamie, would Julie *ever* have said the things Jamie claimed had provoked him?

Any normal woman, any woman not having to deal with the law, would probably not even get to that point. Her question would be: So what if Julie did say harsh things to him? *What bloody difference should it make?*

THE COURT adjourns for lunch. We have not met before but Dunn wanders over to me and begins to chat, apparently idly. Then he gives me a sideways glance and leans forward confidentially. 'You know, after the committal we had all these people phone us up.' He pauses to see if he has my attention. He has. 'One woman was saying Julie Ramage had had an affair with her husband. A man said she had broken up his marriage. Another woman rang saying Julie was a nymphomaniac.' He shakes his head slowly, his voice sympathetic. 'I don't know what was happening with that woman, but she must have been very unhappy for a very long time.'

I don't know quite what to say to this. 'Yes, I had heard that lawyers play up the sexuality of women killed by their partners' does not seem quite the ticket. Pretending to play along with him, even less so. I am saved by Leckie, who has spotted the approach and decides to run interference. He crosses over to our side of the room and leans back in a bench, his arms spread languidly across its top bar. He chuckles in his most comradely fashion. 'Portraying her like she's a trollop screwing the world,' he says, gently but reprovingly to Dunn. Dunn protests his innocence, also laughing.

Move and countermove; no hard feelings.

On the way back to the office, I think about the 'trollop' defence. This is a line of provocation argument better known in vulgar newspaper parlance (ever a tautology) as 'the dud-root defence' or 'the small-dick defence'. The male court reporter who explained it to me put it this way: Charlene tells her boyfriend Darren that she has been sleeping with Jason because Jason is a better lover. Darren, outraged at the attack on his manhood, kills Charlene. In court, he claims she provoked him to do it. His defence is that he 'lost it' when she told him that Jason was a better lover; when she told him, in effect, that he had a small dick.

In the end, it's all about male pride. And there's another name for that kind of crime: honour killing.

BACK IN court after a sandwich, I glance over at Jamie Ramage and wonder what happens about his lunch; whether he has any choice or whether the petty dictator has now lost all control over the minutiae of his life.

Leckie begins to talk about the way Julie had mentioned the head-butt to two counsellors she saw with Jamie the week before she died. 'The matters which concerned her were active in her mind even days before the assault upon her and are capable of speaking volumes as to whether or not she would venture the sort of conduct and words to her husband in a position where she is alone with him.' This, he says, overcomes Dunn's argument that the head-butt was too 'remote in time' to be relevant.

The judge takes the point. 'It might be said, if one goes to the next paragraph – "Recently she had just been saying whatever, agreeing with James, instead of fighting, which built up hatred inside her" – that it's all part of the one narrative.' But Osborn is still concerned that the actual head-butt was a long time ago and that airing it would be prejudicial to Jamie. Leckie points out that if the jurors don't have the full story, they will only be able to speculate as to what had happened and will not understand the depth of feeling it had created in Julie. The fact that she was frightened for her horse 'does indicate that she still has a concern about the level of his ability to control his anger'.

The judge suggests that the violence and the control aspects of Jamie's behaviour should be separated out. Leckie resists: 'You can't divorce the controlling aspect from the violent aspect . . . How you may exercise your power over someone may be in a number of different ways, and most likely a combination, and the violence is part of that.'

Leckie wants the claims about sexual domination in. He argues that Julie gave in to Jamie's persistent sexual demands because of her underlying fear of him. The judge is concerned the jury will find it hard to put this inflammatory material in perspective. Osborn says, 'The law has always taken a different view to evidence about an accused and a victim and that may, in one sense, seem unfair, but the risk that is seen in evidence about an accused is that the jury will treat it as propensity evidence.' Osborn also points out that the evidence about sex is hearsay, and that Julie did not speak of it to counsellors she saw with Jamie in the week before she died.

It's hard to imagine a woman raising sexual matters on a first visit to a stranger, even a professional stranger; especially if the woman has her partner sitting next to her. It's even harder to imagine her doing so if, like Julie, she has no intention of resuming the relationship and is going to counselling just to hose down her ex. The law's analysis treats all these marital revelations as if they are equal; the reality is that some are far more emotionally loaded than others. For both parties.

LECKIE ARGUES that the evidence about the 'slut' remark should go in. (Earlier, Dunn had said Jamie absolutely denies having used that word in the row.) Leckie says 'slut' is important because it 'would be part of the history of why she would be wary about what she would say to him, when in recent times he was prepared to react during the course of an argument about how they should deal with their daughter by calling her a slut'. But Leckie concedes many of Dunn's objections, including evidence by the horse-riding friends that they had seen Julie with a black eye. He says this is because Julie herself did not say the black eye was due to violence from Jamie.

Leckie also concedes that many times Julie said of Jamie, 'He will kill me.'

FINAL WORDS

Day three
Wednesday 6 October 2004

COURT TWELVE has a small vestibule that one passes through to enter and leave. This morning as I arrive Jamie is in it. He stands mute and still, head bowed, as a small woman in uniform, who barely comes to his shoulder, unlocks his handcuffs. The man with a disdain for women is now subject to one.

In court, Dunn strides up to Ramage and greets him with a booming, '*Good* afternoon, James, how are you?' Even though it's morning. He does it often; one of his little jokes. Dunn drops his voice and they murmur confidentially to each other.

The interminable legal argument begins again. Jamie has given up on the note-taking for now. He leans back, gazing at the curlicued ceiling.

LECKIE APOLOGISES to the judge for a document he has submitted that he fears is not what it should be. 'It was done on the run. I think there are some difficulties with the process in the sense that I got the brief fairly late on. I was involved in a long-running committal with police corruption until a week before this, and then I had to absorb this brief.'

Dunn has had the brief for months, and Dunn himself cross-examined all the witnesses who testified at the committal. He is familiar with the terrain. Here is another problem for Julie's case: the State, in the form of the Office of Public Prosecutions, cannot offer what a hospital would call 'continuity of care' – that is, the same professional devoting himself to the case all the way through the process. Leckie did not do the Ramage committal. And Crown prosecutors are more rushed and pressured than defence counsel, with less time to prepare. The scales of justice are starting to look decidedly out of whack.

LECKIE SURRENDERS on 'slut': 'I cannot see an argument I can sensibly advance to you in relation to that matter.' Osborn agrees: 'Yes, the vice is that she may have used that phrase to encapsulate or emotionally describe different words that he used.'

Leckie argues for photographs in which debris can be seen in Julie's brassiere, showing that she was near topless when buried. I can see a photograph of her curled up in foetal position with her back bloodied. Leckie argues for an autopsy picture that shows haemorrhaging in the muscles of her right forearm and dissection pictures of her shoulderblades that show deep haemorrhaging there. In this day and age, he argues, a jury can deal with such graphic images. I wince at a glimpse of a pale, shaved head and an autopsy incision that goes the width of it. Poor, poor Julie. This is about a *death*. The lawyers seem to feel the same. They are sombre and their voices unusually muted as they deal with the pictures. Osborn leans forward, both hands on the crown of his wig, as he thinks the questions through.

DUNN RISES to have his final say. It becomes clear that he *is* a jury-address man. You can see it in his air of authority, his relentless building of point upon point and his zoom-lens style of rhetoric, which sweeps grandly from the general to the particular and back again.

He accuses Leckie of trying to place before the jury a 'juggernaut' of impermissible evidence 'relying upon social chitchat, horse-riding conversations or conversations between lovers as being the basis for saying what this woman's state of mind was'. He points out that state of mind is not a static thing, 'and it is artificial in the extreme for the Crown to say we can rely upon something that happened in 1991 as indicating a state of mind in July 2003.

'The fundamental pieces of principle are these: that when the Crown and the defence lead evidence, or when the defence cross-examines and the Crown leads evidence, different rules apply. The Crown has to lead evidence which is relevant to the case that they are trying to present. They cannot attack the character of the accused or lead propensity evidence, or indeed lead hearsay evidence, except in certain clearly defined cases and exceptions. The defence, on the other hand, are permitted to attack the credit of the witnesses and, indeed, the deceased, if they wish to, but they are confined to what is relevant and what is not scandalous and objectionable.'

He argues that Julie's revelation of the head-butt in an interview with a therapist 'did not emerge until at the very end and in the course of a response to a direct question. If you go through witness after witness after witness, not one of them says she was leaving her husband because of acts of violence. They all say [it was because] she'd gained in confidence, she'd seen the solicitor, he was domineering, he nitpicked, he was controlling, she'd wanted to leave for ages, she wasn't in love any more, they'd grow old and grow isolated, there was tension about the horse-riding. *None* . . . say . . . she was leaving because she was (a) frightened of him, or (b) thought he would belt her if she left.'

Leckie has a problem because there is *no* example of contemporaneous violence, says Dunn. 'He has to slide the argument into one of being, "Well, it's control I'm talking about, and control therefore equates to intent and then I link that back to violence."

And that is slipping away from authority and slipping away from what the courts said you can do.'

As for the claims of sexual domination: 'There is no evidence that [Jamie] knew what she was thinking... There is no evidence to suggest that he was told that she didn't find sex with him anything other than entirely normal or that he... was a rapist. But to suggest to the jury that he is, is most powerfully prejudicial.'

Osborn adjourns the court until Friday to prepare his ruling.

THE JUDGE'S CUT

Day four
Friday 8 October 2004

I ARRIVE to a silent tableau. Jamie, the lawyers, the tipstaff and the judge's associate sit waiting for the judge, the only sound the rustle of paper. The young associate has her hair up today, wrapped with a headband twisted from a grey scarf.

They rise for his entrance. Osborn does not read his ruling but hands it down in 25 typewritten pages. He has decided that these items are 'out': the head-butt, the allegations of sexual dominance, the 'slut' claim, the many times Julie told people 'Jamie will kill me', and the specifics of Jamie's controlling behaviour.

Jamie pushing Julie out of bed is 'in'. So are Julie's affairs with two lovers, Adam and the family friend. Osborn admits all the photographs Leckie had wanted except the one showing deep haemorrhaging below the shoulder muscle, which he says is too graphic and potentially shocking. He allows Dunn's picture showing 'frontal lividity'.

The result is legally sound. The purpose of this trial is not to fully describe the Ramages' marriage and the reasons for its breakdown. Legally, the trial should touch only on the elements of the marriage that are relevant to points of law. But the picture that will be painted as a result is lopsided. This was a marriage where both behaved badly, but Julie was far more sinned against than sinning. The jurors won't discover this until they see the massive burst of publicity after the trial.

THERE IS another picture of Julie Ramage of which I caught an illicit glimpse during that voir dire. It is a photograph of her face that forensic investigators took at the gravesite. At least from a distance, it is unexpectedly lovely. Her delicate features are visible but the soil has not yet been brushed away from them. The greyness looks like stone, as if this is the carved face of a goddess being unearthed from some ancient site; an archetypal image of a woman. Julie Ramage was no goddess. She was all too human. But the image crystallised what was about to happen to her memory. Under the defence of provocation, she would be dragged through the dirt.

THE CASE BEGINS

Day five
Monday 11 October 2004

IT IS time to choose the jury. The courtroom has been cleared and observers sent upstairs to the overhanging visitors gallery to allow room downstairs for the pool of about 30 potential jurors. I wonder how the twelve will finish up. What chance a radical lesbian feminist? Or an angry male black-shirt? A fundamentalist Christian is statistically more probable.

What is not probable, it turns out, is women like Julie.

The judge begins with an address to the jury pool. He describes the charge against Jamie of murdering Julie. Then he lists 49 potential witnesses by name, telling the potential jurors that they must excuse themselves if they know any of the participants or have personal knowledge of events. They can also be excused if serving would make it difficult to care for young children, the sick or the elderly, or if it would place some other intolerable burden upon them.

Several are excused. One woman must care for a grandchild two days a week. A scientist says he cannot be spared from a work project. One woman has a mother with Alzheimer's; another woman's husband is due to be called for an operation. One younger man excuses himself on the grounds of potential bias: his father had spent time in hospital and was due to appear in court as the victim of an aggravated burglary. A man who works as a commission-based salesman says serving would cause him financial hardship. Two women with pre-school children are excused, as is a man who works at night: 'I think I would be half-asleep most of the time, your honour.' A casual worker says his employers would not be obliged to pay him.

Women are excused because they are society's carers. Middle-class people such as scientists and businessmen can be excused because they cannot be spared from work. Lawyers and doctors are permanently excused. Friends of Julie sitting vigil in the courtroom would later express their dismay that the selection process seems to weed out People Like Us in general and younger women in particular. In the demographic sense, Julie would not be judged by a jury of her peers.

Next, the judge's associate stands up in her place under the judge's box. She is at the front of the room and Jamie Ramage at the back. They lock eyes. In a firm, clear voice, she says, 'You are charged that you did at Balwyn murder Julie Anne Ramage. How do you plead?'

'Not guilty,' says Jamie, quietly.

Still looking at him, she says, 'You must challenge any potential juror before they take a seat in the jury box. You may challenge six jurors without cause. If you wish to challenge after that, you must provide good cause for your challenge.'

Her next warning has a swashbuckling air to it: 'Look to your challenges!'

Both lawyers are on their feet now. It is they who will decide whom to challenge. The only information they will have is the potential juror's occupation and appearance. A woman who works in 'product control' makes it to the box, as does a retired female teacher. A woman who describes herself as a 'retired journalist', and who is also a well-known political activist from an establishment family, is challenged by Dunn. He then challenges four others, all younger women. The judge's associate has been keeping count; she warns him he has only one peremptory challenge left.

A woman who is an integration aide makes it to the box, as does an older man who is a pensioner. A taxation auditor also makes it. A female receptionist is challenged. Dunn is told he has now exhausted his peremptory challenges. The next juror to make it is a middle-aged male bus driver. Now that Dunn's challenges are exhausted, a young woman who looks to be in her twenties who is a manager completes the walk to the box. She will be one of only two younger women – the other looks to be in her thirties – in the final line-up of five women and seven men. All twelve jurors choose to make their oath on a Bible rather than make an affirmation.

The judge's associate tells the jurors that James Stuart Ramage has pleaded not guilty. 'He has placed himself upon God and his country, which country you are.'

THE JUDGE sends the jury away to elect a foreperson to speak for them. How decisive is this group? How quickly will they come to a decision? And how conservative will their choice be? They spend twenty minutes. They choose a middle-aged man in a grey suit with thinning hair and glasses. He takes the seat in the front row nearest the judge's bench.

IT IS Osborn's custom at this point to tell the jurors a little about their task. He says they are engaging in the ultimate form of community participation, and that they are now the judges of the facts in this case. He talks to them genially and with respect, emphasising their right to be here, as if trying to help them relax in this unfamiliar setting. He describes the basic principles they must apply.

'The first is that the burden or onus of proof of all the elements of the offence charged is on the prosecution. The accused man, like any other person charged with a crime, does not have to prove *any*thing.

'The second principle is the standard of proof of which you must be satisfied before you would convict Mr Ramage: the standard is beyond reasonable doubt. That is a concept with which you will all be familiar and you have the combined human experience and commonsense of twelve people to help you apply it.

'The third basic principle to remember is that you must decide the case on the evidence. The evidence is not what the barristers may say to you by way of argument or what I may suggest by way of comment. It is what the witnesses will tell you from the witness box.'

Most of the evidence will relate to facts observed by witnesses, but there might also be evidence that the Crown invites them to draw inferences from; that is, to form conclusions about what must have happened. But 'although you can draw inferences, you can't just guess or speculate as to what happened. If you did that, you would not be satisfied beyond reasonable doubt'. He warns them they must stay dispassionate and 'decide the case objectively and carefully and not in accordance with feelings, emotions, sympathies or perhaps prejudices'.

Finally, he warns them they must not be affected by anything outside the courtroom. They must not talk to others about the case, and they must try to avoid media reports. 'You've got to decide the case on the basis of the evidence, not on the basis of what someone who hasn't heard the evidence says to you.'

The jurors listen attentively, their faces turned towards him. The young woman has rather an anxious expression. A grandmotherly woman with white hair has a conscientious set to her face. A large, soft woman with short dark hair and small gold hoops in her ears looks troubled. An olive-skinned man with grey hair and a large moustache listens with his eyebrows raised. An older woman with short hair and glasses wears an unreadable expression she would maintain throughout the trial. The foreman, too, looks closed.

This is one of the biggest responsibilities they will ever have to bear and there is no reason to think they approached it with anything other than seriousness. You can't help but feel sorry for them, plucked out of their normal lives and plunged into this high drama. Jamie Ramage's burst of deadly rage would affect so many lives.

LECKIE STANDS and looks directly at the jury. He goes through the charge: that on Monday 21 July 2003, Jamie murdered Julie. 'He was 43 at the time; she was 42.' He explains that they were separated when it happened and that the marriage had had 'a history of unhappy incidents. It included some violence which had precipitated fear in the mind of Mrs Ramage, and it culminated really with her deciding or coming to the conclusion that she could no longer live with Mr Ramage'.

When she left the family home Julie had left a letter for Jamie. Leckie reads it to the court. The letter is undated and neatly typed on to one long page. It misses a few apostrophes and misspells a word but what it lacks in grammatical precision it makes up for in clarity and emotion. This will be the only time we hear Julie's own voice.

Dear Jamie,
After a lot of heartache I have decided to leave you because too many things have gone on over the years with you and I feel we would both be happier on our own.

I know that you would really try to do anything to keep us together but that is not the point because it's what is truly in your heart that matters and I know that you can't help yourself and the real you bubbles to the surface and I don't like that person.

I feel I need to be my own person and that I let you run my life too much and that I'm stifled. If you said I could do anything I wanted I couldn't because I have become conditioned over the years to always worry about what your reaction will be to the things I do and say and therefore am never fully relaxed.

I think doing the renovations brought everything to a head because I just couldn't get enthusiastic over something that should have been fantastic to do. I still feel young and gregarious but you are so stayed [sic] and conservative and people only get worse as they get older. I'm not really saying that you are a bad person or the way you want to live is wrong it just isn't right for me.

I really don't want to hurt you but know that you really wouldn't like the real me and that we would have constant fights and life would be miserable for the kids if I just stayed and did what I wanted regardless of you. You have often said you would be happier on your own with a nice sports car, apartment and not such a great financial burden as us.

If you do care for me, please let me go without a horrible fight for the kids sake. Lets prove to them that we are better than all the other separated couples that we know. I could hate you so much for some of the things you have done and said to me over the years but I also understand that you are a good person and that you work hard and most importantly that you love our kids very much.

I know you will be mad when you realise I have left for good, but please be reasonable and hopefully see that it could be a new and exciting life for you too without the stress I seem to cause you.

The kids both love you very much and nothing will change with them. I want them to share more great times with you and know that we will be decent to each other because of them.

I hope you will understand that in order to live I needed to take an advance on some of our funds so I have transferred some money out and also used the Visa to buy some things. I feel very insecure at the moment leaving the house, beach house and all our other assets in your hands and I hope you won't do anything stupid that will hurt the kids. Please, please be reasonable and amicable and I promise I won't do the wrong thing by you.

I have asked Sam to come with me as it would be so hard to be on my own at a time like this, she is VERY upset and isn't choosing me over you. Matthew is old enough to make up his own mind. We will discuss what's best for the kids later. I have not gone into great detail with them as to why I am leaving and certainly haven't said anything to make them take sides and never will.

Please talk to your friends and think things through before going crazy. I will talk to you on the phone if you are reasonable and don't carry on and on about the situation or make threats. I hope you don't mind that I am taking Archie [the family poodle]. I have tried to leave the house clean and tidy and prepared a meal for this evening.

Take care,
Julie

It's the 'Dear John' letter from the perfect wife. She's cleaned the house and cooked him a last supper. It's a letter that swings between firm and appeasing. Julie shows that she has considered staying and trying to make things different but has decided this won't work: *I know that you can't help yourself and the real you bubbles to the surface and I don't like that person.* She points to the fact they are still parents together and promises to be a good girl: *Please, please be reasonable and amicable and I promise I won't do the wrong thing by you.*

There is a sense that she is trying to use the children as a shield against Jamie's anger: *If you do care for me, please let me go without a horrible fight for the kids sake. Lets prove to them that we are better than all the other separated couples that we know.* And she expected him to be enraged: *Think things through before going crazy; Don't carry on and on about the situation or make threats.*

Maybe that's why Jamie got a letter instead of a face-to-face talk. *I know that you would really try to do anything to keep us together.* Julie Ramage was frightened that Jamie would not take 'No' for an answer.

There is one tooth-cracking nut in this tender confection: it would turn out that Julie had lied when she claimed she had not said anything to make either of the children take sides.

LECKIE PAUSES briefly to allow the import of the letter to sink in. He continues: 'During the weeks that followed that separation, the accused tried to persuade his wife to return to the marriage ... [He] seemed unprepared to accept the fact that his wife now wanted to live her own life. He consulted with many friends of both his wife and himself, trying to work out what had gone wrong, how he could perhaps modify his behaviour so that he would be more acceptable to her.' Julie agreed to see him with joint sessions with some of the counsellors, Leckie says, even though she was not seriously considering returning. She was 'trying to let him down gently' – the phrase that would become the riff of this trial.

He tells the jury that in her six weeks of freedom, Julie met Laurence Webb and became deeply attached to him.

This is the countdown to death described by the Crown: On Saturday 19 July 2003 – 'two days before she was murdered' – Julie and Jamie travelled to Geelong together to watch Matthew play football. They talked for a long time, and Julie told Jamie that her relationship with Laurence was serious. The following day, Julie went horse-riding with Laurence. Jamie spent that Sunday morning rowing with his daughter Samantha. He questioned Samantha about Laurence. That Sunday evening Jamie saw a friend, Nick Farley, and told Farley he knew Julie was seeing someone else. He told Farley he was angry with Julie.

The Monday of her death, Julie drove Samantha to school in the morning. She told her daughter that she was going back to the family home in Marock Place at lunchtime to look at the renovations. Then Julie went to work.

At 12.10 pm she left work and drove to Marock Place. Leckie warns the jury, 'What we know of the events that then follow is largely based on what Mr Ramage has told the police. And in this case, whether that's the truth – the full truth! – about the matter will be for you to determine.'

Jamie says that he got to the house about 11.30 am. He wanted to clean up a little before Julie got there. He moved a small kitchen table out of the laundry area, where it had been sitting while the renovations were going on, and set it up with some chairs in the kitchen/family room. He had bought some rolls for lunch and laid them out with glasses. Jamie says Julie arrived and they talked about the renovations and their relationship.

Leckie has decided that Jamie will speak for himself as to what happened next. He is going to play to the court a part of Jamie's videotaped interview with police. It was made with Detective Senior Constable Darren Wiseman in a homicide interview room at police headquarters in St Kilda Road at 11.30 am on Tuesday 22 July.

This will be one of only two times that the court hears Jamie's own voice.

WE TURN expectantly to the blank wall opposite the jury. The images are flashed up there, soft and fuzzy but still clear enough, like the home movies projected on to the lounge-room walls of my childhood. Jamie Ramage sits on the left of the screen in a dark jumper. In front of him is a desk, with a detective facing him from behind it. Jamie looks boxed in and pale under the fluorescents of the small interview room. His face is blank. He would turn out to have a gravelly voice with a faint working-class English accent; a slight clipping of his 'I's', the English 'ah' in words such as 'chance'. His tone is flat and apparently unemotional but he must be anxious because many of his sentences are disjointed.

Leckie has chosen this as the starting point:

Jamie: 'On – on – with the – when I talked about the renovations I said, "Look, you don't know how hard it is getting to keep this going" and so on, and she sort of made that sort of, you know, wank-wank sort of sign' – *his right hand jerks rhythmically up and down to illustrate* – 'and, you, know, "you didn't have to do it" sort of stuff.'
Policeman: 'Mmm.'
Jamie: '"We should've done these renovations years ago. You – you've had enough money," and so on. So that hurt a lot.'
Policeman: 'Mmm.'

Jamie *(he is talking quickly now)*: 'Because I put so much into doing the renovations, and so did my son, and to – to at least get it to where it was and also again, having a go at, I suppose, with me – with having a go at what I've done with the business, the – the family sort of stuff's important to me and so on.'
Policeman: 'Yeah.'
Jamie: 'And that's why all this, us splitting up, has been so hard because the family's so important to me.'
Policeman: 'Mmm.'
Jamie: 'So, do you want me to carry on with the conversation or . . . ?'
Policeman: 'Yeah. Obviously she said things that have hurt you, you said?'
Jamie: 'Yeah. Look, I'll – I'll go through bits. I mean, there may – there may be others – other things but the things that stick in my mind – after that we – we had that funny thing' – *he plucks imaginary fluff from his sleeve* – 'then we – we sat down and I really just talked out of it, you know, but I suppose I just pleaded with her, "What do I have to do? What – what can I do?"'
Policeman: 'Mmm.'
Jamie breaks eye contact with the detective and drops his gaze to the table: 'And she sort of said, "You don't get it, do you? I'm over you. I should've left you ten years ago." Those sort of things. That sort of stuff. We changed the subject, or I changed the subject, I suppose. We talked about rowing. I went rowing with my daughter yesterday.' *He draws an audible breath.*
Policeman: 'Mmm.'
Jamie looks up and meets the detective's eyes again: 'And she mentioned again that Sam wasn't happy because I kept talking about her and "I – and I don't know whether she wants to go around and stay with you as much" and so on, so that – apart from Julie leaving me, she also took my daughter and the daughter's really important to me . . .'
But, he says, he cleared that up with Sam: 'I spoke to Sam about that last night about Julie saying that about her, and Sam said

that's not the case, she's fine with coming around and so on. And, I mean, Sam was – I've talked to Sam about it and – and one thing I want to make sure is that the kids aren't involved.' *He looks at the detective*: 'I mean, yeah, Matt's still seeing his mum and all that sort of thing . . . You know, I wouldn't say to my son, "You don't go and see your mum."'

Jamie says he then told Julie that Samantha was not happy about 'this guy' – *Laurence*. 'And I – I – I just said, you know, "Sam's not happy." And then she said, "It's none – none of your fucking business. I'm – I'm not with you any more."' *Jamie pauses a moment.* 'I said, "Well, how, you know, how serious is it with him?" And she said, "I've had sleepovers with him," and – and that really, really hurt.'

Policeman: 'Mmm.'

Jamie: 'And we talked about – you know, she talked about how much nicer he was' – *Jamie pauses and breathes heavily* – 'and, you know, he rides horses and – and cares for her more and all that sort of stuff.' *He sighs, as if defeated.* 'And – and – she talked then – she talked about then that she's going to the Cumberland or something, Marysville or the Cumberland with him for a weekend. And that upset me – upset – upset me because, I suppose, it's sort of like saying – it was just – just – she was just – just being really hurtful.'

The policeman continues to encourage him quietly, with the calculated minimalism of the professional listener: the 'Mmm' of the lawyer, the therapist, the journalist, the cop.

Jamie: 'And through the whole th–, I dunno – I don't know why unless she decided – and it also upset me because I know my son would be really – because he – she promised him that she wouldn't see anybody else or do anything that . . . at this stage too. And the sh–, then she said – the sex with me and, "It repulses me"' – *he holds his hands up as if warding something off* – 'and screwed up her face. And whereas he knows all about what – she sort of said that – she said how much better he was and he knew what – that he was caring and so on and then sex with me repulses her. And

then she sort of got up to finish the conversation or finish the – you know, like, we finished the food and so on.'
Policeman: 'Yes.'
Jamie: 'And that's where I lost it.' *He looks helplessly across the table.*
Policeman: 'How did you lose it?'
Jamie: 'As she stood up, I – I stood up and I hit her.'
Policeman: 'Mmm.'
Jamie: 'And then – then I just wanted it to stop and that's when I strangled her and' – *he looks down and sighs and wipes an eye* – 'and you don't know how much I wish I could change that.'
Later in the interview, the policeman asks: 'Did you strike her?'
Jamie: 'Mmm.'
Policeman: 'Do you remember which hand you – you've hit her with?'
Jamie: 'Yeah, this one.' *(His right.) They discuss its current state; the scratches on it are from his morning rowing with Samantha, Jamie says, but the swelling is from punching Julie.*
Policeman: 'How many times did you hit her at that stage?'
Jamie: 'Look, I – I had lost the plot. I remember hitting her once or twice and then just strangling her. I can't – I – it all – I just don't' – *long pause* – 'it just all becomes a –'
Policeman: 'How hard do you think you hit her?'
Jamie (*softly*): 'I think reasonably hard.'
Policeman: 'Mmm.'
Jamie: 'I just wanted it to stop, just . . .'
Policeman: 'When you struck her did she fall to the ground or on to the table or what did she . . . ?'
Jamie: 'She sort of fell to the ground and then – then I grabbed her by the neck.'
Policeman: 'All right. Did you pick her up or did you get down on the ground with her and strangle her?'
Jamie: 'Yeah.' *He looks at the detective and puts his hands out in front of him and makes a small indecipherable noise.*
Policeman: 'All right. Were you able – your knees, or . . . ?'

Jamie: 'Yeah.'

Policeman: 'I'm just trying to picture it, that's all.'

Jamie: 'I can't remember.' *He puts both hands out in front of him, thumbs and fingers spread and curved as if wrapped around something circular.* 'I just remember holding her neck.' *There is a long pause, and he takes another deep breath.*

Policeman: 'What was she doing at that stage?'

Jamie (*muttering*): '. . . She couldn't speak or anything 'cos I was holding her neck.'

Policeman: 'Was she fighting? Did she . . . ?'

Jamie: 'She did for a bit, but not for long.' *His voice is low. He looks tearful. His mouth tightens and he brings the fingers of his left hand to his forehead.*

Policeman: 'Mmm.'

Jamie: 'I just can't believe –'

The policeman is not interested in his disbelief.

'When you had her around the neck and you said she's fought you for a bit, how did she fight you?'

Jamie: 'I really can't – I can't remember. I can remember getting off . . .'

Policeman: 'Did she scratch or punch at you or try and kick out, anything like that?'

Jamie: 'I think she held her arm up. I – I can remember hitting her and then I remember holding her neck. I can't remember anything else.'

Policeman: 'All right.'

Jamie: 'I just can't. I'm sorry.' *He closes his eyes and puts a hand over his face.*

Policeman: 'All right. When did you actually go or get up off the ground?'

Jamie: 'I got – yeah, I got up off the – and I couldn't believe what I'd done and I wandered around and then I dunno, it was just stupid. Then I . . . clean up and then I gotta go and put her somewhere, or something – just stupid. And all the time I'm thinking, "I might as well go. I might as well just call someone."'

Policeman: 'When did you actually realise that she was dead?'
Jamie: 'I dunno. I suppose I just – I just thought because she wasn't moving she was dead.' *He shakes his head and buries his face in his hands.* 'I took her – when I took her out to the car –'
Policeman: 'At that stage, when you first realised, did you check for a pulse or any breathing or anything like that?'
Jamie's fingers are over his mouth as if to steady it: 'No, no, I just . . .'
Policeman: 'Did you attempt any sort of CPR or first aid or anything like that to try and revive her?'
Jamie: 'No.'
Policeman: 'Did you contact anyone else at that time?'
Jamie: 'I just realised – stupid, I should have done something.'
Policeman: 'Was she bleeding or [were] there any injuries that you could see to her?'
Jamie: 'She had some blood on her face.'
Policeman: 'Mmm. And . . . what caused the blood, do you know?'
Jamie's voice drops again. He says the hardest things in his softest voice. 'I don't know; probably me hitting her.'

THERE WAS something *adolescent* about Jamie's manner in that interview; he was like a schoolboy being carpeted in the principal's office. He seemed co-operative but sullen, like one who knows he must not create more trouble for himself but who feels aggrieved to find himself here because it's not really his fault. He kept saying how hurt he was, as if Julie had inflicted the first injury. He never said he was angry, much less furious or vengeful. He did not even admit to squeezing her neck; he was 'holding' it. Leaving his wife to die on the kitchen floor, to die without aid, was not callous but 'stupid'.

There was nothing adolescent about the legal implications of Jamie Ramage's claims, though. His story contained many elements of 'provocation': Julie had attacked his worth as a businessman, a husband, a lover and a father. She had done this through words, gestures and facial expressions.

Jamie Ramage had offered police minimal descriptions of his own rage and his physical attack on Julie while laying solid ground for a provocation defence. But two things were missing: sorrow and remorse. He expressed no affection for Julie or sadness over the loss of her, and no remorse for what his actions had meant for *her*. Those oversights would come back to bite him. And, like Julie, he had lied about not using his child against his wife. Months later, I would learn that Jamie *had* initially tried to stop Matthew seeing his mother in the hope this would pressure her to return home.

LECKIE RISES as the film ends. He points out Jamie's coldness. 'He didn't lend any assistance to his wife, who he said he loved, he didn't render any assistance to her when he . . . realised she was motionless. Instead . . . he then starts to cover up the crime and dispose of her body.'

Leckie goes through the rest of Jamie's afternoon step by step. Jamie half-dragged, half-carried Julie out to the boot of the car. He tried to clean the kitchen floor. 'He packs a change of clothes and shoes and puts them into his Jaguar car, where he's put the body of his wife in the boot. He gathers up her handbag . . . and takes that in his Jaguar as well.' He packs the cloths he had used to wipe up Julie's blood and the shovel he would use to bury her. At 1.16 pm he checks the message bank for his mobile phone. At 1.19, as he's travelling with Julie in the boot, he rings her mobile phone number. The man who had such trouble thinking clearly during his police interview apparently had no trouble doing two things at once after the crime.

Eventually, Jamie Ramage turns off into some private property. He digs Julie a shallow grave. He drags her body over to it, forces her in and covers her with dirt. Then he further camouflages the site by pulling bits of tree, bark and shrubbery over it.

The judge halts Leckie's relentless account. 'Mr Leckie, is that a convenient time?'

WE BREAK for lunch. It has been a big morning. Leckie's opening was brilliantly structured. His delivery might be more restrained than Dunn's but he has proved to have as fine a sense of narrative power: setting the scene with Julie's gentle, pleading letter, contrasting it with Jamie's throttling of her, pounding the message home with a barrage of detail about the calculated cover-up. The chill of Jamie's cold-bloodedness is in the air as the jurors file out of the room. They must be wondering why he hasn't pleaded guilty to murder. What's to decide? But it's early days yet. If Steve Pica is right, and this is a jury-address case, it will be won or lost at the end, not the beginning.

LECKIE PICKS up his thread after lunch. According to mobile phone records, those thoroughly modern monitors, these were Jamie's movements: by 2.25 pm, he has left the bush gravesite and rings Acropolis Marble. About 2.50 pm, he stops at a petrol station in the outer suburb of Diamond Creek. At 3.17 he is continuing on with his journey and is near Bundoora; he calls his work. At 3.28, he calls Acropolis Marble a second time to tell them he has been caught up in traffic. He arrives there about 3.30 pm.

Leckie says, 'When he leaves there, there's a period of time where the prosecution is unable to know his movements, that is between something like 3.45 in the afternoon and 5.06. However, we know at 5.06 he checks his message bank because of his phone.' By 6.15 pm, Jamie Ramage is back at Marock Place.

The following day, Tuesday 22 July 2003, an autopsy was performed on Julie. The pathologist identified twenty injuries on her, Leckie says, and found that the cause of her death was 'compression of the neck'.

Leckie moves away from Jamie's actions to offer a legal explanation of 'the elements of murder' that the Crown must prove. The accused must have caused the death of the deceased; there is no argument about that in this case. Secondly, the act that caused the death must have been conscious, voluntary and deliberate: 'He wasn't sleep-walking or on drugs so far that he didn't know what he was doing.'

The Crown must also prove that Jamie attacked Julie with the intent of either killing her or of causing her really serious bodily injury. 'Either of those two intents is sufficient for murder.'

Finally, the Crown must prove that the killing was without lawful justification or excuse. A lawful justification might be self-defence – something that is not being claimed in this case. But the jury might have to consider whether Jamie had an 'excuse'. After hearing the evidence, the judge will decide whether the jury will be asked to consider the excuse of *provocation*. That means they will have to decide whether it is possible Julie did, in fact, say the 'provoking' things that Jamie claimed she did.

If the jury is not satisfied beyond reasonable doubt that Julie did *not* say those things, they must go on to assess two more questions. Did Jamie lose self-control? And would an ordinary person in the same circumstances have lost self-control in this way? Says Leckie, 'Throughout all of this the onus of proof is on the Crown, and the standard by which the Crown must prove all of this is beyond reasonable doubt.'

Suddenly, the case against Jamie Ramage seems fraught with difficulty. I wonder how you prove a negative. How can the Crown possibly prove that Julie did *not* say those things? Beyond reasonable doubt?

At secondary school I had taken legal studies. I had written essays full of youthful idealism and certainty supporting the presumption of innocence on which the principle of 'beyond reasonable doubt' is based; better that nine guilty men go free than one innocent man be unjustly convicted. I understood the hearsay rule: of course people should only be allowed to testify to what they saw and heard themselves and not what they heard from others – look what happens with office gossip and Chinese whispers. But I had never imagined that it could turn out like this. What Julie told others about Jamie was hearsay and could not be used as evidence. What Jamie said about Julie in that final encounter was an account that came from him alone. He would not have to take an oath that he was telling the truth, and he would not have to testify or be cross-examined in court. But Jamie's story had to be accepted unless the Crown could disprove his claims beyond reasonable doubt.

The dice seems loaded against victims even in death.

NEXT LECKIE takes the jurors through their 'jury books', which have maps of the relevant sites, floor plans of the Ramages' house and photographs. He warns them that some of the post-mortem pictures of Julie will be confronting. He takes them shot by shot through the first 100 or so images, starting with the approach to the bush block and the uncovering of the grave. 'The next shot will be of the deceased's body where they've uncovered the dirt.' The jurors turn to it. The large soft woman swallows and puts her hand to her mouth as if to stop herself being ill. An older male juror with fierce eyebrows shoots a piercing glance at Jamie over the top of his glasses. Jamie stares at the carpet.

When he gets to the autopsy pictures Leckie takes a sip of water to fortify himself. This is what was discovered on the body of the woman Jamie Ramage had promised to love and cherish: a wound on her nose, a black eye, abrasions on her lip, purple bruising on her neck and around her chest and collarbone, deep bruising in one forearm and smaller bruises on her hands. There were abrasions on her leg and scrape marks on the top of her buttocks and on her shoulderblades – the latter is accompanied by a dissection photograph showing the scrapes were severe enough to cause bleeding into the muscles of her shoulders. We come to the lump on her head that Laurence Webb saw when he identified her body. When the doctor examined the scalp beneath it, he found 'there was haemorrhaging almost on the whole left side of her head'. Leckie repeats it: 'It was on the whole left-hand side of her head that he found haemorrhaging.'

Philip Dunn might be right. The police did not turn up any firm evidence of severe violence between Jamie and Julie in the previous decade. Perhaps Julie did not spend most of her marriage as a battered wife. But she most surely ended as one.

WHEN LECKIE stops, the judge offers the jury a short break. It is 3.15 pm and a lot of ground has been covered today. Dunn rises and asks to raise 'a matter of minor concern'. It turns out that, at lunchtime, a man stood in the path of Jamie Ramage as he was being led from the courtroom. When Jamie returned from lunch, the man positioned himself in the anteroom, where Jamie stands to have his handcuffs removed, and then stood in the doorway as Jamie was brought into the court. Dunn says indignantly, 'I stood between him and the accused in case there was some problem which I'm unaware of. I understand this man to be the husband of Mrs Jane Ashton.'

He has gestured to a balding man with a dark moustache sitting at the side of the courtroom. Jane and members of her family who are witnesses may not sit in court until after they have given evidence. Howard Ashton is their representative in the meantime. He lives with Julie's bereaved twin sister. Jamie Ramage put his hands around the throat of a woman who was almost the image of Howard's wife.

Howard looks up at the judge intently. Osborn points out that, with only one entrance, such events can come about quite innocently, but he notes that Jamie's passage should be unimpeded and free from harassment. Dunn repeats his concern again. Osborn ends it tartly: 'I understand what you've said, Mr Dunn.'

IN THE short break that follows, Leckie turns to me. (The tipstaff has moved me to a table just behind both lawyers.) 'Now, is that a reasonable letter, or is that a reasonable letter?' he asks of Julie's note. He turns back to his associate. 'I wanted more young women!' he murmurs of the jury.

THE JURY returns at 3.30 pm and it is Dunn's turn to open. He says Jamie Ramage is not denying that he killed his wife but he is denying that he is guilty of murder. 'The law recognises that when one person kills another it isn't always murder. The law recognises that there are different levels of responsibility . . . I will be urging you that you should, as you would with most things in life, try to keep an open mind until all the material is before you because, like a coin, this case has two sides.'

Dunn flags his argument: that, firstly, the Crown cannot prove that Jamie *intended* to kill or seriously injure Julie. Alternatively, that he was *provoked* to attack her, in that Jamie's actions 'could have been brought about by what Mrs Ramage did and said'.

He says, 'There had been some instances of violence and aggression in the marriage but in recent years that's not so.' In 2002, Jamie pushed Julie out of 'the matrimonial bed' and she went off and stayed at her sister's. 'You'll also hear that around that time Mrs Ramage had commenced this relationship with [Adam], but that was unbeknownst to her husband and certainly to her son Matthew.' Dunn takes them through a potted history of the rest of the marriage and the break-up.

He tells the jury they will hear from several psychologists and marriage guidance counsellors whom Jamie Ramage sought out. 'In the course of doing so, he shouldered a degree of responsibility for the break-up, saying that perhaps his wife was right, that he was too controlling, nitpicking and, I think, staid, conservative, grumpy and wasn't listening, and generally was controlling. What will be important for you is to see what those psychologists and therapists say as to his emotional state. Was he rational and calm or was he becoming emotionally fragile? Psychologically vulnerable?

'The plan, you will hear, between Gilda, her sister Jane and Mrs Ramage was to tell Mr Ramage that there was a chance that the two of them would get back together again, whereas in fact there was no chance. The plan was to "let him down gently". So Mr Ramage set about trying to improve himself and the house, as you will hear, and when talking to various people was told by the confidantes of Mrs Ramage, "Yes, there is a chance you'll get back together again but she needs time and space."' The sequence of communications over this became very important in July, says Dunn, the month that Julie met Laurence Webb. As the relationship blossomed between Julie and Laurence, an unknowing Jamie was calling her best friend and her sister asking about his chances and was being told there was still hope for him.

On Tuesday 15 July, only six days before her death, Julie attended not one but two marriage counsellors with Jamie. She told the second therapist that there was no one else in her life, and the Ramages made future appointments to attend together. 'Julie Ramage told her husband in [the counsellor's] presence that she wasn't going anywhere and that they were going to continue with the counselling. And so there was a degree of optimism.'

On Friday 18 July, Laurence had told Julie that he was going to get a divorce from his wife (whom he had separated from several years earlier). On Saturday 19 July, there was the footy match at Geelong where Julie told Jamie about Laurence. On the Sunday, she and Laurence went horse-riding and he gave her some lingerie, 'and then,' says Dunn, 'they talked about planning to start living together. I think they'd met each other, what, seven times and had known one another for less than two weeks. Mrs Ramage rang her sister and said that this man was the love of her life on the Sunday night. At a time on the Sunday, Mr Ramage also rang Jane Ashton and asked her about the man Laurence, and Mrs Ashton will tell you that she told him that it was a perfectly innocent relationship, there was nothing in it, that Laurence was a friend of hers and that her sister was committed to counselling.

'So you then come to the events of Monday 21 July, and on that morning Mrs Ramage told her work friends, at least one of them, what she had told her sister on the Sunday night: that this man Webb was the love of her life and that there was going to be no more lies. And so that would be a question for you to ask yourself: *What were the lies that there was going to be no more of?*'

FAMILY HISTORIES

Day six
Tuesday 12 October 2004

THE FIRST person to step into the witness box is Julie's identical twin sister, Jane Ashton. Jane has long, straight honey-coloured hair, expertly tipped and layered at the bottom. She has Julie's blue eyes but, unlike Julie, she wears a fringe. She is in mourning clothes: a ruched white shirt and black pants with a tailored black knee-length jacket, her only jewellery gold studs in her ears. She has a pretty face but today it looks ravaged. Her eyes are red and her face sags with tiredness. She looks like she has been up crying all night. She is a walking billboard of grief for her sister. And, of course, she is the image of her sister. The jury can gaze at her and see Julie. Jane is a witness for the Crown before she even opens her mouth.

Opening her mouth is the part Jane has trouble with. Her voice is almost a whisper. Several times Leckie gently asks her to speak up. As she listens to questions her mouth works and she swallows nervously. Her husband, sitting in a side pew, does not take his eyes from her face. The tipstaff brings her a cup of water. Asked her occupation, she stumbles a little: 'Home – house – housewife.' The next few questions are easy, though; yes and no answers. And I realise that this is how Leckie will lead his witnesses safely through the mire of material that has been objected to; he will state a fact taken from their statements to police and ask them to agree to it. They are to be kept on a tight leash. The result for the listener is staccato; fragments will be laid out before the jury piecemeal, and it will be up to them to try to weave the story together as they go.

> Leckie: 'Did she meet [Jamie] through a friend?'
> Jane: 'Yes, he was going out with . . .'
> Leckie: 'Did they then start seeing quite a bit of each other?'
> Jane: 'Yes, they did, yes.'
> Leckie: 'Did it become known to you that he was planning to go to Australia at around this time?'
> Jane: 'Yes, he was.'
> Leckie: 'And work with an old friend of his father's?'
> Jane: 'Yes, that's correct.'

And so they went through the history of the marriage. A rift developed between the Garretts and Julie and Jamie after Samantha's birth, Jane agrees. 'Now I don't want to have the details of it,' warns Leckie, 'but just the fact that there were some disputes or arguments.' As a consequence of the falling out, Julie and Jane saw less of each other. At this point Jane's face looks like it might crumple but her voice remains steady. She takes a sip of water. Later they did see each other more again; they caught up over horse-riding once Samantha joined a pony club. Julie became more confident after she got her job at Eco-d, Jane agrees: 'She wanted more freedom and it became quite strained [with Jamie] as she became more mature.' Leckie asks Jane about the growing problems in the Ramages' marriage but cautions her that she must be careful because of the hearsay rule. Jane has clearly been forewarned about this and just as clearly is maddened by it; she raises her eyes heavenwards but nods.

Julie had spoken to Jane several times in the six months before her death of her desire to leave Jamie. She had decided it would be safest to do it when he was away but at that stage was going to wait out Matthew's VCE. Then came a serious fight that left Julie distraught. Jane spoke to her on the phone on 6 June 2003: 'She hadn't planned to leave that early but she had to, and she was concerned that Matt was in the middle of his VCE and she was going to try and make things as smooth as possible while trying to get away as safely as possible.'

'Did she say anything about her growing strength or confidence about being able to make such a move?'

'She felt that she had the strength to do it. She sort of realised that – that there was a lot to life; that her life wasn't normal. And she – she was ready to go.' Julie looked around for a rental property that was near the children's schools and took the first one she found. Her father booked her a removal truck and she began moving the following Thursday. 'She stayed at Balwyn on the Friday night, and Jamie had rung her from Sydney Airport . . . She told me that she told him that she wasn't going to be there when he came home, and did he want his brother to come and meet him, and he said "No, that was fine." He took it quite calmly and she was so happy.'

How did it go after that? 'She told me that he was calling her constantly, and that she was being very careful of what she said to him because she didn't want him to become *violent*' – Jane gets one over the net – 'and that she was going to let him down gently and just be very careful.'

Jamie rang Jane during the separation and asked if they could have coffee. They met at the Yan Yean Golf Range. 'He seemed upset. He was frustrated. He wanted some insights into how to get her back, probably more than [asking for insight about] what he'd done to instigate [the break-up].' Jane was surprised to hear that Jamie had been to see 'an anger management professional'. 'He said that he realised that he'd been petty and nasty for most of his life and that despite material gains, he'd not enjoyed life very much.' He nagged at her about his prospects with her sister: 'He continually wanted to know out of ten, marks out of ten, what chances I gave them of getting back together or her coming back to him. Continually asking.'

Jane ducked the question but did manage to serve Jamie a few home truths. 'I remained pretty vague and tried to suggest that she's just – you know, she'd been married to him for a long while and that she needed time, she needed some space, and that who knew what would happen in the future . . . I did explain to him that she'd become more sort of sure of her own mind and that she was more confident now and that she hadn't communicated particularly well with him because she'd learnt not to, that her opinion was never taken on board and that she felt intimidated by him . . . I did point out that he'd been controlling and manipulative of her for a long while.'

Jamie telephoned Jane several times and also visited her home one day. He told Jane that he and Julie had come to an understanding that they would not see other people at this stage: 'He was still making up the rules, how they were going to behave.' Jane did not challenge his belief in such a deal: 'I said to him that I felt the last thing Julie would want, having been in the relationship for twenty years, would be to get hitched or have a serious relationship with another man.'

The weekend before he killed Julie, Jamie rang Jane again, this time to question her about Laurence. 'He said that he understood that Laurence was like him: he was English, he played rugby, he was a businessman. But that he was a nicer version of him . . . Jamie's perception of it was that this was, if you like, more serious than, say, having dinner with Simon.'

Jane says this added to Jamie's growing realisation that he was not going to get Julie back. 'He'd already spoken to the counsellors and he realised that she probably wasn't coming back. That this was a serious relationship was another hurdle . . . I tried to play it down and reassure him that . . . she was just spreading her wings, that, you know, she hadn't been on her own since she was seventeen and she was just out there having some fun.'

Jane spoke to Jamie about the counselling sessions he had been attending, some of which Julie had gone to as well. 'He said that [the counsellors] told him to leave her alone, that the marriage was over. And he rang me and said, "I've shot myself in the foot," because it wasn't the result he wanted.'

From Julie's perspective, 'She was going to let him down gently. She didn't want to trigger any incidents of violence, and she just hoped that he would accept her decision and that, you know, he'd get used to the idea.' Jane is now near tears again. She says Julie had been reluctant to attend counselling – 'she felt it might bring things to a head quicker than she wanted' – but Jane persuaded her to go. 'I thought it may give her a structure where she could, you know, deal with him safely and in front of independent people and that he may listen to them and take on board what they said.'

In those weeks of separation, while Jamie was beginning to fall apart, Julie was blossoming. 'She had the freedom to come and go. I saw more of her in that last six weeks than I'd seen of her in months. She was happy. It was as if the weight had been lifted off her shoulders, and I had my sister back.'

Jane and Julie spoke on the phone on Friday 11 July. Jane warned Julie not to tell Jamie too much about her relationship with Laurence. 'She said she wasn't going to lie to him again but that she wasn't stupid. He was no longer going to control what she did but, you know, she was still cautious.' At this point, says Jane, Jamie knew that Laurence and Julie 'were planning a commitment some months into the future and it was serious'.

Jamie Ramage is staring at his pad and writing earnestly.

Jane saw Julie for the last time on Wednesday 16 July. 'She was good. Very buoyant.' The tears have finally started to run down Jane's cheeks. She finds Julie's brief burst of happiness even more sorrowful than her years of distress. It is the poignancy of so little, so late that has made Jane crack. The tipstaff refills her cup.

Jane last spoke to Julie on the Sunday night before she died. She tells the court about the flurry of calls the following night, the Monday, when it was realised Julie was missing.

Leckie has finished. There is a ten-minute break. In the waiting area outside the courtroom, Jane is consoled by a woman from the court's witness-support program. As the jury rose, I noticed that the young female juror is all in black today. Perhaps it's because she now has some idea of what she is facing.

AT 11.50 am the jury re-enters. Dunn rises for his cross-examination. I expect him to take it easy on Jane. Why rouse the jury to even more sympathy on her behalf? But Dunn does not see it that way. From the first his tone is challenging, as if he means to turn even inconsequential questions into accusations. He begins by asking her about the phone conversation with Julie the night before she died. Their exchange flares almost instantly into combat. His tone ratchets up from challenging to belligerent.

> Dunn: 'During that conversation she told you, did she not, *that she had met the love of her life?*'
> Jane: 'She said that she and Laurence were in love.'
> Dunn: 'Did she tell you that she had met the love of her life?' *They fence tautly over whether she had agreed to this phrase at the committal. A few sentences later Dunn is accusatory:* 'You've changed your evidence, haven't you, here in court in front of this jury, about what you've said in the past, have you not?'
> Jane: 'No, I haven't.'
> Dunn: 'We'll come to that. Let me just go back to the Sunday – and obviously you loved your sister?'
> Jane: 'Yes. Yes.'
> Dunn: 'You disliked James Ramage?'
> Jane: 'Yes.'
> Dunn (*voice rising*): 'You disliked him for many, many years?'
> *Jane stares away from him and responds with steely calm*: 'Yes.'

Dunn is trying to paint Jane as an unreliable witness who had her own barrow to push. Jane does not seem rattled by this; but then, she was forewarned by their encounter at the committal hearing.

Dunn gets her to acknowledge that on the Sunday night before Julie's death, she told Jamie that there was nothing serious in the relationship with Laurence Webb, and that Julie was committed to counselling with him. Dunn starts in on Ray Garrett.

> Dunn: 'When your father discovered they were having an intimate relationship he asked your sister to leave school?'
> Jane: 'Correct.'
> Dunn: 'Your father was a strict disciplinarian?'
> Jane: 'Yes.'
> Dunn: 'Conservative?'
> Jane: 'No.'
> Dunn: 'Old-fashioned in some of his views?'
> Jane: 'No.'
> Dunn: 'When he discovered your sister was having an intimate relationship –'

Leckie breaks in with an objection. Dunn argues that the fact that Julie was pulled out of school for having sex as a teenager goes to her state of mind. Leckie retorts that it is hearsay and ancient history to boot. The judge instructs Dunn to move on.

DUNN TAKES Jane to her sister's marital separation in 1984 and manages to slip in a reference to a lover from back then.

> Dunn: 'Did she tell you that the reason she separated, she'd met a man called Chris?'
> Jane: 'No.'
> Dunn: 'Did she discuss with you a man called Chris?'
> Jane: 'Yes.'

He asks her whether Julie ever complained, in the years 2000, 2001, 2002 and 2003 that her husband punched her or did anything like that. Jane, who had earlier been trembling and close to tears, has now rallied.

Jane: 'Sorry. Could you repeat the dates?'
Dunn: 'Yes. She never suggested to you that her husband punched her?'
Jane: 'The dates, please.'
Dunn: 'I know you say he does –?'
Jane: 'No, *the dates*.'
Dunn: 'But she never suggested to you –'
Leckie objects. 'My learned friend is talking over the witness.'

Later, Jane agrees that Julie had told her that after seeing the solicitor, she was confident that she could leave Jamie without being financially impoverished. And that she had been surprised by the solicitor's aggressiveness about securing her a fair share of the money. It is not in Dunn's interests to raise the obverse of that point: was Jamie's desperation to get her back related at least partly to the realisation that half his worldly goods might disappear with her?

Dunn moves on to contrast Julie's infidelity with Jamie's longing for an intact family. Had Julie told Jane she was having dinner with her lover 'Adam' the night she moved out of the Balwyn house? 'No.'

'He told you, did he not, that he was devastated by the departure of his wife?' 'Words to that effect, yes.' 'He asked you, did he not, to help him get the family back together again?' 'Yes.'

Dunn hammers her about whether she had thought Laurence Webb was a likely beau for her sister and suggests Jane should have known better. He says accusingly, 'Did you suggest . . . to Laurence that perhaps he should slow down a little bit, because your sister had just come out of a very long-term marriage after 23 years and the *last* thing she should be doing was hitching up with another man?' 'No.'

Later, Jane will take some comfort from the realisation that she did not sob, and she did not rage back at Dunn. Jane had feared Dunn would put her under pressure so that *she* would 'lose it', which the jury might interpret as evidence that her sister Julie could have exploded on that fateful Monday. Jane felt that her self-control on the stand would deny Dunn what he needed.

In fact, Dunn retired satisfied. He did have what he wanted for his Rational Alternative Theory (RAT): an admission that Jane had told Jamie *on the Sunday night* that there was still hope for him with Julie.

The right to silence means Jamie Ramage doesn't have to suffer the ritual humiliation of cross-examination. That is reserved for the people he has hurt.

LECKIE, IN his re-examination, asks Jane Ashton what was behind the plan to let Jamie down lightly. Jane finally gets to have a say: 'She wanted to let him down gently so that it didn't make him become violent, so we were very careful what we said . . . I wanted to protect my sister. I didn't want to aggravate him, and he was not somebody that I would be honest with or trust . . . [Julie] was concerned that he'd be violent towards her if she told him anything, and she'd learnt not to do that, not to antagonise him.'

Why had Jane disliked Jamie so? Jane's anger is now visible but contained; it shows only in her tight face and tense voice. 'He'd isolated her from me and my family, and I believed that he was manipulating and controlling her continually and that she was not allowed to be her own person and that he had abused her physically, verbally – and she's my twin . . . He's a very clever man.'

Her words hang in the air as the jurors file out for lunch.

RAYMOND GARRETT is a thin man with clear blue eyes and a shock of white hair. His face is narrow, with a strong nose and chin and a ruddy complexion. He has come to bear witness for his daughter in a grey suit. He is composed but a little nervous; he blinks rapidly and clears his throat after taking the oath. He still has his English accent and gives his occupation as 'retired'.

Despite their difficult relationship, Jamie had called him, too, to ask advice during the separation. 'He asked me if there's anything he could do to sort of rectify the situation, I suppose, and I said, "I don't think so. I think it's gone beyond the point of reconciliation." And that he was a young man. You know, good-looking bloke, had money, he should try to find himself another life, because I don't think there was a lot left in this relationship with my daughter.'

Ray Garrett is clearly a plain-speaking man. There *were* people who told it straight to Jamie. It will be interesting to see how Dunn manages this witness.

Ray Garrett had known about Laurence: 'Her relationship with this gentleman was – he just made her very happy. He was a very ordinary sort of chap, and I think she was – they shared a lot of interests and she was very, very happy. She was, you know.' He says it almost pleadingly. His chest and shoulders are visibly rising and falling as if his heart is pounding.

He goes on to paint his view of the Ramage marriage. 'At one time, she did love her husband, and she had her children, and she was a very good mother and hostess and housewife and everything. And her way was to try not to rock the boat. And she didn't want to hurt him excessively [with the separation], but she wanted to take care of the children and see that it all went, you know, as best as these things could go. And her attitude was caring. She met Jamie on numerous occasions. They went to watch Matthew play football. She was in contact. She didn't isolate herself from him.' He points out that Julie had left most of the furniture and belongings in the family home, which she had not wanted to strip.

He and his wife had wondered, given Julie's situation, whether they should put off their planned driving trip to Queensland. 'We thought that we should be around here, but my daughter reassured us, "No, Mum, Dad, everything's fine, you go ahead."' He speaks briefly of the phone calls from Jane on the night of Julie's death but Leckie cuts him off from describing their content. 'We travelled back immediately.'

Leckie sits down. Dunn says briefly, 'No questions.'

This is as much as Raymond Garrett will be allowed to say about his daughter's life and death. He will later torment himself over what was left unspoken. He would have tried to say more if he had realised there would be no cross-examination. But he didn't know.

THE JUDGE calls in Matthew and Samantha Ramage. Matthew turns out to be tall and lean. He has brown eyes and wavy brown hair that is ruffled in the front into a cross between an Elvis quiff and a Tin-Tin fringe. He has come in smart casual: a blue-and-white striped business shirt that is open at his tanned neck, navy pants and polished black shoes. He is attractive, in a soapie-star kind of way, even though his chiselled features are not quite regular. He looks young; the kind of age where he would be called a youth rather than a man. Dunn would point out that he is nineteen, the same age as Jamie was when he married Julie. Impossibly young.

Samantha is now seventeen. She is dressed for the fine spring weather, which is warm, rather than the situation, which is chill. The motherless girl has come to her father's murder trial in an aqua singlet top that bares her arms and shoulders – her bra straps are visible – and a short white rah-rah skirt that shows off her brown legs. Her build is smaller and more rounded than her brother's; her tummy has a slight curve. She has long, straight, black hair, and her almond-shaped eyes are dark under finely plucked brows.

Samantha scans the room curiously but Matthew looks straight at the judge. He stands like men in the royal family often do, with one hand clasped over the other in front of him. Osborn offers each of them an exemption from giving evidence. They both decline the offer, Samantha with a flashing smile. She is sent to wait outside while her brother enters the witness box.

MATTHEW JAMES Ramage makes an affirmation rather than swearing on the Bible. He says he got home from football about 6.30 pm the night of the day his mother died. He and his father chatted about the day. Over dinner, Jamie initiated a talk about goals. Matthew says, 'One of mine was to move on with our lives, even though Mum had left, and one of Dad's was [also] "Move on from Mum."' Matthew is taking deep breaths.

About 8.15 pm he heard his father talking to Samantha on the phone. He was distracted with his homework but gathered there was some sort of a problem. His father came over to him. 'He said, "I'm just going to go over and pick up Sam. Mum hasn't come home, or something, from work."' Samantha called Matthew 45 minutes later to say her father had not arrived.

Leckie backtracks. Had Matthew known about Laurence? 'I became aware of it on the Saturday before Mum's death when my father told me about it after they'd been down to the football . . . He only thought Mum could have been interested in this person, he didn't know the full extent of their relationship at that point in time. I think Mum had just told him that she'd met someone else and they'd, you know, gone out for dinner a couple of times.'

They return to the night of 21 July. By 9.15 pm, Matthew was getting concerned. He called his sister again, tried his mother's mobile and then his father's. They both seemed to be turned off. He rang his sister another couple of times and his Aunt Jane. Gilda Pekin arrived with her son.

Matthew told the court his father rang at about 10.40 pm. 'He sounded, I suppose, a bit jittery and worried; yes, a bit of a wreck.' Matthew keeps swallowing, nervous himself now.

Leckie takes him through the history of his parents' marriage. Matthew says his mother had told him she was leaving his father because 'he was too controlling, was a nitpicker, had become boring in some respects'. Was Matthew aware that there had been a serious argument some years before?

'They had arguments, like all people,' he says flatly.

Had Matthew ever seen any violence between his mother and father? 'No.'

What was his father's response to his mother's leaving? 'His first response was to try and get back with Mum through making himself a better person, through improving all the qualities that Mum disliked about him and going through that methodically. Like, it was – I spent about four weeks with Dad every night going through everything that he could do to improve himself.'

Julie was not the only parent to relegate her son's VCE studies to secondary importance.

Next, Matthew drops a small grenade. It seems to go unnoticed by most present; they are not yet aware of the importance to Dunn's case of that final exchange between Jamie and Julie before he killed her. Matthew says that on the Friday night before she died, 'Mum, as she'd told me all along, had said that there was still a chance of Dad getting back . . . On the Sunday night she basically told me that – that Dad didn't have a chance of getting back with her, that she was very keen on Laurence and was seeing him, and *I basically tried to persuade Mum to tell Dad that. She said she'd think about it.*'

Matthew has just provided a new motive for Julie to have challenged Jamie on the Monday. Did she abandon caution and tell her husband the full truth because her son had begged her to? Could her protective instincts about Matthew and his VCE have overcome her wariness about Jamie? I look over at the jury. A juror with a tuft of hair on his chin who has been sneaking glances at the clock is taking yet another one.

Matthew has another piece of news. He says that on the Saturday after football, his father still did *not* know how serious Julie was about Laurence: 'Dad didn't know whether they'd slept together, the full extent of their relationship.'

'Did he say anything about it being obvious that [his relationship with Julie] was totally over?'

'No, he didn't.'

Leckie challenges him. 'Are you certain about that? Think about that carefully, please.'

Matthew turns pink. He fingers his face. He accepts Leckie's offer to refresh his memory by looking at his police statement. Leckie asks him to read the last line above his signature, then asks him again what his father had told him about his mother that weekend.

Matthew still can't quite get it out: 'Yes. I suppose that over the Saturday and Sunday, when we found out, we talked about it a lot, and I suppose he might – yes, he would have said those things.'

Leckie persists, civil but stubborn. 'Will you tell us *what* he said, please? Having refreshed your memory from a document, could you tell us what you remember he said, his comments in relation to his relationship with your mother and whether it was totally over or not?'

'Yes, he said – said in the statement, "It keeps getting worse and it's obviously totally over."'

Leckie has no further questions. He has just blown a great hole in Phil Dunn's argument. Jamie knew on the weekend that his relationship with Julie was over. No claim could be made that Jamie lashed out in that final encounter because his hopes of reconciling were suddenly and brutally dashed. Jamie knew his fate on Saturday. Monday was about his refusal to accept it.

DUNN BOUNDS out of his chair as if propelled by pent-up fury. 'You've been asked questions about a statement that you made to police, and the prosecutor has showed it to you. Is that a statement that you made to police at 4.45 am, quarter to five on the Tuesday morning after you've been told your mother is dead?'

'Yes.'

Dunn accuses Leckie of having cross-examined Matthew. He and the judge debate the issue. Dunn asks Matthew, 'On Tuesday morning 22 July, could I ask you, were you feeling well-balanced and settled at that time?'

'No.'

'Have the police been back to ask you questions since then?'

'No.'

I HAVE begun to realise that the criminal justice system is like a series of funnels. Witnesses are asked to make a statement to police, and that statement sets the boundaries for what they can be asked about in court. That is the first funnel. Then there is the second funnel of the voir dire, where a lot of material in the witnesses' statements can be thrown out, including evidence that is uncorroborated or hearsay or contradicted by others. No attempt is made from that stage onwards to call people back and try to check out those holes or contradictions, to open up the information to a continuing search for what really happened. Then there is the trial itself, which further narrows down the information that can be extracted from witnesses according to the rules of examination and cross-examination.

By the time a case is played out in court, the truth is a trickle.

DUNN ASKS Matthew about his phone call to his mother on the Sunday night. Matthew rang 'to have a chat, but I also asked her questions like, "Seriously, Mum, is there any chance of you getting back with Dad? And what's the story with Laurence?" She said that it was pretty much over with Dad, or that it was over with Dad, that she was really keen on Laurence.'

Matthew says he did not tell his father this 'because that would hurt him and that would be a hard thing to do and I thought, I suppose, the best person to do that would be my Mum'.

He says again that he asked his mother to tell his father. 'I was getting tired of every night coming home and talking to Dad about "Why won't Mum come back?" Yes, I was tired of dealing with a Dad who was – all he thought about was, "How can I get my wife back?" I just kind of wanted her to tell him to stop it. The general gist was, "If there's no chance of you getting back with Dad, can you tell him, because it's emotionally draining on me and I've had enough."'

Jamie told Matthew about his visits to counsellors. Asks Dunn, in an unwittingly comic touch, 'And did he write himself notes and say, "I've got to relax and be more carefree?"'

Matthew doesn't smile. 'Yes, I suppose, like he wrote up lists and things, the things that were bad about him, and I suppose went methodically about how he could work on those things. He went to counsellors for little things. He was trying to work on his spiritual side, trying hobbies and exercises and all that kind of stuff.'

Later, Dunn asks whether Jamie made up CDs of songs to send to Julie. Matthew curls his lip: 'He just gave me the lists and I ended up making them up.'

Matthew says his father wasn't sleeping well and would be up walking around the house at three or four in the morning. One Saturday night Jamie came home crying. 'I sat with Dad and talked to him until 3.30 in the morning and he was just in tears the whole time, and there were a few occasions when I remember speaking to him, him being in tears, and also hearing him in tears.'

IT WOULD soon unfold that Jamie had talked obsessively with many, many other people about his troubles. He was not isolated; it was not as if he had no one else to turn to. But he still insisted on inflicting his distress on his son, who was trying to complete his crucial final year of schooling.

Later, I would read that it is a fallacy that abusive and controlling men are 'out of touch with their feelings'. They prioritise *their* feelings. It's other people's feelings they cannot accommodate.

THE JURY and Matthew Ramage are asked to leave the courtroom. Leckie and Dunn are stoushing over a line of questioning. Dunn has been asking Matthew about how his father talked to him about goals over dinner at Colombo's. The fact that Jamie had originally planned to have this conversation in November, and had moved it forward to that night, indicates that he had already decided to hand himself in to police, Dunn argues.

Dunn is also fuming about an aside Leckie had made earlier in an exchange about admissibility of evidence. Leckie had mentioned that they had spent a week talking about this already. Dunn says indignantly, 'Your honour, I take considerable exception to the jury being told audibly there's been a week's argument and this evidence has been ruled out. It's almost sufficient to discharge the jury, in my view, because it's intimating to them that there are matters kept from the jury . . . It can't be inferred to the jury that there's something they're missing out on, that there's something that . . . by some magician's trick it's been put out, and it took a week to get there, because it's grossly misleading and unfair.'

It turns out that Leckie's quietly spoken aside is legally more worthy of reproof than Dunn's bellicose style with witnesses. The judge reprimands Leckie.

The jurors, those representatives of the community, are not only *not* seen as mature enough to be able to discard their prejudices and judge on the facts; they're not even allowed to know that this is the case.

The judge decides Matthew can be questioned about dinner. If the Crown wants to use the dinner to argue that Jamie was maintaining an appearance of normality, the defence must be free to argue that it was not a normal dinner but a farewell.

A new argument begins over whether Dunn will be permitted to question Samantha about the 'slut' row between her parents. Dunn wants to make clear that Julie and Jamie argued over the fact that Jamie wanted Samantha to have a midnight curfew and did not want Samantha to go to Noosa with her boyfriend the following September. Leckie argues that this gives the wrong flavour to that argument because the jury will not get to hear that in this exchange Julie was also called a 'slut'.

Osborn says, 'Mr Leckie, the difference is that the evidence that Mr Dunn at this stage seeks to adduce is direct evidence. The evidence that you sought to adduce was hearsay.' The jury will hear only one half of the crucial argument. 'Slut' remains off-limits.

Osborn rubs his wig back and forth on his head as the jurors file back into their box.

MATTHEW RETURNS to the stand. He talks about how his father had planned to take him to the final of the Rugby World Cup in November.

At Colombo's, Jamie told him, 'There is something I've been planning. I was going to tell you in November, at the Rugby World Cup, but I'm going to tell you now.' Jamie told Matthew that he was as perfect a son as a father could have; that he was nearly grown-up now, approaching eighteen; and that he loved him and was very proud of him.

He had a final word of advice: 'In terms of what you're doing over the next few years . . . go to university and study hard. I don't want you getting involved in Thermoglaze [Jamie's business].'

Leckie re-examines. What problems in his personality had Jamie been trying to fix? Anything about being controlling?

'Yes, in terms of controlling Mum. Like, things like controlling the horse-riding, what Mum wore, the money that Mum spent, things like that.'

The lawyers have finished with Matthew. Court adjourns.

OBSESSION

Day seven
Wednesday 13 October 2004

THE CASE has begun to take off in the newspapers. Osborn begins the day with a warning to the jury about deciding the case 'on the basis of what you hear in the court and not what you may see in the paper at the breakfast table'.

Ray Garrett, in a blue-and-white-checked gingham shirt and glasses, sits in what has become the family pew at one side. He stares stonily in front of him. Matthew is back too, in a white polo shirt and jeans and soft camel slip-ons. He looks as if he hasn't slept well.

Samantha Jane Ramage is called. Like Matthew, she walks past her father without looking at him. Today she is in stonewash jeans, a white cardigan with a front zipper and a long strand of fake pearls. Samantha chooses to make her oath on the Bible and tells the court she is a student at Lauriston Girls Grammar School. She thanks the tipstaff for her cup of water with a small smile. She gazes at Leckie watchfully as he questions her; she is not anxious, exactly, but wary. At one point she glances up at the gallery, where some of her mother's friends are on vigil. So is her Aunt Jane.

If Matthew was his father's confidant, Samantha was her mother's. The court hears that Julie had told Samantha months earlier that she planned to leave after Matthew's VCE. Samantha says she knew that Julie wasn't confiding in Matthew about her secret plans. Matthew was closer to Jamie, and Samantha was closer to Julie, she agrees. Her voice is curiously lifeless.

Both children had been recruited to the war of the sexes in this family, but both tried to set proper boundaries between themselves and their parents. Matthew asked Julie to sort things out with Jamie. Samantha resisted Jamie's attempts to quiz her about whether her mother was sleeping with Laurence: 'I just said it was between him and Mum, and I didn't answer really.' As she says this Samantha puts one hand up, palm forward, and turns it from side to side in a fending-off gesture.

There is sadness in her eyes as she tells of the many times she tried to call her mother on that Monday night. Talking about how her father sounded 'just normal' when he told her on the phone that her mother was probably with Laurence, she rests her chin in her hand, her little finger in one corner of her mouth in the gesture of a small child. She goes on to describe how she went to Felicity Holding's house when her father didn't turn up for her. Back in the pew, Matthew is bent over, his face hidden. He looks down and plays with his hands.

Samantha's account finishes with both the newly orphaned children going to Gilda Pekin's house for the night. Leckie lets her go.

DUNN ASKS Samantha to confirm that before she went to Lauriston's country boarding school for a year in 2002, everything seemed to be normal between her mother and father. Samantha agrees: her parents argued sometimes but there was no violence.

But Julie had confided to Samantha that her father was too controlling and that she wanted to leave. Samantha knew all about

Julie having seen a solicitor and about the way her mother had begun to photocopy family documents. More surprisingly, Julie had also told her daughter that she was having a relationship with another man. Samantha kept this, too, secret from her father and her brother. Jamie Ramage didn't know it, but his family was divided long before his wife left his home.

Samantha agrees with Dunn that her father was a man who liked routine. He liked the whole family to sit down to dinner together, and he liked Samantha to be home by midnight. She talks about the Noosa argument; Julie had told Samantha she would try to talk Jamie around. And Samantha confirms that she, too, was under instructions from Julie to let her father down gently. She was told not to tell her father that there was no chance of a reconciliation. When asked about Laurence, she told her father she knew nothing.

Samantha leans over the witness stand to murmur to the tipstaff. He goes to the judge's associate, who passes the message to the judge. Samantha has asked for a break. Court adjourns for ten minutes.

WHEN SAMANTHA returns to the witness box, Dunn questions her about Saturday 19 July, two days before Julie was killed. Samantha had stayed at her father's house that night. She says Jamie was very upset: 'He was crying and asking me what to do, and he was just really distraught.' *Distraught*. Such an adult word. But Samantha responded in a little-girl way. She climbed into bed with Jamie and gave him a hug to comfort him. As Samantha recalls this she rocks, ever so slightly, back and forth.

On the Sunday night, at home with Julie, Samantha asked her mother if she had told her father about Laurence.

'Did your mother tell you that she hadn't told your father everything, not the full story?'

'Yes.'

'Did your mother make it clear to you that she'd said something about Laurence but not the full detail of their relationship?'

'Yes.'

Had her mother told her she was planning to start living with Laurence? Samantha corrects him: 'That they were making plans of spending more time together.'

'Did you tell your mother to slow down a bit?'

'Yes.'

Dunn is not satisfied. He wants to firm up his claim that Julie and Laurence were planning to live together. He takes Samantha back to her evidence at the committal. 'Were you asked this question, "Did she tell you she was planning to spend – they might live together and spend more time together?" And did you answer, "Well, yes. Yes."'

'Yes.'

On the Monday morning of her death, Samantha says, her mother had said that she was not going to hide Laurence any more.

'Did you again say things to your mother like "Slow down" or "Take it easy?"'

'Yes.'

'I mean, she'd only known this man for what, less than two weeks?'

'Yes.'

IN LECKIE'S re-examination, Samantha says she had advised Julie to be careful with Jamie. 'She told me about [Laurence] and I just said I didn't think she should tell him anything, really.' Leckie asks Samantha why her mother had not wanted to tell Jamie it was all over. Samantha says, 'She didn't want to, like, kick him when he was down.'

Why her mother had chosen to leave her father secretly? 'Because he would just try and persuade her to stay if she didn't leave when he was away . . . she was worried he might get angry.'

'Yes, worried that he might be angry, and anything else?'

Samantha doesn't hesitate. 'That he'd do something to try and hurt her, like, I don't know, kill the horses or steal the horse float or control the money or something like that.' Leckie persists and she elaborates: her mother had feared that her father 'might control the money or maybe be violent towards myself or her – or her, really'.

It is somehow shocking to hear this from Samantha. The fact that her voice and gaze are steady, that she speaks of it so calmly, makes her loss of innocence even more confronting. This young girl knew that her mother feared this kind of violence from her father. This is old news to her; it has been part of the reality of her world a long time. She speaks of it as if it is to be taken for granted. In her family, it clearly was.

DEBATES ABOUT the way the Ramage children positioned themselves in the court hearing would be conducted over coffees and chardonnays all over town. People wondered about the painfully divided loyalties they must be feeling. I heard a lot of gossip about how Matthew and Samantha got on after the killing and it will not be repeated here. They were both under-age when this catastrophe tore their lives open and they should be allowed to get on with the rest of their lives in privacy. It's not hard to sympathise with their loyalty towards their father. He had always been loyal to them, in his own way; no one doubted that he loved them. And all children have a terror of complete orphanhood.

But it is also important to point out that the Ramage children had grown up in a family where the father was an unusually powerful figure who was accustomed to marshalling his family around his goals and unused to brooking defiance. As one of Julie's friends pointed out, 'Look what happened to the last family member who crossed Jamie Ramage.'

IT IS time for Dunn's hoped-for 'bleeding hearts'. The first therapist to testify is Peter Fullerton, a tall, spare man with straight iron-grey hair and deep-set piercing eyes. He is wearing a navy suit and a dispassionate air. His voice is husky and he pronounces his words with an almost-English precision. Fullerton is a Jungian psychoanalyst and a marital psychotherapist. It seems an unlikely choice for the bombastic Jamie Ramage: depth psychology? Hours on a couch wrestling with dreams, memories and childhood emotional wounds? But Jamie was referred to Fullerton by the wife of his touch-rugby friend Rob Moodie; her father is a psychoanalyst.

Jamie saw Fullerton for a total of three sessions in June 2003. Jamie wanted to talk about his marriage – or lack thereof. They began by looking at the letter Julie had left for him. He told Fullerton he could recognise much in what she had written and that he understood that she had been experiencing him as pushy and demanding. He admitted that at one point he had pushed Julie out of bed during an argument. Jamie had also spoken to Matthew about his pushiness, and 'that led him to think more about how not just his wife, but the family might have experienced him as being pushy', Fullerton says.

Leckie pauses to study the statement in front of him. Fullerton remains utterly still but relaxed; he has the therapist's comfort with silence. Jamie Ramage is looking down at his lap.

In the second session, says Fullerton, Jamie talked about being the boss at work, 'where he expected people to do what he said because he was paying them, and he realised that part of what [Julie] was raising was that this was not an appropriate way for him to engage in his personal relationships, so he was thinking about making a distinction between being a partner and a father and an employer'. He sought no guidance from Fullerton regarding any problems with violent behaviour: 'I got the impression that he didn't experience himself as being, you know, a violent person.' His main concern was to get his wife back. Fullerton saw him for another session to help him with his anxiety but told him that if he wanted to keep open the option of couple-therapy with Julie, there was a limit to how many sessions he could have on his own.

DUNN RISES. Within minutes, he has Fullerton agree to the following propositions: that a person whose long-term partner has left him spends a lot of time thinking about it, often takes on blame for the failure of the relationship, and can become locked in a state of anxiety that undermines his ability to cope and makes him psychologically vulnerable. Dunn hammers it home: 'If you have five weeks or so of anxiety, coupled with mood swings, where a person is tearful and crying, has difficulties concentrating on work, suicidal ideation, things like that, these are all signs that somebody is psychologically vulnerable?'

'Yes.'

I glance over at Ray Garrett. He is staring straight ahead with an unyielding glare.

As a person's ability to cope is reduced, his ability to cope with further shocks or stresses is also diminished? 'Yes.'

'And that's quite clear from psychological study and understanding, isn't it?'

'I think so.'

Dunn asks Fullerton to define 'adjustment disorder'. It is a crisis in a person's life where they have a big change but long to go back to a familiar, pre-existing situation.

But Dunn is not to have it all his own way with this 'bleeding heart'. Fullerton spends his working day helping people understand how they have contributed to their own messes. Dunn asks, 'What would happen if somebody is anxious or depressed and they were then confronted with something which cut them to the very core as a father, a husband, a lover; how would they react in that situation?'

Fullerton says, 'Well, presumably it would depend somewhat on the extent to which the individual is conscious of their having contributed to the situation as it evolved.'

'People can behave irrationally, though, can't they, in that situation?'

'Indeed so, but they are more likely to behave irrationally if there's no notion in that individual's mind of being a contributor to a developing relationship situation.'

SO, A man like Jamie is more likely to 'lose it' if he blames his wife for everything and fails to take responsibility for the way he, too, has damaged the marriage. Outbreaks are more likely where there is lack of insight.

I wonder whether any of the men on this jury have ever hit their wives, or fantasised about killing them; whether any of the women on it have ever been knocked around. I remember reading once about a long-married couple being asked the secrets of their success. Had they ever considered divorce? The wife laughed. 'Divorce? Never. Murder? Frequently!'

LECKIE ASKS Fullerton whether Jamie ever complained to him of any of the symptoms raised by Dunn, and whether he had diagnosed any disorder other than anxiety in Jamie. 'No.'

After Fullerton retires, the jury asks its first question. The tipstaff, who looks after the jurors, has relayed it to the judge: How much experience does Peter Fullerton have in his field? They are told that he completed his first degree in 1975 and has been working as a Jungian analyst and marital psychotherapist since 1988.

ROB MOODIE should not be here today. He has been lined up to testify with the therapists, probably because he carries the title of doctor. In fact, he is involved in this case not as a professional but as a family friend. He is dark and boyishly handsome, with a deep voice that carries the authority of the successful man who is accustomed to being heard. He carries a briefcase and a laptop bag.

Jamie spoke to him often about Julie's leaving. Leckie asks, 'Did he speak about the possibility that his marriage might be at an end?' 'He did, but he didn't want to accept that reality, if it was going to be a reality.' Jamie kept saying he wasn't coping. Moodie referred him to two counsellors: Rosemary De Young and Pauline McKinnon.

Moodie says Jamie was frustrated that, at that stage, Julie was refusing to attend counselling with him. Moodie visited Jamie a couple of times, including the afternoon of Sunday 20 July, the day before Julie's death. He found Jamie beside himself over the news that Julie was in a new relationship. 'I was sort of trying to advise him on the notion that maybe it wouldn't be possible for him to change Julie and her actions and what she wanted to do, and that was something he would have to look at, maybe accepting that reality.'

Jamie tried to recruit him to the cause, asking him if he could contact Julie and intercede on his behalf. 'I felt I couldn't at that stage.'

Jamie Ramage was like a king tottering on his throne, desperately seeking envoys to put his case for him.

DUNN DRAWS out more background. As well as heading VicHealth, Moodie is a professor of public health at Melbourne University and a professor at Monash University. As well as their children being friends, the Moodies and the Ramages socialised at their beach houses over holidays and shared New Year's Eves and New Year's resolutions with each other.

'Your reaction to the separation?'

'We were surprised.'

On Sunday 20 July, 'Did it cross your mind that he was suicidal?'

'It did.'

'Had his situation travelled, from an emotional point of view, downhill when you saw him on 20 July?'

'Certainly that was the most distressed that I had seen him.'

Jamie was angry as well as upset, Moodie says, over 'not knowing where he was, not having, I guess, a clear vision of whether it was going to stop or where the relationship was going to go'. But no, he had never expressed any wish to harm Julie.

LECKIE RISES. The doctor in charge of promoting public health in Victoria is about to get the blowtorch to the belly. Leckie's voice is sharp with accusation. 'Did you, in that meeting, having observed him and talked to him, suggest to him that he should go and see one of his counsellors or psychologists that night or the next day?'

'No. I can't remember actually advising that at that point.'

'And by the end of that hour and a half, what was your view in relation to leaving him at that stage? Were you content to leave him at the house and go off on your way, or what was the position?'

'This had, I guess, been going on for five weeks, and I had been watching him go up and down. I was more concerned – that's why I was concerned, I guess, the next day, to follow up with the outcome of [Jamie's meeting with Julie].'

Leckie won't let go. 'I was just trying really to understand the comment that you made that you were concerned that he might commit suicide – what you did . . . in relation to that, you being the medical practitioner and he is a friend of yours and you are there?'

'I didn't take action at that time. It had crossed my mind and that's why I was so keen to follow up the day after.'

'Well, did you ring him first thing in the morning or anything? Was there a follow-up?'

'I was – I thought of it in the afternoon. I didn't ring him first thing in the morning, no.'

Leckie takes him back to Jamie's anger. Moodie confirms that Jamie was angry not only about his confusion over the future but over the timing of the separation, and over the news that Julie was seeing someone else. (Dunn's team will leave crestfallen tonight. This was the friend they had relied on to build a sympathetic portrait of Jamie's emotional state. Moodie had not said anything about anger at the committal.)

Leckie is done. Moodie has kept his face impassive throughout but he must be relieved to be off the stand. Like Jane and Laurence, he is a person whose innocent actions – or inactions – have been painted as contributing to the build-up of this Greek tragedy that no one saw unfolding. Jamie Ramage, unrecognised Man on the Edge, must have triggered a tsunami of survivor guilt.

SHARON MARCUS is a small, glamorous woman with big hair. She is wearing a straight black skirt, a ruffled white blouse and a nervous smile. Marcus is a counselling psychologist and family therapist based in Surrey Hills. She saw Jamie for two sessions on 26 June and 8 July, 2003. Leckie begins with the usual string of questions, to which she answers 'Yes' in her cultured, lightly accented English.

Jamie told Marcus that Julie had told him he was petty and nasty, wouldn't listen, did what he wanted but was cold and disapproving if she came home late, didn't like her going horse-riding and put her down. He admitted that he had once exploded and thrown a glass during an argument with Julie. As with Fullerton, Jamie presented to Marcus as stressed and anxious, preoccupied with getting his wife back. Did Marcus detect any state other than anxiety? 'I thought he was grieving.'

In the second session, Jamie reported that he'd spoken to Julie on the phone every day; that they were good friends, and the nastiness had lessened. But Julie would not come to counselling because she would be doing it only because Matthew had asked her, and she felt this would be the wrong reason to go.

Asks Leckie, 'Did he tell you that Julie had said things like, "I couldn't imagine having sex with you?"'

'Yes, he did.' (So, the fact that sex with Jamie repulsed Julie – another prong of Jamie's provocation defence – would not have been news to him that Monday.)

'Did he tell you that every time his wife Julie ridiculed him as a businessman, anger would build up?'

'Yes, he did.' (So this, too, Jamie had heard before. The flip side of this plays to Dunn's defence: Julie knew how to wind Jamie up.)

'And did he then state something along these lines: he stated that he is righteous and would react angrily?'

'Yes.'

Jamie told Marcus he had sent Julie flowers with a note saying, 'Forgive me. Find it in your heart to talk it through with me.' And he told Marcus that he hated the whole idea of 'the single thing'. Julie had been his confidante, his good friend, his girlfriend. Julie told him he had been fantastic through the situation, and Jamie said that he believed the way he had acted over the last three weeks was the real him. From his point of view, they had had a happy family and marriage for 23 years, and he felt frustrated that he hadn't addressed the problems in the relationship six months ago.

Marcus says, 'The only advice that I gave Mr Ramage was that he should check with his wife whether she would be happy to receive the phone calls from him that he said he wanted to make. He said he wanted to call her often and he wanted to see her often and my advice to him was to check with her, whether that was okay for her.'

Jamie booked another session for 21 July but later rang to cancel, saying Julie refused to come with him.

And no, he had never spoken to Marcus about problems with sleeplessness or suicidal thoughts.

I HAD been waiting for Rosemary De Young. According to the transcript of the committal hearing, she was the only therapist who used her evidence to point out the power dynamic in the Ramages' marriage. Dunn had asked her then, 'It's not uncommon to read in the newspapers that men kill wives or kill their children after the break-up of a long-term relationship. Are you familiar with that?'

'Yes. But there are a lot of men that don't,' she pointed out.

'Is there some phenomenon which you're familiar with in your studies or your practice that explains this?'

'I think it's *the break of the control.*'

'What happens?'

'[These men] don't cope very well when they don't have control of the external environment.'

Later, she actually rebuked Dunn: 'I feel that your questions are very general and if you wanted to give me something more specific I'd be happy to answer it.' Perhaps wisely, Dunn left it at that.

I wonder whether Dunn will have trouble getting 'fragile' and 'vulnerable' past such a no-nonsense witness. But Dunn has learned his lesson; he does not let her anywhere near 'control'.

De Young turns out to be a small ash-blonde woman with a deep fringe, a self-possessed manner and a calm, pleasant voice.

She is wearing a sober flecked grey pantsuit, a sky-blue top and glasses and looks like a schoolteacher. De Young is a psychologist based in Hawthorn and has been in practice for eighteen years. On 15 July, she saw Jamie and Julie together – at Jamie's request – for a one-off session to clarify whether there was any hope of saving the relationship.

Julie had come to the session because Matthew blamed her for leaving and wanted her to talk. She told De Young the marriage was virtually over and that she was over Jamie. She had been unhappy for ten or fifteen years and Jamie was controlling and mean. She had left him a month earlier because of some final insulting remarks and since leaving she had felt lighter.

Jamie had said that he wanted the marriage to survive. He reminded Julie of the good times they had had, said he'd had personal counselling about his anger and tried to convince Julie to try again. Julie again said No and repeated that she was over him.

De Young pointed out their competing agendas: Jamie wanted to get back together and Julie emphatically did not. As there was no goodwill on Julie's part to revive the relationship, there was no point in marriage counselling. De Young suggested that they remain respectful towards each other and reminded them that they were always going to be parents to their children. Julie, De Young told Leckie, 'was very reluctant to be there'.

DUNN ASKS De Young, 'After [Jamie] suggested that it would be best if his wife spoke first, he sat there politely and listened?'

'Yes, he did.'

'Did she tell you that she'd had affairs throughout the marriage?'

'No, she did not.'

'Did she tell you that she had an affair immediately prior to the marriage ceasing?'

'No, she did not.'

'Did she tell you if there was a man in her life at that time?'

'No, she didn't.'

'A Mr Laurence Webb?'

'No, she didn't.'

And later: 'She had no difficulty in your presence in describing the things she didn't like about her husband, apparently?'

'Yes.'

De Young says Julie also complained that she had to withdraw money secretly to pay for feed for her horses, and that she felt like she had to be the super housewife and mother and had also to work hard and earn money while staying the attractive wife.

And she told De Young that recently, she had just been saying 'whatever', agreeing with Jamie instead of fighting – *which built up hatred inside her*.

JULIE HAD her say at De Young's and Jamie, at least outwardly, copped it sweet, but he must not have liked what he heard. The very same day that they saw Rosemary De Young, he took Julie to *another* marriage counsellor. Scotch College parent Rhonda McMurtrie had said that Jamie was known at dinner parties as someone who would not let an argument rest until he got the answer he wanted to hear. He always had to have the last word. Was his pursuit of Julie about that same stubbornness? Or was he utterly panicked about being on his own? His persistence was tragi-comic: *If you should leave me, can I come too . . . ?*

COURT ADJOURNS for the day and Dunn drifts over. 'Ah, twists and turns and permutations!' he says ruminatively in that rich, deep voice. 'The problem with what we do is that I have one brief from one party and he has one brief from another and often they don't meet . . .'

I reply, 'It sounds to me like the typical bad marriage. There is her marriage and there is his marriage, and their different experiences have nothing in common. But it shouldn't end like this.'

Says Dunn, 'Oh no, nothing is worth this. I have another case, a young man who hit a man in a pub here' – he gestures to my jaw.

'He fell over and died.' He looks at me. 'And every life around him is ruined.' He turns and strides off, dragging his wheelie case of documents behind him.

Is that what he thinks this is? The chance result of a single impulsive moment?

SEX v DEATH

Day eight

Thursday 14 October 2004

THE AGE newspaper ran a headline about Jamie as a 'killer husband' this morning. Dunn greets me gushingly: 'How are you, young lady?'

I wince, feeling every one of my 40-something years. 'That's a relative term,' I reply.

Matthew has moved today; he is sitting beside his grandfather. The day begins with the prosecutor requesting some time to attend a relative's funeral the following morning. Osborn decides that given the continuing burden for the prosecution of such a complex case, Leckie should be allowed the whole day. When the jurors enter Osborn tells them, 'Because of personal matters affecting one of the participants in this trial, we will not be sitting tomorrow. We'll be adjourning today, and going over to Monday . . . We'll try and sit a bit longer today, but we won't be sitting tomorrow.'

It seems a clear enough direction, but it would lead to the jury asking for clarification. Some of them must have failed to understand a simple instruction about taking the day off. What chance would they have with the Dickensian cast of characters and complicated legal argument that is to come?

THE SECOND counsellor the Ramages saw together was Tom Paterson, a Hawthorn-based psychologist who has been a relationship counsellor and therapist for 37 years. He is a tall, thin man with glasses, ruffled grey hair and one of those beards that has no moustache. It gives him the look of an Amish elder.

Jamie had initially made an appointment for 30 July but had later rung Paterson and begged for other names so that he might see someone else sooner. Then Jamie rang again and asked to be fitted in to the first cancellation as 'he was not travelling as well as he thought he would'. Paterson phoned Jamie the day they saw De Young, 15 July, and offered him a vacancy that had arisen due to a cancellation. Jamie grabbed it.

When Jamie had originally contacted Paterson, he had said that Julie had told him she was 99 per cent sure she didn't want to come back to the marriage.

In the session together, Julie had told Paterson that she and Jamie had had problems early on, and that he had been violent a couple of times. Then she left him for six months in 1982. After they reconciled, they had two children and there was another incident of violence. After this, Jamie realised she would not tolerate any more violence but he continued to intimidate her with actions such as breaking glasses during arguments. She had felt she couldn't leave because of the children.

Jamie accepted that most of the marital problems were his fault and said that he would not even have agreed to see a counsellor if Julie had not left. He was very anxious that Julie not begin a new relationship. He asked Paterson whether it was a good idea that neither of them saw other people at this stage; Paterson agreed.

Jamie said that if Julie had felt able to stand up to him earlier in the marriage, this would not have happened. He and Julie were very similar but he hadn't put enough into the marriage or spent enough time on people. He had concentrated too much on the good-provider role and was not happy with the business he was in.

Julie said Jamie had had a fight with her father that had gone on for far too long. When she had threatened to leave two years earlier, Jamie had finally made up with her family. She told Paterson that the way Jamie controlled her affected all their relationships and if they grew old together, they would be very isolated.

Jamie pointed out that his previous business, which he had had for ten years, had great problems, and for three or four years it was all he thought about. At the time, he had not told Julie he was on the verge of bankruptcy.

Julie said she had left him a few times and gone to stay at her sister's. She said he had treated her very badly while he was working at Country Road and studying full-time. Jamie explained that at that time he was frustrated and not where he wanted to be; the house they were living in was not renovated and was a bit of a dump.

Paterson asked them what had led to the violence. Jamie said he became upset when Julie questioned him about being a good husband and family man. Julie said that when they were out in a big group, Jamie would get argumentative, and she would tend to side with other people because she did not want to be identified with him. But she had been impressed that Jamie had not done anything hurtful after she left. She had been afraid that he might hurt her horse or punish her.

They made three more appointments with Paterson. The following day, Jamie rang Paterson to ask what he thought of their chances of getting back together.

Jamie Ramage hadn't wanted a therapist. He wanted an oracle.

IT'S THE kind of story marriage counsellors hear every day. He's caught up in work and money because he doesn't know how to connect emotionally at home, so it suits him to cling to traditional role models. But because he is over-invested in work, he thinks he's a failure as a man if he does not live up to his role. She resents the way he neglects her emotionally and expects her to play her traditional role perfectly, because her role requires a lot more work than his does and has less status. And anyway, why should she have to play wifey, waiting on the man of the house, when she is out earning money too?

That's the problem with male fantasies of a little woman who will make him feel like a big man – women are bigger than they used to be.

DUNN KNEW from the committal that Paterson would be a key part of his RAT. He takes him through his qualifications and the fact that he has taught other counsellors for many years and knows his craft well.

Paterson says he was surprised at how relaxed Julie was in the interview: 'She was not afraid of him, did not show any fear of him at all.' Later, he says that this must have been because Jamie was so contrite: 'She felt very safe with him being very willing to admit his mistakes and accept his responsibility for what had gone wrong.' Paterson did not know they had seen another counsellor earlier in the day, or that Julie had told the other counsellor that the marriage was over.

Had Jamie reacted badly to the home truths at De Young's? Or did his very persistence – his taking her to see Paterson – suggest to Julie that she needed to pull back? Because this is what she told Jamie in front of Tom Paterson: 'Jamie, I'm not going anywhere!' She said, 'Jamie was, and still is, my friend.'

Matthew turns his face away from the body of the court as Paterson says, 'It's unclear, of course, whether she recognised, as I did, that James was certainly not ready to accept the idea that the marriage was over. Frequently the person in Julie's position will go along with a contract [to attend more sessions] because they want to find a way out of the relationship without too much . . . hurt.' He tells Dunn it is not delusional for a man to still have hope four weeks after his wife has told him it's all over: 'People in his position, it takes them often a long time to accept and come to terms with that possibility, and it seems to me important not to try to force the person to accept what they're not ready to accept.'

Paterson says they both left looking buoyed up. 'I didn't – didn't get any signals at all that it was a dangerous situation . . . I would have done something quite different if that had been the case.' Paterson says that even considering that Jamie had not expected to lose his 23-year marriage, 'He was unusually agitated and worried and anxious.' But he doubted that Jamie was depressed. 'He was making plans for the future. He was really looking very seriously at his life, and so on, which was not so consistent with being depressed.'

And then Paterson put the cherry on Dunn's cake. Would he conclude that Mr Ramage may well have been emotionally fragile? He answers eagerly. 'Very, very much so. I would also think, given that he admitted himself he's a very controlling man, who wants to know what's going on, that . . . it would be harder for him than it would be for many other people moving out of a long-standing marriage.'

So, says Dunn, it would be harder for Jamie because he had a controlling personality and ran his own business and was used to making his own decisions? 'Yes.' For such a man, losing the hope he is clinging to so desperately might well trigger desperate action, Paterson agrees.

Dunn asks about such a man hearing that his wife is having a sexual relationship with another man, with whom unfavourable comparisons are made. Paterson replies: 'I would have to say that that's a dangerous situation. He'd be extremely overwhelmed by something like that . . . This was a situation where, for safety's sake, it would have been important to take things slowly.'

Dunn turns his attention to Julie. 'A woman who's been in a long-term relationship may well be vulnerable to being swept off her feet quite easily?'

'Yes. It's not unusual when people are considering leaving a relationship, or leave a relationship, to sort of see how attractive they are; things like that.'

'They affirm to themselves that they're still desired or wanted?'
'Yes.'

'In that situation, they may form inappropriate relationships if they're not careful?'

'Yes. And they're often short-term relationships.'

So it's not a good idea for either party to get hooked up with someone else? It's their decision, Paterson says, but that was his advice.

He agrees that Julie, having been married to Jamie for so long, would know exactly how to upset him. He points out Julie had been careful for a long time not to say things that upset him, but agrees with Dunn that she had gained confidence because of Jamie's contrite attitude.

And then, Dunn goes over it all again. He takes Paterson once more through every point that fits with his RAT; every comment that paints Julie as newly confident with Jamie and unwise to have begun a new relationship; every point that paints Jamie as a fragile, grieving, obsessive man unable to cope with any further shock. Dunn is like a teacher revising at the end of a lesson; he is saying to the jury, Now, did you note this? And this? And this?

LECKIE TAKES Paterson back to Julie's civility towards Jamie. Yes, she had spoken confidently but she was in no way provocative, abusive or vindictive towards him. 'She was being very constructive and open and clear,' says Paterson. I glance over at Jamie. He has a faraway look in his eyes.

Could Jamie's anxiety have been related to his fear that he wouldn't get his own way? It could, agrees Paterson. There was also talk in the session about how angry he got when he didn't get what he wanted. 'She said he would be upset if she wasn't at home on time and that she could do things herself provided that it didn't disrupt his life and so she had to be very careful not to inconvenience him . . . And it appeared that he didn't have to do very much for her to be very conforming after a period of time in the relationship.'

Julie Ramage must have gotten so tired of being a good girl.

THE JURY has a question. There is another simple point they have not understood. Originally, they had been told that Jamie had said he was 99 per cent sure Julie didn't want to come back. This has been corrected, and they were told that Jamie had said that *Julie* had said she was 99 per cent sure she would not come back. Through the tipstaff they told the judge they were still unclear about it. Paterson's evidence is read back to them again.

It's hard to know whether to be relieved that they are paying attention or dismayed at how difficult they are finding the proceedings. Jury duty is like parenting: a crucial job for which one needs no qualifications.

DR KATE Clark is another family friend who seems to have slipped into the line-up of therapists because of her professional title. She tells the court she is a friend of both Jamie and Julie. Clark is a small, pale woman who looks to be in her late 40s, with dark hair that she has swept up and back with a crocodile clip. She is wearing dark-rimmed rectangular glasses and a plain brown coat. Her voice is so soft it sounds shy, but the determined Clark has spent a lot of time thinking through what she wants to say today, and she will prove surprisingly successful at getting it out.

She says that Jamie had a subtle power over Julie that was obvious in their day-to-day life. Julie was not quite 'submissive', she says – 'Submissive's a difficult word to use. But something along those lines. He was always in control. Julie never, *ever* was in control.'

Kate Clark was one of the people Jamie phoned obsessively in the weeks of the separation; sometimes three or four times a day, and for as long as 40 minutes at a stretch. The theme was always 'whether I could suggest some ways of getting her to come back, to seeing the mistake she was making . . . He often would ring me about what happened that day. What did I think about something that she'd said? Did I think that this perhaps meant that she would be coming back soon? Did I interpret it as meaning she would never return? Did I think I might be able to perhaps persuade her to change? What if she were to meet somebody?

'There were lots of questions, but really, especially in that early time, it was about how to help exert some pressure to get her to return.'

Her advice to him was shrewd and blunt. Kate Clark told Jamie, 'You need to *back off*. You've got to stop applying all this pressure to her; you've got to stop doing what it is that she's trying to get away from . . . You are suffocating her. You have got to stop suffocating her *because this is why she's gone.*'

She damages Dunn's portrayal of Jamie as a fragile man disabled by grief. Her vision is of a cold man whose determination to have his wife back was almost autistic in its lack of emotion: he was convinced that Julie had to return because it was structurally 'necessary'. 'It was like a building block in a house, something important that was required to be returned to its position . . . It seemed that he wasn't sort of talking about missing her, but rather the state of the family requiring a particular structure.'

Kate Clark advised the Ramages to see Tom Paterson. They both had the idea that marriage counselling was about retrieving the relationship but Clark explained it could also help people through a break-up. She hoped that if Jamie was getting help, Julie would be allowed to get on with her life. Jamie became impatient when he couldn't get an appointment straight away: 'Like everything that James would have as a plan, he would be dissatisfied if it couldn't be executed immediately.' But when he did see Paterson, he was pleased with the session; he had been unhappy with his experiences with other counsellors.

Forget the mantras about counselling and self-growth; for Jamie Ramage, counselling had to be a way of getting Julie back. He was like the great and powerful Wizard of Oz exposed by the pulling back of the curtain to be a small, anxious man. Jamie didn't want to probe his anxiety. He wanted Julie back so the curtain could be closed again.

But Julie, says Clark, was very happy in her new life. 'She never said anything really bad about James; she was very loyal . . . She just had this very sunny, nice outlook on life, was very positive about it. There was nothing reckless that she was going to do; she was just looking forward to this continuing of this great happiness that she felt.' And Julie told her that she didn't think that Jamie could ever change.

Clark last saw them together at the football in Geelong on the Saturday. 'They both looked very distressed and uncomfortable. James was standing in that way he had, which I can picture very clearly, because he often did it, but it looked more solemn and heavy than usual. He would stand behind Julie's shoulder, as if guarding her or keeping her.' On the Sunday morning, Jamie rang Clark and told her that Julie had said she was seeing someone else.

THE LAST counsellor is Pauline McKinnon, a family therapist and meditation counsellor who runs a meditation centre in Harp Road, Kew – the street that also has the hotel where Jamie confessed, and the police station where he turned himself in. McKinnon is beautifully coiffed, her short brown hair upswept, and she has the enunciation of an ABC announcer. She specialises in clients with symptoms of anxiety: insomnia, panic attacks, agoraphobia. Jamie had demanded of her, too, that she provide an appointment quickly, and when she first interviewed him, he told her that his current anxiety rating was ten out of ten and that he had trouble sleeping.

He told McKinnon he had possibly developed an angry attitude and this might have been due to striving too hard in his work and lacking the balance of a more altruistic focus. He seemed 'heartbroken, I would have said' over the break-up of his marriage. McKinnon explained to him that personal change would not necessarily bring Julie back but that it might improve his own life, and it was possible this would lead to her return. Jamie signed up for sixteen one-hour meditation sessions. He did not make it to any of them. The first one was scheduled for the morning of the day after he killed Julie.

WE BREAK for lunch. There are now three of us following the trial from what has become the journalists' table: myself, *The Age*'s Supreme Court reporter, Peter Gregory, and a young woman from the *Herald Sun*. As the courtroom empties of non-participants Dunn, ever-determined to foster team spirit and lighten the mood of this grim proceeding, grabs himself a lolly from the jar under the tipstaff's desk and offers some to the rest of us. He promises the tipstaff, who is raising an eyebrow but holding back a grin, that he will replace them. The tipstaff quips, 'What – "Trust me, I'm a barrister?"' The lawyers and the journalists laugh. It is the camaraderie of fellow travellers around a small campfire in a dark landscape.

AFTER LUNCH Dunn wafts in singing 'Oh Dunnie boy' to the tune of the old Irish melody. Matthew is already here, on his own in a pew next to the witness box reading a paperback. He has doubled the book over with its spine bent back. Further along in the side pew is a cool young blonde with heavy make-up, a business suit and a notebook; it looks like TV is now on to the story. The judge's associate pops her head out of the door behind the bench and asks the tipstaff to get the jury.

The first witness is the much-discussed best friend, Gilda Pekin. Gilda Pekin is short and solidly built. She has unfussed short brown hair with a soft wave, and her face is bare of make-up. For her day in court she is wearing a black suit and carries a backpack. In a low, croaky voice that sounds as if she has a cold, she tells the court that she is a certified practising accountant and a lawyer, and that she first met Julie in 1985 when they were both visiting the local baby health centre.

Gilda went out with Julie and her lover 'Adam' in March 2003. Julie later became very worried – 'hysterical', recalls Gilda – that her husband would find out about Adam (this was about the time Julie accidentally turned on her mobile while she was with Adam). Gilda's advice to her was to choose: 'I told Julie that the circumstances of her meeting [Adam] were silly, and the fear that she had that she might be caught out was a ridiculous situation to put herself in, and she should make up her mind about whether she wanted to stay in her marriage or go.' Julie told Gilda that she would wait until the children's school fees were paid and she could manage financially. In May, Gilda referred her to family lawyer Caroline Counsel. A week or so later, Julie insisted on meeting Gilda in a car. She again expressed terror that Jamie might find out about her affair. On Friday 6 June, Julie told Gilda that she had had a bad argument with Jamie. She was weeping.

A week later she moved out of the house. Julie was anxious not to take too much furniture because she did not want to anger Jamie or disrupt the family. 'We discussed every item she was going to take or not take,' recalls Gilda. Gilda and Adam and Julie had dinner together that night.

Jamie called and came to visit Gilda several times during the separation. He wanted to know whether Julie had anybody else. 'I knew she hadn't planned to leave him *for* anybody, and so I told him that she hadn't been planning to leave him for somebody; there had been nobody else.' Gilda did tell Jamie that Julie had met a man called Simon at the Botanical Hotel on the Friday after she left, with whom she had had a casual dinner. Julie was cross with Gilda for having said this and told her that she feared Jamie knowing about any men in her new life. Julie told Gilda that Jamie was continually asking her around to see the renovations. Gilda warned her against it.

On 17 July, Julie and Samantha came to dinner. Julie told Gilda that she had told Jamie about Laurence. 'I said, "Have you really told him what Laurence means to you?" and she said she had done that . . . because she wasn't going to pretend any more that she was going back, and she didn't want the pretence of conducting a relationship while she was still married. She said she felt quite free . . . She was absolutely ecstatic.'

Cross-examined by Dunn, Gilda acknowledges that Adam had been sending love letters to Julie care of the Lorne Post Office over the summer holidays in 2003, and Gilda had minded them for Julie. She kept them for six months but gave them back to her at dinner on 17 July. She acknowledges she knew of an affair Julie had had with a man whose children were also at Deepdene Primary.

Dunn questions Gilda hard about the degree to which she had helped cover up Julie's affairs and about the way she had reassured Jamie that there was no one else. He has her repeat again that Julie had said she would no longer hide her relationship with Laurence. Gilda answers with her arms folded and her eyes staring sightlessly away from him.

THE NEXT witness is the mystery lover whom I have called 'Adam'. For legal reasons, he cannot be named or described in any way that might identify him.

He met Julie in September 2002 and they became friends. She confided in him about the problems in her marriage and told him she wanted to leave her controlling husband. By October, they were lovers. The sexual side of their relationship ended after she separated from Jamie: 'She basically said [it was because] I was a married guy and there was no future in being intimately involved with me. We remained very good friends, even to the day that she passed away, and we spoke and still maintained that friendship, but she said that she would start to date or, you know, see other men, and I accepted that.'

He spoke to her on the morning she died, as he did on most mornings. 'We caught up on what she had done, what I had done, just general banter; two close friends catching up with each other.' Julie told him Jamie had made the footy trip to Geelong horrid: 'She said it was a particularly difficult journey there and back and even at the ground. He isolated her from their friends and the other parents and badgered her and kept going at her all day.' Adam reaches forward and grips the top of the witness box with one hand.

Julie revealed to Adam that she had told Jamie that day that she had met someone else and the marriage was over.

How concerned had Julie been to keep the affair with Adam from her husband? 'She was fearful of her life.'

WHERE LECKIE is trying to keep the jury focused on fear and death, Dunn interposes sex. Cross-examining Adam, he heads straight for the bedroom: You and Julie were strangers when you met? You were married? She was married? You began an intimate affair? You wanted to keep it secret?

And he throws in another line of questioning that reveals a strange titbit: police discovered that Jamie Ramage had called Adam's phone the afternoon he killed Julie. Adam had never given Jamie his number, and Adam says he did not receive the call.

As Adam leaves the courtroom, his eyes on the exit, Jamie Ramage shoots him a hard look.

WAS JULIE Ramage ever without a man in her life, really? The affair with the man at Deepdene Primary was followed by the affair with Adam. She met Simon at the Botanical Hotel around the time she dropped Adam. She cancelled a date with Simon to have her Friday night with Laurence. She seems to have been an emotional trapeze artist, swinging from one man to the next, frightened of the empty space in between.

But it sounds like her fear of being alone went with a kind heart. Julie had managed to hold on to Adam's friendship; it must say something.

Months later, I would wonder about *what* it said. Dunn would tell me that defence counsel routinely seek any police records of witnesses. He found that a woman had once taken out an intervention order against 'Adam'. Another source told me that the complainant was a married woman who had ended an affair with Adam but who felt harassed when he continued to pursue her.

Maybe Jamie wasn't the only man Julie was letting down gently.

THE JUDGE warns the jury that Adam's evidence about what Julie told him is just evidence about her state of mind. They cannot take it as fact that what she told Adam about what she said to Jamie was true. 'Now that may seem a bit artificial, but there are very good reasons for that rule, because whereas when Julie describes something in Mr Ramage's presence to the counsellors, he has the opportunity to contradict or say what he says happened; when Julie is speaking to someone else, he's not there, and it's hearsay of the underlying facts. So you can see that in terms of those underlying facts, the law says that's not admissible evidence.'

Let's hope the jury make more sense of this than they did of the news about their day off.

Matthew leaves court during the afternoon break without looking at his father. Jane Ashton, in a smartly tailored olive green pantsuit, stands talking outside. She must be watching the trial from the upstairs gallery. Coming back, Matthew is just behind me. I hold the door open for him rather than have it close in his face. He meets my eyes. 'Thanks,' he says courteously. I feel another stab of sympathy for him. What an initiation into manhood the kid has had.

LAURENCE WEBB is called. The journalists reach for their pens. They have been waiting all day for 'the lover'. He is in a dark suit, his hair clipped short above his square face. Like Adam, he is self-contained in the face of courtroom scrutiny. He has a direct way of talking and an upright bearing that is almost military.

Laurence explains how their relationship began and says that on Friday 18 July, three days before Julie's death, he spoke to her more seriously about their future. 'My wife and I had agreed when we'd separated some two and a half years before that we would not seek to get a divorce immediately. We wanted to do the minimum to upset the children. But as soon as either of us entered into a serious relationship, then we would seek a divorce at that time. From the day after our first day, [Julie and I had] entered a relationship where we weren't seeing anybody else.' They planned to spend more time together while each maintaining their own homes, 'particularly being sensitive to our daughters'.

He spoke to Julie on the phone in the morning and the evening of the Saturday she had gone to the football with Jamie. Julie told him that Jamie had come into her house and seen notes relating to a vacation she planned to take with Laurence and their daughters during the September school holidays. On Saturday, she had decided to tell Jamie that it was serious with Laurence, that 'she was not going to lie any more. And he'd asked a lot of questions about me'.

Laurence spoke to her again on the Monday morning. She was going to call him back with the travel arrangements for Noosa, which she was keen to finalise. She never did.

DUNN TAKES Laurence through his dates with Julie and itemises in detail what they had done on each evening and which nights they had slept together. By this stage you'd now seen Mrs Ramage for what, *five or six days*, and you had decided in your mind that it was a serious relationship? You suggested that the two of you may start *living together*? At this stage you were *unemployed*? At one point he barks at Laurence like an old-time schoolmaster: 'If you would attend to my question, please, *sir*!' Laurence's face reddens but he refuses to bite. He corrects any inaccurate assumptions and they move on.

Julie had told Laurence on the Friday that both the counsellors had advised Jamie that he had to let her go. She told Laurence she felt Jamie had finally come to terms with the fact that the marriage was over.

Laurence agrees that he had been enthusiastic in his approaches to Julie. He had emailed her some of his poems and bought her lingerie. 'The main reason for that was that she was embarrassed that the lingerie she wore when she was with me was from Target.'

MONTHS LATER, over a long lunch and a bottle of pinot noir, Philip Dunn would tell me that the Ramage case reminded him of the Akira Kurosawa movie *Rashomon*, in which three different people see an incident in the forest, and each comes away with a different account of it. 'The central theme is that incidents occur and [how it is perceived] is very much in the eye of the beholder. It's a very subjective thing, what you take away from it. So how Jane Ashton describes the marriage is different to how Matthew describes the marriage which is different to how Dr Clark describes the marriage.'

And how Jamie saw the counselling sessions is different to how Julie saw the counselling sessions, which is different to how the counsellors saw the counselling sessions. Jamie took away hope that there could be a new beginning, and Julie took away confidence that he had accepted an ending. The counsellors saw a couple in which the man was meek and contrite and there were no signs of danger.

This story is riddled with miscommunications of Shakespearean proportions. Does anyone ever really hear anyone else?

LINDY WEIR, a horse-riding friend, tells the court that Julie's attendance at the club became more erratic in 2003. Julie rang Lindy early in the year and asked her not to tell Jamie that she hadn't been coming to horse-riding. She was in 'considerable fear' of what might happen if he found out. At the time, Julie's moods were up and down, and she seemed not to be herself. Julie confided in Lindy about the marriage; Lindy told her to leave if it was violent.

'Did she tell you that she was seeing a married man instead of horse-riding?' asks Dunn. 'Did she mention a man called [Adam]?' No.

BEFORE COURT adjourns for the three-day break, Leckie asks Osborn, in the jurors' absence, whether the judge could tell the jury not to make a moral judgement about the sexual evidence. Leckie wants this evidence to be assessed only in terms of whether Julie would have said something provocative to her husband on the fatal day.

Osborn demurs. He talks again about how the law has different rules regarding evidence about the character of an accused and evidence about the character of a victim. 'I understand that the dignity of the deceased is a proper concern. I understand that it is not appropriate for her character to be blackened in this court. But I am charged with the duty to ensure that the accused man gets a fair trial.'

Leckie is tenacious. He is like a knight at a joust, charging with a lady's colours tied to his lance. He argues that there is huge prejudice in the way the evidence is being used and that it will distract the jury from the true issues. Osborn refuses him. The jurors are entitled to see this part of the relationship evidence and make their own call.

The lady's champion has been unseated.

THE WORKMATES

Day nine
Monday 18 October 2004

SITTING DOODLING before court begins, I realise there is something addictive about this show. It is a cross between theatre-sports and melodrama. I missed it over the break. I also wonder, with a tickle of shame, whether I'm the one feeling close to *Schadenfreude* now. The fascination as the tale unfolds is almost pleasurable, in a ghastly sort of way; so is the relief that I am an observer, not a participant. Storytellers plunder other people's emotional treasuries while keeping their own shields up.

Dunn arrives as Leckie is already laying out his papers on the bench. Leckie responds to his greeting with a cheerful 'G'day Phil. What shocks have you got for me today?'

Among my papers is a clipping of a news story from a broadsheet newspaper at the weekend. It's headlined 'Real estate killing in death houses' and talks about how hard it is to sell houses in which there have been murders, and how there is a push to force real estate agents to disclose such histories to potential buyers. One

Sydney couple had demanded their deposit back after putting down $80,000 on the North Ryde house where triple murderer Sef Gonzales slit his mother's throat and stabbed and bashed his father and sister to death.

Perhaps I'm not the only one to have clipped the article. Or perhaps it's coincidence. But after more argy-bargy over the admissibility of evidence, Dunn brings this very topic before the judge. 'The former Ramage family home has not been sold. The money from that sale will go to Samantha and Matthew. There has been some concern articulated to me [about media references to the address] rather devaluing the house, which has an impact, of course, on whatever it is that the children will get from the sale of it.' Could his honour request the media to refrain from mentioning the address?

Osborn says he is not willing to make a formal order but he welcomes consideration from the press.

This case must be the ultimate in middle-class crimes. Jamie Ramage kills his wife, and now his QC asks us to protect his property values. Is this what is meant by *petty* bourgeoisie? One of the other reporters mutters under his breath about the unremarked fate of addresses owned by killers in Sunshine and Reservoir, two of Melbourne's working-class suburbs.

ANNETTE LUCKMAN is the first witness today. She has come in a black leather jacket and dark casual pants. In her late 40s, she wears no make-up on her pleasant, countrywoman's face, and her fair hair is wavy and fly-away. She is a personal care worker and a member of the Hurstbridge Adult Riding Club, she tells us in a voice that is rather breathless with nerves. Most of the other witnesses adopt their best businesslike manners when being examined. Luckman is simply her own self.

Julie had confided in her about the marriage. She knew there had been several 'distressing episodes', and that Jamie disliked Julie's horse-riding and wanted her to play golf with him instead. Several weeks before she actually left Jamie, Julie told Luckman that she was leaving. Then she rang back and said she had changed her mind because of Matt's VCE. She wasn't riding much and was very distracted when she did turn up. When she finally did leave, she told Luckman that she felt like she was a teenager again; she was having a good time.

On that last Monday morning, Julie was open and happy in a phone call with Luckman: 'It was the first time I'd seen Julie like that for months.' Luckman begins to cry, quietly; not so hard that she cannot speak but the tears are visible. Julie had told Luckman she'd had a romantic weekend with Laurence and that she'd found her perfect match. 'She was happy.' Luckman turns aside to hide her tears and then shrugs, embarrassed.

Cross-examined by Dunn, Luckman says Julie had introduced her to Laurence the previous Wednesday and suggested that the local riding clubs should have a poetry night with him and other poets at the Warrandyte Hotel. On the Monday morning, she and Julie talked about making up a flier to advertise it. She looks puzzled at Dunn's intense questioning about this, as am I; where could this be going? Dunn's tone suggests the poetry-night plan is somehow guilty behaviour. He clearly wants the jury to note it.

Julie had told Luckman there were difficulties between Jamie and Samantha, which she was finding it hard to deal with. She found it distressing when they fought. Julie also told her that she had tried to include Jamie in her horse-riding; she bought him a saddle and would bring him to events but he was very remote and didn't mix well.

JEANETTE FARLEY is a primary school teacher and librarian. She wears dark-rimmed glasses and an olive green jacket. She speaks in a clear, confident tone and comes across as brisk and organised; it's not hard to imagine her shushing naughty children in the library. She had known the Ramages for thirteen years, since their children started prep together at Deepdene Primary School. They socialised often: 'Julie was a girl I liked a lot and we were quite good friends. She was lovely.'

In 1997, Julie had told her that she was having an affair with a mutual friend. 'He and his wife, we were all friends together.'

The first Jeanette Farley knew of the separation was when Jamie rang to cancel a dinner date because Julie had left. Farley, too, became another brick in Jamie's wailing wall; he came around to see her one night even though she suggested he wait until her husband was back from a trip. He quizzed her about whether Julie had left him for another man. Could Jeanette please try to persuade Julie to go to counselling with him? He would ask Jeanette Farley to intercede for him every time he saw her in the next few weeks. That night, he was also angry that Julie had left during Matt's VCE and angry that he had found out about the separation when he rang from the airport. 'He also told me that it would be easier if she'd left him for another man than the way she'd just left him.'

COULD THIS be true? Jamie Ramage sounded like a possessive man. By his own account, he killed Julie in a rage that was at least partly fuelled by jealousy. Would he really have accepted it so easily if she had left him for another man? It is true that he was a man who loved certainty, and this would have offered him finality. But it is also possible he was being manipulative, telling people that knowledge of another man would calm him so that they would tell him the truth about any affair.

The complications of this marriage would lend themselves to a speculative board-game. Would he . . . ? Would she . . . ? What if . . . ?

THE FARLEYS had dinner at Julie's place in Toorak on the Friday night before she died. She told them she was meeting Jamie but always in public places where she was surrounded by other people. 'I was under the impression she was meeting just to make it easier for him, not because she intended to go back to him.' She told the Farleys that she had told Jamie about Laurence during the week, and that Jamie knew that she wasn't coming back to the marriage.

She thanked them for having been supportive of Jamie and helping him through this difficult time.

Jeanette Farley says she never saw Julie being unpleasant or provocative to Jamie in any situation: 'Never, never in the entire time I knew Julie. No, never ever.'

JEANETTE FARLEY'S husband, Nick, is a primary school principal. He has grey hair and a grey beard and his eyebrows are raised in a questioning look for most of his testimony. His manner, like his wife's, is direct, and his tone neutral. Jeanette was closer to Julie and he was friendlier with Jamie. They played golf and talked politics, sport and business. Jamie was far more dominant in his relationship with Julie 'than my own married relationship with my wife,' he says. Farley suggested to Jamie at one point that he try to get in touch with his 'feminine side'.

Jamie tried to recruit him to the cause of reunification, too. 'He asked me, I guess it was in inverted commas, to "spy" for him at an evening meal we were going to have with Julie with another couple.' Jamie asked him to report back secretly on any impression he got as to how Julie was feeling about him. At the dinner, Julie told them that Jamie was basically a nice bloke but he was too controlling of both her and Sam; he would put her down and wouldn't give her any space and had a chauvinistic attitude. He was home at 4.30 every day and expected her to keep him company and have his dinner on the table by a certain hour every night.

Jamie phoned Nick Farley on Saturday afternoon and they arranged to meet Saturday night. Nick told him that Julie was happy and doing great. Jamie asked him about Laurence. 'He asked me if they had started a sexual relationship and I said I didn't know. I did know, but I didn't feel it was appropriate to give that information out.' Jamie said that he'd been out himself socially with a friend and they'd met some girls but he wasn't interested. He said he had to make a decision now as to whether he would have Julie back. Yes, Jamie was down: 'He was upset, like I've seen a lot of people upset in the same situation.'

Nicholas Farley leaves the court without a glance at his old friend.

THE NEXT witness's evidence would raise as many questions as it answered. Graeme McIntosh was the family builder. He had done jobs for the Ramages on and off over the years and had worked for the Ashtons and the Garretts too. He takes the oath and gazes around the courtroom with a furrow between his brows. A middle-aged man, he has a red face and dark curly hair and has come in working-man's clothes, jeans and a windcheater. He answers questions carefully, as if he is concentrating on getting it right.

He was the tradesman doing the Ramages' kitchen and family-room extension. After Julie left, Jamie told McIntosh that he was seeing counsellors. He told the builder that Julie was 'ranting and raving about everything she wanted to do', and that he was worried that she didn't want to get back with him. On that Monday 21 July, Jamie phoned him to tell him that Julie was coming around at about 12 o'clock. He asked McIntosh to leave at about 11.40 am and asked him not to make a mess. He told the builder to take the afternoon off. McIntosh said he had to go to another suburb to buy washing machine parts and could be gone for a couple of hours. He offered to come back and to wait in the street if he saw Julie's car still there. Jamie said no. He insisted McIntosh take the whole afternoon off.

Others would later wonder whether this meant Jamie Ramage had planned his crime. That does not make sense: a man as perfectionistic as he, as pernickety about detail, would have developed a foolproof scheme if he had planned it in advance. And he would not have told others he was having Julie to lunch if he planned to kill her in the house. But disposing of the builder for such a long period does seem curious. How long could one conversation take? What was Jamie expecting – a romantic rendezvous? Sex?

Dunn suggests he wanted to have a private chat with his wife. As a family friend, he asks McIntosh, you understood why he would want some privacy? McIntosh concurs: 'Well, I think anyone would want a bit of privacy, wouldn't they?' So McIntosh did not return to the house that day. The first he knew of trouble was when he turned up to work at Marock Place the following morning.

THIS CASE has so many characters with different sensibilities from different walks of life. Jamie Ramage's crime has rippled through a genuine cross-section of the city. Anthony Brady, his business partner, turns out to be a tall, thin, dark man; he looks urbane, in a Clark Kent sort of way, with his fashionable glasses and thin tie. He has a gentle voice. I would hear later, through someone who knows someone who knows him – the village again – that Anthony Brady had been devastated by Jamie's killing of Julie.

He tells the court that they knew each other primarily as business partners, although the Bradys would be invited to 'milestone events' such as Julie's fortieth birthday. From such a distance, it looked to him like the Ramages had a strong marriage. He had never heard them argue. Jamie didn't confide in him much about the personal side of things but he does recall that once, 'about three weeks into the separation, he said "There's a small part of me that would like to say 'To hell with it; I'm a good-looking bloke, I can find someone else.'" But he then said, "But there's a very large part of me that would like to get her back."' Another time, 'He told me that if she had spoken to him face to face about leaving, he would have been able to talk her out of it.'

On Monday 21 July, Jamie seemed a bit down, but he had been that way for weeks. They talked business for half an hour. About 11 am, Brady went into the office they shared and found Jamie had left a Post-It note on his desk that said, 'I'll be back around three-ish.' At 3.17 pm, Jamie phoned the office and said that he wouldn't be back because he had to see the granite people about his kitchen. They talked about setting up for the following day's manufacturing and about Jamie preparing tax statements. Jamie did seem a bit odd, says Brady: 'He sort of mumbled at the start, when he was telling me why he couldn't come in, and I sensed he wanted to get off the phone fairly quickly.'

After work that night, Brady played tennis. He got home around midnight to a call from Jane Ashton: 'She thought James and Julie may have been at the warehouse and then described what she thought may have happened.' He rang her back an hour later and heard that Jamie had turned himself in.

DUNN ASKS about their business history. 'You thought that he would be a good person to be in business with because he was hard-working?'

'M'mm.'

'Conservative?'

'Yes, yes, conservative.'

'Obviously honest?'

'Yes.'

Leckie leaps to his feet in that swift, silent way of his; he is halfway through his sentence before I even realise he is standing. He objects. 'If my learned friend's seeking to lead character evidence he's permitted to do that, but it's got to be in a particular form, and a personal assessment is not that. As I understand character evidence and the law in a case like this, he can give us what his reputation in the community is but not his personal assessment.'

Dunn takes the rebuke with uncharacteristic meekness. 'Yes, I follow the objection. I think I follow the objection, your honour.'

At the time, the exchange would seem to be of little import. It was only later, talking to Dunn and friends of Julie, that I wondered about it. Julie's friends and sister would tell me indignantly that several people had been approached to be character witnesses for Jamie. All had refused, they said, appalled even to have been asked.

Dunn would have a different story. He would tell me that the defence at one stage had three or four people committed to testify on Jamie's behalf. They all pulled out. They said their position was untenable because they had been telephoned and warned that they would be ostracised if they spoke for Jamie.

I HAVE not been able to see Jamie Ramage's reaction to any of these witnesses. We three reporters are now seated at the 'informant's table' – a bench behind the lawyers' bench, usually assigned to the police running the case. It offers a ringside view: I am directly opposite the judge and midway between each lawyer and can easily see the witness stand, the jury box and the pews where the public sit downstairs. But I cannot see Jamie Ramage. His pew is behind me. He must be angry to see strangers noting every smirch on his family's dirty laundry.

At one point during a break in the trial, I express curiosity as to where he is kept before and after court and during the lunch break. I want to know what his day is like. It turns out that one of my listeners is someone who can show me. I am offered a tour of 'the cells'.

The broad bluestone steps to the Supreme Court cells lead up to a narrow modern corridor with the feel of a suburban police station: terrazzo floor, bland wall. On the left is a big lunchroom with wardens eating their sandwiches and watching telly. Directly outside their room is a tiny corridor that has three narrow visitors booths. Each booth has two purple seats. In front of them, a clear screen goes all the way to the ceiling. It has a small metal vent along the bottom with tiny holes for voices to go through. Lawyers huddle here to consult with their clients; there is no privacy from the guards or other prisoners, and often the lawyers are reduced to whispering through the vent.

There are six cells, three up and three down. They are Spartan in their bareness. The walls are a sickly mint green and the floors brown. The only seating is a hard plastic bench built into the wall. A stainless-steel sink and toilet bowl are also built into the room and must be shared by however many prisoners are being held in the cell. All hanging points have been removed and a Perspex screen sits in front of the bars on the high, tiny window. The air is close and nose-wrinkling, like the air in shopping-centre toilets. Prisoners are offered a choice of chicken loaf or cheese sandwiches for lunch;

they may also request a salad sandwich. I wonder that they have any appetite at all.

This is where Jamie Ramage sits in his perfect suits waiting for his daily summons. From the Balwyn house and the pistachio Jag to this. What a fall from grace.

AFTER LUNCH Janis Kean, Thermoglaze's bookkeeper, is greeted in cross-examination by Dunn's exaggerated courtesy. It is easy now to tell how he regards the value of each witness to his case: he flags it in his tone. Yes, Kean agrees, Jamie was a fastidious, perfectionistic man who insisted that all the bookkeeping and records be done precisely but who was always pleasant to her during her monthly visits. On Monday 21 July, however, he was snappy when she made a feeble effort at a joke. After he went out that morning, she had to call him with an accounting question, and he gave her an incorrect answer. He had also failed to register Thermoglaze's superannuation fund for the GST, which she found surprising because he was normally so organised.

Jamie was not paying his usual attention to things.

THE NEXT clump of witnesses would be Julie's workmates. Young Tarsha Warren wears a ponytail and a self-conscious smile as she enters court. She is the 'expediter' for the Eco-d fashion chain. She has a pert nose, perfect skin and streaked blonde hair and is wearing a pale mushroom top and dark-mushroom-coloured pants.

Julie had been afraid that Jamie would be very angry about her leaving, Warren says. Julie felt terrible about the pain the separation would cause him and the children. She had said she wanted to ease Jamie out of it gently, and that Matthew was angry with her and that she had tried to see him on his own. She confided in Tarsha Warren about Laurence and showed her his photographs and emails.

Asked about the day Julie died, Tarsha's small, polite smile disappears. Julie was in the kitchen making coffee when she arrived at 9.10 am. Julie said she had told Jamie that she was seeing somebody and that she wanted everything out in the open, and that there had been no reaction from Jamie when she told him. At 12.10 pm, Julie dropped by Warren's office and said, 'I didn't have any breakfast and I'm popping out to get something to eat. I won't be long.' Warren was on the phone; she said briefly, 'No worries. I'll see you later.'

Julie didn't return, even though she had a 1 pm meeting with her boss, Felicity Holding. Warren tried calling her on her mobile at 4 pm but there was no answer. She turned off Julie's computer at 5.20 pm.

DUNN CUTS to the sex again – had Warren known about Adam? – and then moves on to money. Had Julie told Tarsha that she'd removed $125,000 from the family business's mortgage account, and that she spent $15,000 on a Visa card setting up her new place in Toorak? This was not news to Tarsha, but it is to the reporters, who begin scribbling furiously.

He pounds her over what Julie had claimed to have told Jamie on the Saturday. Tarsha Warren sticks to her story: that Julie had said she told Jamie on Saturday that she was seeing Laurence and that the marriage was over.

THE JUDGE then calls a short break. Dunn turns to me and says lightly, 'It's love, actually.'

I am confused for a moment. This is such a tangled family diagram. 'Whose love?' I ask blankly.

'Her love for Laurence gave her confidence.'

'To be provocative and vindictive?'

'To be blunt. Wait and see how it unfolds.'

JOANNE McLEAN was hired by Julie as a contract fashion designer for Eco-d. McLean looks to be in her thirties. She, too, is a glamorous blonde, with shoulder-length straw-coloured hair and wide eyes. She is carrying a Louis Vuitton bag and wearing a little black dress and black spike-heeled shoes with embroidered toes. She is one of the few witnesses to look over at Jamie. Everyone treats him as though he is invisible, and he sits there, remote and still, as if he wishes he were.

McLean tells the court of a farewell party for one of the staff at a restaurant in a bayside suburb on 5 June 2003. The following morning Julie was very distressed at work. She had had a serious argument with Jamie the night before and had decided to leave while he was overseas: 'She only felt safe to leave while he was away.' Later, despite intense questioning by Dunn, McLean holds fast to the fact Julie was terrified of Jamie: 'I *know* she was.' She stands with one hand holding the witness box and the other on her hip. Dunn hurries on; he's not finding these blondes pushovers.

On Monday 21 July, when Julie told her she had told Jamie about Laurence, Joanne McLean replied, 'You're mad, saying that to him.' McLean was concerned about Julie's safety. She also advised her to take it easy and not get too serious with Laurence until she knew his character. 'I never spoke to Julie again.'

THE JOURNALISTS snap to attention when Julie's boss, Felicity Holding, takes the stand. She commands it before she's even said a word. She is fifty-ish and small-boned – another stylish blonde, in a black three-quarter length coat and pants, a ruched cream top and pearls. Her diction is almost prissy in its precision and there is an imperious tilt to her head; she listens to the lawyers with her shoulders back and her chin up. She is literally looking down her nose at them. The reporters scent the promise of sport.

She becomes more and more irritated. At one point she apologises for not remembering a date but while the words are placating, her tone is angry: 'I'm sorry, I was only given about four hours notice that I was on today, [or] I would have read it up.' She continues in a snappy, businesslike tone to describe how frightened Julie was when Jamie turned up one morning at the shop unannounced.

The fury spills out when she recalls talking to Jamie on the phone on the Monday night. Holding was looking after Samantha at the Toorak townhouse while Julie was missing. She says, with icy outrage: 'He was very, very cold and he said he'd seen Julie and that I didn't know what had been going on in the last month.' The contempt in her voice is now unmistakeable. Her eyes are blazing. 'I said I didn't care what had been going on, because I've got a 16-year-old [sic] daughter that's very, very frightened about what's happened to her mother and no matter what has gone on between you two, you've got to come and look after your daughter.'

YOU DON'T know what has been going on in the last month: *On the Monday night, after seven hours in which to have become grief-stricken – or at least guilt-stricken – over what he had done to Julie, Jamie was still furious and still blaming her. Where is the regret here? Where is the remorse?*

No matter what has gone on between you two, you've got to come and look after your daughter: Holding was demanding that Jamie behave like a responsible adult, not a wounded child. He agreed to come and pick up his daughter.

But this idea panicked Samantha. 'No, he can't come here, don't bring him here!' the girl begged. So they decided to leave Julie's place and wait together at Felicity's house. Which raises the question: *Why was Samantha so frightened?*

I can't wait to see how Dunn will handle this captain of Julie's Praetorian guard. I suspect Felicity Holding will fry him for lunch. So, apparently, does he: 'No questions, your honour.'

MONTHS LATER, Dunn would confess to me that the testimony of Felicity Holding, like that of Rob Moodie, had been a nasty blow to his RAT. At the committal hearing, 'She said that they loved one another. "It's all a misunderstanding. He loved her, she loved him." She'd done a U-turn. I don't know where she came from. She was cranked up at a million miles an hour. I wasn't going near her.'

He steeples his fingers, drumming their tips gently against each other, and looks vaguely off to one side. 'Was that a witness?' he inquires, with mock innocence.

FROM THE GRAVE

Day Ten
Tuesday 19 October 2004

ARRIVING AT the Supreme Court, you must pass through security. Handbags and briefcases go through an X-ray machine and people through a metal-detection unit like those at airports. This morning, there is an impromptu party at one of them. A young woman with long dark hair is swaying her hips and waving her arms like a dancer as the unit beeps its protest; her friend is standing laughing to one side. 'It's my keys,' cries the dancer joyously, wriggling to intensify the jangle of her bracelets with such genuine good cheer that even the security guards are smiling. 'No, it's not,' retorts her friend, grinning. 'It's money. Money!' The sudden outburst of life and spontaneity seems incongruous in this formal place. Most people who walk into the court complex lower their voices and pull into themselves like snails into shells. I like their refusal to be cowed. We take different corridors but it would turn out that they are witnesses in this trial.

In Court Twelve, Jamie Ramage is sitting motionless in a dark grey suit. As usual, he is ensconced before his lawyer arrives. With his black robe flowing behind him Dunn flaps into the room like a large, cheerful bat. Julie's father is in the downstairs public pews, wearing his customary air of restraint and surrounded by a group of elderly friends. Jane Ashton is centre-stage in the upstairs gallery, flanked by two women friends and a class of teenaged schoolgirls who have come to watch justice at work in the *Queen versus Jamie Stuart Ramage*.

The first piece of business is Leckie tendering to the court Julie's letter to Jamie. It had been found in Jamie's briefcase.

The first witness is Julie's cleaning lady, Milka Glendza. Glendza had been working at another house in Marock Place on that Monday and had seen Julie arrive. Julie exchanged greetings but said she couldn't stop and talk because she had to go into the house. The second witness is a neighbour, Deborah Webb, who saw Julie's Mini and Jamie's Jaguar still in the driveway at 1 pm.

Next are the two young women who had been laughing at the security entrance. Despina Panagakis, receptionist at Acropolis Marble, had been the girl dancing through the metal detector. Her friend Magdalini Tzimas-Koroi is not laughing now; she testifies with an unhappy expression and a frank, forthright manner. The smile comes out only briefly when she is asked whether she is normally called Lina: 'That's right, it's a lot easier.'

Jamie had phoned Acropolis Marble at 9.30 am on that Monday and cancelled an appointment to look at the granite. He phoned again at 2.35 that afternoon and said that he was in Balwyn and would be over soon. He phoned once more before arriving a little after 3 pm. He told them he'd got stuck in traffic. Panagakis noticed that he was playing with his fingers and a bit fidgety, but other than that, both women thought he behaved normally.

He told them he wanted the best part of the granite used for the island bench in the kitchen and he described how he wanted the side panels joined to the bench-top. They marked out which parts of the granite would go where. Jamie bent over at one stage to remove one of his boots and fix his sock. He was polite, well-mannered, gentle, says Tzimas-Koroi; he showed no sign of being agitated or upset.

NEXT IS a string of police witnesses who confirm different aspects of the investigation. Dunn presses the first one about what Jamie Ramage said when he escorted him to the toilet. Jamie had asked about the whereabouts of his children and was told they were being looked after. Did the officer get the impression that his answer had put Mr Ramage at ease? The policeman refuses to play ball: 'I didn't get any impression as to how he was thinking. He was fairly emotionless; there was no real response.'

THE JUDGE calls a mid-morning break. As the room empties of onlookers, Dunn turns round to me and asks, 'What's the difference between a cowl neck and a roll neck?' This one, at least, does not catch me off-guard. I know that Julie had been wearing a roll-neck jumper when she died. A roll neck, which would have sat up around her throat, would have provided a layer of wool between her skin and the means of strangulation. A cowl neck might have meant direct contact between her flesh and whatever was used to throttle her. It is the kind of question that might be used to debate autopsy findings on her injuries. 'A cowl neck sits down on the chest more,' I tell him, wondering whether he really needs feminine input to work this out.

'Let's have a look,' he commands. He strides over to a brown paper evidence bag that had been brought in by the prosecution. I watch in disbelief as he hauls out a blue-grey woollen. It is the jumper Julie died in. It's the jumper she was *buried* in. He comments on the smears of dirt upon it and grimaces in distaste. The prosecutor's instructing solicitor looks alarmed at this impromptu display but tells him where he can find a rubber glove with which to handle the jumper. Instead Dunn lays it down on the rich, red carpet and calls me over to look at it.

It is only a few steps from my seat to where he is standing. I use the distance to remind myself of other frightening things I have managed to look at calmly as a reporter: a tiny premature baby having a tube put down its throat; a man's heart beating in his open chest during surgery. But this is different. Those encounters were about life; this is about death. My stomach churns as I look down at the soft blue jumper with its telltale smudges of brown around that neck. I feel horror and pity for the woman who wore it to her death. If Dunn is trying to help me gain a forensic distance – to draw me into a cool legal perspective on the case – the attempt has failed. Distance would feel like desecration.

'It's a deep turtle neck; not a cowl,' I say briefly. And walk away.

POLICE CONTINUE to detail their exchanges with Jamie. As one officer describes how he gave Jamie his rights, Jane Ashton wipes tears from her eyes. I wonder what it must be like for Jamie to be looking every day at this grieving woman who is the image of the wife he killed. By the time a policeman is describing how he found the boot of Jamie's Jaguar slightly ajar, the jurors, too, are staring at Jane, their attention caught by her brooding presence. For Jane and her family, this must be like coming to a funeral every day.

AFTER LUNCH there is more police evidence. The jury hears of the painstaking uncovering of Julie's grave and the bloodstains in the garage and the family room. Jane sits holding her husband's hand. A policeman describes opening the second hole and finding the handbag and bed-ruffle – 'it looks to have been used as a drop-sheet' – and Julie's friend Gilda Pekin tries to sniff back her tears. As the relentless detailing of death continues, in an almost ritual chant of question and answer, I feel an urge that has not come to me for years. I am tempted to cross myself.

AT 2.50 pm, the jury leaves so that the lawyers can argue over the crime-scene videotape. Leckie wants to air it. Dunn objects: there are shots in the tape that have been excluded from the jury photographs, including many close-ups of Julie's face 'after she's been in the ground and bleeding and there are insects buzzing around the face and things like that. They are unnecessarily gruesome and, in my submission, shouldn't be shown'. The lawyers agree to edit the tape to show what is required with the minimum of unpleasantness. Jane and Howard Ashton leave the courtroom with their faces averted. Ray Garrett stays on.

The next witness is forensic medical officer Dr Michaela Marginean. She examined Jamie Ramage after he turned himself in. She has a rapid, machine-gun-like way of speaking. She found a few small red abrasions over the knuckles of his right hand, which he told her he got while rowing with Samantha on the Sunday morning; this could have occurred as he claimed, she says. His right hand was also swollen, 'an acute response to blunt trauma usually caused by the small blood vessels in the region being damaged and therefore allowing the release of fluid into the tissues'.

We are finished for the day.

UNTIL DEATH

Day eleven
Wednesday 20 October 2004

THIS MORNING Leckie is over talking to Julie Ramage's father about the crime-scene video he will show when court begins. 'It's your decision, and it's her decision, but I want you to know it's coming,' Leckie warns. Ray Garrett nods his understanding. At least someone is looking out for the family.

When the trial resumes, the jury has another query. They say they cannot agree on what they heard from Dr Marginean: 'Can we have a summary of what Michaela determined in relation to the injuries that James Ramage suffered? Thank you.' Her evidence is read back to them.

Housekeeping out of the way, the lights are turned down and the crime-scene film is projected on to a side wall of the court – behind and to the right of the pews where Julie's sister and father sit looking straight in front of them, away from the video. For the jury, their faces will be part of the canvas: two cameos at one side of all the images to come. Jamie Ramage stares down at his hands, which are clasped in his lap.

There is no sound but for the hiss of the videotape. The 'credits' flicker on: 'Crime Scene Unit Video: Police use only. 22/7/2003. Deceased Julie Ramage.' The first images are shot through the windscreen of a police car: the long, winding ribbon of country road that Jamie took with Julie in the boot. The only sign of life in several minutes of driving is a lone white bird overhead. The day before, her sister had told me, the heavens had opened, lashing Melbourne with wind and rain. But this day, the morning after Julie was killed, wintry sunshine dapples the unmade road. The paddocks either side of it are winter-green and eucalypts line it like sentinels. The film is grainy and soft, with a dreamlike quality; this could be the lead-in to a romantic film. But the sibilance of the tape and the unnatural stillness of the court's onlookers lend it a discomforting eeriness. Now the road is climbing and the paddocks fall away on the right-hand side. The minutes tick by. If Jamie was 'stupid', he was stupid for a long time. The car slows to walking pace and turns on to a dirt track, passing through a wide wire farm gate. This is a bush block, fenced off but largely uncleared. The lens slowly pans police, trees, a pile of bracken in a particular spot. Then we see the spot again with the bracken removed, and a glimpse of something light and strangely human-looking poking through the newly turned soil. And then we see the spot with its shallow coverlet of earth removed.

There lies Julie Ramage, turned away from the camera on her left side as if she is asleep. Her legs are bent up to fit the small space and her hair is flung back. She is still wearing her trousers but her jumper is off and tangled around one arm. Her pale, slender body is smudged with earth and topless but for her dark blue bra. We see her from the back, so her bruised face is not visible. This is how Jamie Ramage laid his wife to rest: directly in the dirt. I look over at him. He is still staring down and seems not to have moved a muscle.

The camera rests upon Julie just long enough for the image to register. Just long enough to remind everyone that, at the heart of this wordy trial with its interminable debates on points of law, its obsessive preoccupation with the minutiae of the Ramage marriage, lies the dead body of a real woman.

Then the camera moves to the second hole and a pile of belongings: watch, clothes, rope, teatowels. The domestic detritus of a love gone dreadfully wrong.

Suddenly we are staring at another crime scene: the family home in Marock Place. The death house. The first shot is from the street, with a view of the rubbish bin and recycling box still standing on the footpath. The familiar motifs of police dramas – crime-scene tape, a police car and police van – overlay the suburban normality. It looks to be a cold morning; the wind is swishing leaves on the concrete floor of the double garage. Its door is lifted open on to the street. It sits to the right of the house. There are neatly clipped hedges in the small front garden, which has no fence, and stepping stones to the front door. The camera goes first to the garage. It bears the signs that children live here: a basketball hoop over the door and a cricket wicket against a wall. There is a beach umbrella and a carpenter's horse and an old push lawnmower, a stock of plasterboard and a pile of firewood. And there are signs that this is where Jamie bundled Julie into the boot: the camera closes in on a yellow marker with the number '1' on it near a smear of blood on the floor. Julie left traces of her life force all along the route she travelled after death.

The camera tour is ghostly. It moves slowly and in silence, observing without remarking, attentive but distant. The forensic style mimics the kind of technique film directors often use to try to portray a spirit returning to survey its earthly home. It's like Julie's tour of Marock Place.

The camera's lens returns to the house. The front door swings silently open. There is a short hallway with pale grey-green carpet, a small antique table and a Persian rug. The camera veers right, into the lounge room. Matt's guitar is sitting where he left it. There are papers on the coffee table and a wineglass next to a studded leather armchair near the fireplace; Jamie's chair, a friend would later tell me, the only really comfortable chair in the place. It's clearly a house being renovated: Jamie's ironed shirts hang on a rack near the antique dining setting with its balloon-backed chairs, and boxes of kitchen stuff – casserole dishes, saucepans – clutter the floor. A sheet hangs in the doorway separating the front of the house from the back.

We go through to Julie's dream family room and kitchen, the one Jamie felt he had made a huge concession over: he had allowed her to choose the look. He'd wanted an old-fashioned kitchen but Julie wanted it modern. She had chosen shiny white cupboards and stainless-steel German appliances. The fridge and dishwasher and rangehood are in place and all it lacks is the infamous bench-top. This is what Jamie had so wanted her to see; this is what he had been convinced would win her back. Men buy off unhappy mistresses with jewellery and unhappy wives with whitegoods. The sun is streaming through the new floor-to-ceiling windows at the back of the room, making it look warm and light and homey despite its bareness. But the next shot is a close-up of a floorboard with a small red speck on it. Then another. The small table and chairs over which Julie and Jamie had their final argument in the family room are now in the white-tiled laundry where he and Matthew had been eating while the renovations were being done. Another part of Jamie's post-death tidy-up?

The camera shows us a downstairs powder room and Jamie's study. His computer is on a computer table but he seems to have worked on his papers at a round antique table with French polish. This is starting to feel like a surreal real estate tour. Upstairs is the master bedroom; the bedroom in which, according to Julie, Jamie had insisted upon soulless sex every morning. It has a large white bed with metal railings and a burgundy coverlet, and the curtains are floral. A white piece of clothing is draped over one bedpost; whether it belonged to Jamie or is a memento of Julie is impossible to tell. Unexpectedly, a Tim Winton novel sits on the bedside table.

Winton's novels are delicate and nuanced, preoccupied with the poetry of landscape and the flows and eddies of his characters' interior worlds. Reading this kind of book does not fit with the image of Jamie given by Julie's friends. Is there another side to him that they have not seen?

We move to what seems to be Samantha's old room: a single white bed in a white room with pink curtains and a blue rug with a red heart on it. Matthew's room has dark bedlinen and an air of boyish energy; a sports bag and computer bag are strewn on the floor, and there is a ghetto-blaster on his desk.

The master bedroom has an en suite and the main bathroom upstairs is separate from the toilet. There would have been no rows over the bathroom in this house. The place is a suburban dream, or would have been when it was finished. But on this film it has the air of an ancient house of Pompeii preserved by lava during the eruption of Mt Vesuvius. Like them, it has been abandoned abruptly in the middle of everyday life due to sudden, overwhelming disaster. It stands testimony to life as it was, and as it never will be again.

THE LIGHTS come back on. It has been an intense interlude. The judge decides the jury deserve a ten-minute break. This time it is me who approaches Dunn. I had been wondering about Jamie Ramage's consultation with Pica before turning himself in to police. What if Jamie had confessed but resisted turning himself in? What is a lawyer's first responsibility – his client's confidentiality, as it would be with a Catholic priest, or the law's right to be informed?

Dunn smiles. 'We were discussing this just last night,' he says. It was exactly what happened to him when Maritza Wales-King confessed in his chambers. 'You can't permit him or her to destroy evidence or change things around. You would be obliged to contact the police. If someone came to me – as happened recently with me – I would just say, "Go to the police." I said, "Let's telephone them right now." You can't aid a crime being committed or furthered, despite confidentiality, but people do have to be free to take advice. There is a bit of a fine line, a grey area.'

Another time, I asked him about what a lawyer would advise in such a consultation. How directive would he be? To what degree does he help shape his client's story? This is the only time I see Philip Dunn genuinely angry. He arcs up like sheet lightning. Apparently my question touches on professional impropriety. A lawyer does not help 'cook up' the facts of a defence, he declares; never, *never*. It would be absolutely unethical. And no lawyer would ever risk it; there's no guarantee the client would keep quiet. If the client later revealed it, that would be the utter ruination of the lawyer's career. Yes, lawyers advise, but they work only with the story they are given.

THE NEXT witness would do handsomely in any television show about people who study corpses for clues. Dr Matthew Lynch has black-Irish good looks and appears younger than he must be, given that he has been a pathologist for fifteen years and a forensic pathologist with the Victorian Institute of Forensic Medicine for eleven. Lynch is also a senior lecturer in forensic medicine at Monash University. His short dark hair is spiky on top and his manner is commanding.

On 22 July 2003, the day after Julie Ramage died, he performed her autopsy. She was lying on a yellow body bag. He noted dirt on her body and dried blood on the right side of her face. Julie weighed 67 kilos and was 172 centimetres tall with light brown hair. She was wearing nail polish and her nails were not broken. Her blue brassiere was secured at the back but the top button of her blue, jodhpur-like trousers was undone. She was wearing R. M. Williams boots with navy socks and light blue underpants. He would conclude that the cause of her death was compression of the neck.

Lynch found blood in her nose, a small split on the skin on one side of her nose and a bruise on her mouth. He saw a bruise on her upper right eyebrow, a black eye on the left of her face and a yellowish-brown bruise just under the jawbone on the right. He also found a spotty red band of discoloration of the skin, about 6 centimetres long and 2 centimetres wide, extending from the midline of Julie's neck to the right. There were also scrapes, bruises and abrasions around her Adam's apple and bruises on the left of her neck. Questioned by Leckie, Lynch acknowledges that he considered the possibility that the neck injuries were caused by a rope because a rope had been found with the body. At this point, several jurors look darkly at Jamie. If Jamie used a rope, the crime is more heinous and possibly involved premeditation. But Lynch goes on to say that he thinks manual strangulation far more likely.

Bruises on Julie's wrist were consistent with 'some sort of blunt force or a grip, a drag, knocking the arm against something'. A patterned injury on her left shoulder was of the kind often seen when clothing has been pushed against the body. There was bruising and abrasion (the scraping away of the top layer of skin) on her upper right arm and hand, and around her waist was a 6-centimetre linear abrasion. On her back, scrapes extended from her shoulderblades to her lumbar region, and there were others on her buttocks. Lynch puts them down to Julie being scraped after death over a surface that was abrasive. There were also bruises on her shoulderblades, which Lynch attributes to her body falling on a hard surface while she was still alive. Surface injuries that also have bruising underneath the skin mean that the injury occurred while her heart was still pumping, he explains. If there is no such bruising, it means she was dead at the time.

The most important area of examination was Julie's larynx. Lynch found she had bruising beneath the skin that extended into four layers of muscles on both sides of her neck, which indicated that at least moderate force had been used against her. But neither of the two bony structures in the neck – the thyroid cartilage or the hyoid bone – had been broken. The damage to her neck was also accompanied by pinpoint bleeding in her eyelids and the lining of her neck called petechial haemorrhages. They are common in people who have died from lack of oxygen. He also found bleeding around the tip of Julie's tongue, 'suggesting that perhaps Mrs Ramage had bitten her tongue in the course of any struggle'.

Julie also had bleeding in both the temporalis muscles, which extend above the ear near the temples, on the right and on the left. There was no evidence of injury to her brain. But on the left side of her head, between the top of the ear and the top of the head, Lynch found extensive haemorrhaging between the skull and the skin. He concluded that she had received blunt trauma to her face and head, which might or might not have rendered her unconscious: 'I wouldn't be surprised if she had been incapacitated in some way. She may not have been, or she may have been deeply unconscious. I can't tell from looking at the injury.'

So we will never really know if Julie was aware as Jamie throttled her; staring into his eyes, choking for air, knowing and fearing her fate. Though hadn't he said that she fought him for a little while, but not for long? That suggests she might have been unconscious soon after she hit the floor.

It is time to break for lunch. Jamie is still staring at the carpet. There is no lawyerly chit-chat as we leave. We are back on Leckie's turf now: the detailing of death.

A PERSON who succumbs to neck compression dies of a combination of factors, Lynch tells us after the lunchbreak. The first is blockage of blood, both going to the brain from the heart and coming from the brain back to the heart. The second mechanism is airway obstruction: 'The pressure on the neck can either push the tongue up so that we can't breathe or, less commonly, it can squash against our airway so we can't get air into our lungs.' The final mechanism, he says, is the most difficult to understand. There is a small nerve underneath the jawbone, and pressure on it can cause the heart to slow, beat irregularly or even stop. The pressures that can cause this include the previous two factors of blockage of the airway or blood supply.

Leckie asks Lynch whether a roll-neck jumper could disguise signs of the means of strangulation, such as fingermarks or ligature marks. Clothing might modify the appearance of some neck injuries, Lynch says. But he holds to his conclusion of manual strangulation.

What's Leckie getting at? Does he think Jamie used a rope?

Dunn is concerned about this too. He keeps pinning Lynch down to the manual finding. Dunn points out that Julie's injuries are consistent with her having been punched and then falling, hitting both her shoulders and her head on the ground. Lynch agrees.

Dunn moves on to the nerve mechanism Lynch had spoken about. Where a defence counsel cannot deny, he must minimise. Dunn's question suggests that the fatal mechanism is all too easy to trigger: 'There are reported cases of people dancing vigorously and someone being grabbed on the neck and literally dropping dead on the dance floor?' he asks. Lynch says, 'The textbooks do contain references to people collapsing on the dance floor, apparently following – I think the expression is usually "a playful tweak" of the neck. What that means, I don't know.'

Lynch concedes that he cannot exclude the possibility that Julie died of 'positional asphyxiation' – that she was alive when she was put in the boot but died because her airway was blocked and she was unconscious and unable to protect it. But Lynch holds fast to the greater likelihood that she was strangled by human hands. He will not co-operate with either lawyer's attempts to prove Jamie's actions are any better or any worse than his original findings suggested.

Dunn asks one curious question. 'Did you find, incidentally, a tampon *in situ*? Was she menstruating when you carried out your post-mortem?'

'I believe so.'

Dunn wants certainty. 'You found . . . ?'

'Yes.'

A possibility flits across my mind. The female-hormones card?

DETECTIVE SENIOR Constable Darren Wiseman, the officer who headed the Ramage investigation, is the next witness. Leckie tenders the videotape of Wiseman's second interview with Jamie and says he will play it in full. This is the same tape from which we have the excerpt where Jamie describes strangling Julie. It will be Leckie's last big hit. Jane Ashton leaves the room. Jamie Ramage's mouth is pushed out into the now-familiar pout. Later, I would learn that one of his brothers was in court today.

ON FILM, Jamie begins in the same pose he wears in court, staring fixedly down at his hands. His voice is flat but he seems a little apprehensive. He is asked how he came to be here. 'I was talking to a friend and then a solicitor and I just really regret what's gone on. I wish I could change it. I wish I could go back and I don't believe that I'm in – in this situation.'

'What was the purpose for us to go out to Kinglake?'

'To show you where I stupidly buried Julie.' He lets out a small sigh.

Wiseman takes him through the night's events and then asks him about his marriage. Jamie says he first met Julie when he was going out with one of her girlfriends. The relationship between them had been 'good going; when Julie left, all my friends were surprised. We had, I thought, a good relationship, as good a marriage as anybody else. We've had our ups and downs'.

Wiseman moves on to the separation. 'Before you went overseas . . . was there any trouble in the relationship?'

'Well, it was fine.'

'Was there any indication that she was gonna move out?'

'Nah.'

'How were you feeling when she told you?'

'Totally devastated. I didn't understand. I didn't know why. I spoke to Gilda and I spoke to her sister. Yeah. And I've spoken to her just to try and understand why. And I've spent the last four weeks understanding why and trying to – trying – trying to fix it.'

Jamie gives them the details of the counsellors he's seen, scratching his ear. As he tries to describe what Julie disliked in him, he moves his outstretched hand back and forth over the table, as if surveying terrain. 'She didn't like the fact that I was grumpy and nitpicking and that sort of thing.' He tries to explain what he thought the counsellors wanted him to do: 'I was supposed to go through everything and try and understand everything . . .' He rubs his temple.

He talks about how he was still seeing Julie, and for this he is able to look steadily at Wiseman: 'We were having dinner on Tuesdays as a regular kind of thing.' He tells about the Saturday at the football: 'We went off and had a walk around the ground, sort of thing. And even to the point we were having a long – we had a long chat about lots of different things. She told me at that stage too that she was – she was seeing somebody else.' He points his finger in emphasis: 'Prior to that Saturday, we had seen another counsellor.' He scratches his head.

He explains that Tom Paterson had rung and offered them another appointment just as they were going in to see Rosemary De Young. 'In the meeting with Rosemary De Young, Julie did get a lot of things off her chest, as far as – you know, what was wrong with the relationship and so on.' He is speaking rapidly now. 'Afterwards I – I asked her if, you know, we could go and see this Tom Paterson as well and she was happy to go and see him, which surprised me at the time. But she was happy to go and see him. We went to see him as it turned out neither of us really liked Rosemary De Young but Tom was very good. And . . . at the end of the thing he came up with a solution of, if you like, me letting Julie go. As being the one way that she would come back.' Jamie touches the table. 'Julie liked that. And I was comfortable working with that.

'So, I suppose we did at least get to a point where there was a glimmer – to – to me there was a glimmer of hope. To Julie it was a possible solution. So, at least it was a bit of a step . . .'

IT IS still unclear why Julie agreed to go to the second counselling appointment. Even Jamie does not profess to understand it. Maybe she hoped for another neutral venue in which an expert would pronounce the marriage dead, as De Young effectively had. Tom Paterson's 'solution' – that Jamie should let Julie be free, in the hope that she would then freely choose to return to him – meant different things to each of them. For Julie, it signified the last rites for the marriage and a blessing upon her desire to move on. For Jamie, it meant rekindled hope. Tom Paterson, with his bird's-eye view, might have understood what was happening for each of them, but they did not understand each other. The fragile peace between them was founded upon mutual incomprehension.

NOW WE hear Jamie's version of what was said in that exchange at the football; the one in which, Julie later told Laurence, she had told Jamie that their relationship was serious. 'We talked a lot about different things.' He struggles to get the words out: 'There's – there – there seemed – there seemed to be less – there's still a chance but less – less of a chance. And she mentioned that she was seeing a guy who she liked a lot and so on, which upset me but that – that's sort of – well, that's the reality of the situation.'

He says they had not argued over her news about Laurence at that stage. Wiseman asks, 'What was your reaction to it?'

'The – the – the – I just – I just – I suppose I thought all – along.' He quickly side-tracks: 'I've – I've just been trying to find out what needs to be done and how to do it . . . Find solace. And I was upset.'

Wiseman asks about that final lunch. It was for Julie to see the renovations: 'We've both been heavily involved in organising them, particularly her, and I suppose I – I found it really hard, the last three or four weeks keeping that going and keeping motivated because we're not together.'

'Mmm.'

'And trying to do everything. I had a week off in the school holidays with Matt and we did a lot of painting and I suppose what I was hoping was when she'd come and have a look, that might help things get back together. We'd organised to do that this week. The – the Tue – she couldn't make it on the Tuesday. So we talked about Monday.' Julie wanted to be home in the evening for Sam 'because she'd been out a few nights and Sam's back at school'. So they decided she would 'pop around' at 9 pm on the Monday night.

Jamie wanted more time; he wanted the chance to put his case again. He says, 'The next day I was able to get out of work, as it were. So I rang Julie in the morning and said "Look, do you want to come around and have lunch? We can have a bit more – than 9 o'clock at night, a bit more of a chance," I suppose, hoping to keeping – like, we did talk a lot on Saturday. And that was fine with her. So, she came on – yesterday.'

IN HIS pew in court, Jamie sits as if carved from stone.

ON TAPE, he talks about why he sent the builder home: 'Because if he was around we wouldn't be able to talk in private but also he – he would involve himself in the conversation.' He talks of buying rolls for lunch and setting up the table and chairs. When Julie arrived, she had a look through the laundry and then they went through into the family room. His speech becomes jerky again. Julie had seemed offhand on Saturday, he says, but she seemed 'harder' now. Then comes the passage we have already seen: the 'wanking' gesture, his pleading with her, her telling him she should have left him ten years ago. Jamie says he then changed the subject, and they talked about Samantha and her rowing. This led to Julie complaining that Samantha was unhappy because every time she saw her father, he would quiz her about Julie. Samantha didn't want to come around to see him so much.

The chain reaction to his meltdown had begun, according to Jamie. He told Julie that Sam didn't like Laurence, and Julie told him that her new life was none of his 'fucking' business, and that she was sleeping with Laurence and he was a much nicer lover than Jamie. She allegedly said that sex with Jamie repulsed her, and screwed up her face. She stood up to leave 'or finish the conversation' and it was then, Jamie says, that he 'lost it'.

HEARING THIS the second time, I realise something I had not noticed earlier. Jamie did not 'lose it' while Julie allegedly hurled abuse and sexual home truths at him. According to his own account, he punched her only when she stood up to leave. The trigger, in the end, was her trying to walk away from him. He attacked her for *leaving*. It was the infantile rage of the abandoned child.

JAMIE TELLS Wiseman that he wandered about trying to collect his thoughts for some time after he killed her; he doesn't know how long. He put her in the car and then went back to clean up the floor. Now he has again the guilty, sullen look of the schoolboy who has been caught out.

When it came to burying Julie, 'I don't know what was going through my head with all that 'cos I remember at the same time thinking – I didn't think – I suppose I could have one last chat with Matt.' He slowly wipes his right eye.

Why did he take the car down to the restaurant? 'It was just a stupid thing. I don't know why I did all of that. I know the whole thing was just stupid 'cos I knew that I would be – so, I'm not even – just – I don't know. It was just stupid.' By now his voice is a whisper. 'Just . . .'

He drove up to Yan Yean because he knew that area a bit. 'Julie rides up there.' He didn't look for any other spots; he went straight to the one he would use and only stayed half an hour. There is a long pause. He shuts his eyes: 'And I – *I just hated myself* . . . I dug the hole and put Julie in it and then hated myself.

'And then drove – drove back – and – and all the way there I was thinking I should just go and – just go and see someone and then – then I was gonna go and see Dyson . . . who's a friend, a family friend. Put me in touch with Steve last night. And then I thought, "Well, I'll go back and see Matt." We went and had a quick meal and then Sam ra – rang up, worried about where Julie was, and that's when I thought, "I'll go and see Dyson."'

It is the end of the court day. It has been a draining one, with the crime brought vividly and, at times, gruesomely 'alive'. Justice Osborn decides this is a natural point at which to break.

LECKIE: IT'S MURDER

Day Twelve
Thursday 21 October 2004

THE NEXT morning Jamie is sitting as immaculately clad as ever in a navy suit and striped tie. Jane Ashton is upstairs in the front row of a now-crowded upper gallery but her father is in the front pew downstairs, within spitting distance of Philip Dunn's end of the bar table. In the same row is a middle-aged blonde woman with a pretty face who has appeared now several times. Her eyes have often filled with tears as she has listened to the evidence. She catches me studying her and smiles. I would later find out she is one of the Ramages' friends from Scotch College, Rhonda McMurtrie. She is one of the few Scotch parents to come to the trial. Most of those who were rounded up for the committal have dropped out now.

Court begins with the rest of the tape. We hear Jamie tell Wiseman that Julie was buried in the clothes she was wearing, the blue jumper and black jacket. (In fact, she was found nearly topless, lying on top of both those items.) But, 'I didn't take any clothes off Julie,' he says.

He tells calmly of the visit to the carwash on the way back from the bush and the trip to Acropolis Marble. After he got home from there, he had a bath and put a load of washing on, including the shirt and pants he had changed into up at the bush block. 'Not for any reason,' he hastens to add. 'I . . . that's what I've been doing, is doing the wash every night, and those clothes went in as well.'

When he met Dyson Hore-Lacy, he told him 'what had happened' and that he wanted to turn himself in and 'do whatever has to be done'. He rests his head on his hand.

Wiseman asks when he last had sex with Julie. 'Just before I went away.'

'And what was the nature of that sexual contact then?'

Jamie looks embarrassed. 'Just normal sort of sex with us.' He mutters something about finding this difficult and looks away.

Had Julie shown him any affection at all yesterday? Had she kissed him or cuddled him?

'No. She was just belittling me.'

Wiseman asks, 'What was your reason for murdering your wife yesterday?'

Jamie's sentences again become spasmodic and, rather than explaining, he rushes into self-justification. He's been so good, he pleads: 'I just – I – I – totally lost it . . . All I've done is try to resolve it and I haven't been angry and I haven't – you can go through, talk to all the – Julie's girlfriends, all our friends – Julie's even said how fantastic I've been and so on with all that's gone on. And even – I – in my briefcase there's some notes or letters. I've written her letters. I've sent CDs. I've sent her roses . . . All of which, trying to understand and trying to get it resolved and get us back together . . . It's been absolute hell, the – you know, every minute of the day, just thinking about wanting to get us back together as a family.'

Yesterday, he says, 'it just hurt so much and then I just lost it. That's all I can say. I mean, I – I regret it. I wish I could go back. I wish I could turn back the clock. I wish I could – I could change it. I – I don't understand – I mean, taking her up to Kinglake and all that. It's just *stupid*.'

The policeman tells him he will be fingerprinted and that they will take a mouth swab for a DNA sample. Then Wiseman says, 'James, at this stage you're going to be charged with murder.'

DUNN RISES to cross-examine Wiseman. It turns out that there is no reference to the Noosa holiday – which Julie claimed to Laurence that Jamie had seen and been angered by – in either her diary or on the calendar found in her townhouse. Dunn goes on for several minutes about the call from Jamie's mobile to 'Adam's' mobile at 5.40 pm on the Monday. Dunn does not explain where he is going with this. He questions Wiseman about letters from Jamie that were found at Julie's place. Did they say things like, 'I miss you and I miss you both?' Was there a poem, 'Sail away with me, my honey, you hold my heart?'

Leckie objects. The jury is sent out. Dunn argues that the letters – signed 'Love always, Jamie' – set out his feelings of affection for her and show how he wanted to be reconciled at any cost, even if that meant moving to Toorak or going to counselling. The letters are relevant to the state of the relationship and to her state of mind when she had lunch with Jamie. Leckie argues that they are merely self-serving. The lawyers compromise: Dunn can refer to them but will not tender them for the jury to read.

Dunn raises the issue of money with Wiseman. Yes, agrees Wiseman, while Jamie was overseas Julie had arranged to take $125,000 from a family trust account. It went into their joint account, and she withdrew it from there. It wasn't actually 'money in the bank' but a draw-down facility, which meant the family trust then owed that amount to the bank. Dunn's tone makes clear his disapproval.

Dunn fires off a string of questions about the contents of Julie's handbag. He buries among them this one: Did the police find a container with some tampons? 'That's right, yes.'

The dud-root defence is going to include a claim of menstrual madness.

JUSTICE OSBORN sends the jury to lunch. Evidence is finished now because the defence is calling no witnesses. The lawyers will soon start their closing addresses, and Osborn tells them that he has decided to leave the question of provocation open to the jury, 'particularly having regard to recent decisions of the Court of Appeal'. He does not feel it appropriate to give reasons for that decision given that the Crown has not opposed provocation going to the jury in this case.

JANE ASHTON and Gilda Pekin have come downstairs to hear Leckie's closing address to the jury, which will take the rest of the afternoon. Jane sits next to her father in the back pew. Matthew and Samantha are nowhere to be seen. Later, the children will reappear to listen to Dunn's defence of their father.

Leckie has a lighter, huskier voice than Dunn, one that is more difficult to project. But we can catch every word because the courtroom is hushed; for once, there are no whispered exchanges among onlookers. Even Jamie Ramage has briefly abandoned his study of the carpet to fix his eyes upon Leckie. This is the prosecutor's big chance to sell his case, and he will be allowed to claim the stage.

Through the trial the lawyers have mostly faced the front as if running this case for the benefit of the judge. Now Leckie turns side-on to the bench and speaks directly to the jury. He takes them again through the elements of murder: the Crown must prove that Jamie caused Julie's death; that his acts were conscious, voluntary and deliberate; and that he did those acts with murderous intent – that is, he *meant* to kill or seriously injure her. The Crown must also *disprove* the defence's claim of provocation. This meant disproving at least one of the following elements: that Julie had behaved provocatively; that Jamie lost all control; or that an ordinary person in his circumstances would also have lost all control. 'If the Crown can prove that an ordinary person in the same circumstances . . . could not have . . . got down on his hands and knees and throttled the life out of her; if the Crown proves beyond reasonable doubt that in your minds an ordinary person couldn't do that, even if *he* might have because of his particular make-up, then again the Crown has proved beyond reasonable doubt that provocation doesn't operate.'

Leckie reminds us that at no stage in his police interview did Jamie say he did *not* intend to kill or seriously injure Julie. He points out that this was a two-stage attack. 'He's not a small man, he's far bigger and stronger than her, and he's punched her to the ground easily.' If he had just wanted to 'stop it', he had succeeded with the punching, which probably knocked her out, Leckie argues. But Jamie went one step further: 'He then proceeds to get on to his knees and choke the life out of her.'

Then he failed to help her afterwards. 'Did he check her for a pulse, to see if she was breathing? He says no. Why doesn't he check her? He doesn't check her because he knows he's completed the deed. He doesn't need to check and he's not interested in checking. The man who loves her so much, who writes her letters of love, who wants her back . . . in his mind, he had decided and wanted to kill her at that moment, and he did.'

In his interview with police, 'Is there any real statement there of remorse for Julie, as to what he's done to her? Plenty of self-pity, you might think, when you read it carefully. "I want to turn back the clock." No doubt he does. He is now in the hands of the police. He realised he was not going to get away with it. But any genuine indication there of remorse for what he'd done to her, the damage he'd done to her, the fact that he had taken her life, the life away from the kids? No.

'The reason, the prosecution say, is because he is a selfish, self-absorbed man. He likes control and that's largely what this was about. He doesn't like it when it is not going his way and we've heard that in the past in this relationship, it has resulted in violence.'

He lists Julie's injuries and says the ferocity of the attack suggests intent to kill. As for having 'lost it', says Leckie – he recites again the methodical way in which Jamie cleaned up the house, got rid of Julie's body and tried to lay alibis for himself with phone calls on the way to and from the bush grave. At 1.20 pm, 'He calls her work. It's only a very short connection, but laying the trail, "Where's Julie?"' Leckie reminds us of the cool visit to Acropolis Marble, and the way Jamie lied to the woman at Acropolis Marble about where he was in the car. He had pretended to his son Matthew that everything was normal. 'Finally, it's the lie he tells to Samantha, his daughter, who's desperate to know where her mother is. He knows what's happened, what he's done, where she is in the bush, and he lies to her. Not just lies that he doesn't know but says she might be with Laurence.'

All of this 'was consistent with a man who knew fully what he'd done and was trying to cover it up'. Each of these elements indicated Jamie had consciousness of guilt of murder, not just manslaughter.

IN TELEVISION courtroom dramas, there is always a build-up to a dramatic moment. A musical cue or a camera close-up warns the observer, 'Pay attention, this is going to be important'. In real courtrooms, where counsel talk for hours and sometimes days on end, the summations can too easily turn into white noise, a background hum while your mind wanders to your shopping list or what to cook for your children's dinner. There is no warning when a rabbit is about to pulled from a hat.

Suddenly Leckie is talking about the blue rope. It was buried with other items that Jamie considered incriminating; it's not suggested that he tied her up, so what role had it played? 'Why did he cut a piece of rope like that, seal its end? Why did he have that available and why did he hide it?' Dr Lynch favoured manual strangulation but he was not able to rule out the possibility that a 'ligature' had been used. 'Whatever way you look at it, we say this is a very incriminating piece of evidence against this man.' The reporters are writing intently.

Osborn intervenes. Court will break for ten minutes. Jamie Ramage has resumed his frozen pose. Having to listen to accounts of what he did seems to send him somewhere deep inside himself.

After the break Leckie resumes. Bear in mind that the only evidence of provocation comes from Jamie, he warns the jury. 'There is no other witness to this account because she is dead.' And remember that he did not just turn himself in to police – 'he spent something like three hours . . . getting legal advice'. Leckie also points out that Jamie does not seem to have told the truth about everything in that interview; he said he had taken no clothes off Julie.

Leckie takes the elements of provocation one by one. Did she say those things? No, she was frightened of him and was always very cautious around him because of previous violence. 'But over the weeks, what the prosecution say to you, is that he lulled her into a false sense of security. It's clear that it was false. Just look what he did to her in the end.' Jamie was anxious and distraught but the real question is why: 'Is it really to get back the woman he loved or did he want back the control in the situation? He was not prepared to accept what was, from her, a civilised way of trying to break [free of] or separate from this marriage.' None of the witnesses were able to say that Jamie had told them, 'Look, I love this woman dearly.'

He urges the jury to look at her letter. 'Is that not a reasonable letter to him setting out what's happened, what she wants to do, what she hopes for the future with the children, that they'll remain friends, that they'll do it better than others around them have done it?' There has been no evidence that Julie was ever spiteful, vindictive or nasty: 'She did not have that sort of nature.'

Now Leckie comes to a delicate matter. He makes the plea he had asked Osborn to make as an instruction: he asks the jury not to be prejudiced against Julie because of her affairs. They don't have to approve of them, he says, 'but don't judge her on that . . . Maybe you can understand that in the sense if she's got a very unhappy situation in her home and getting no true affection or love, that she seeks it elsewhere'. Watching the jurors' faces, it is hard to know what they make of this; none of them respond outwardly.

Leckie then goes to each claim Jamie had made about what Julie said and points out that Jamie had heard each of them before. He had told the psychologist, Sharon Marcus, that Julie had said she could not imagine having sex with him again. Julie told Jamie in the session with De Young that the marriage was over. Jamie had told Matthew that he knew 'it's obviously totally over'.

So, Leckie tells the jury, if they cannot accept the Crown's claim that Jamie made up his story about that final encounter, they should keep in mind that none of this was news to him. This means there was not enough provocation to justify him losing all control. But if the jurors think Julie might have said those things, and that Jamie might have lost control, they must then assess whether an ordinary person of his age and maturity would have 'lost it' in this way.

If Leckie loses, what will it say about 'ordinary men'?

The prosecutor has one more rabbit. 'Julie was got there on a pretext that there would be someone else in the house, and then he organised it so there wasn't anybody else there. What was in his mind? Why did he want it? . . . Whether or not he tried it on again, who knows? Whether something happened and he wanted to sexually approach her and she wouldn't be in it, we don't know. Why were her clothes off? We don't know.'

I had been wondering myself about Julie's near-toplessness and Jamie's insistence on the house being empty for hours. Had he wanted to seduce her – or to submit her to his will sexually again? The only explanation for the toplessness that I can think of, other than a thwarted sexual assault, is that her clothes were pulled off as he dragged her to her grave. Let's assume that she had taken her black vinyl jacket off herself when she entered the house. If her jacket was already off, and Jamie was dragging her by her arms or wrists, say, or even around her middle, would this be enough to pull a roll-neck jumper right over her head? Maybe if he dragged her by her legs, her jumper would have been pulled up and back as the rough ground resisted her progress. But for her jumper to have come right off her body and over her head, and right off one arm, so that only one arm of her jumper remained twisted around one hand? It is hard to imagine. But then, the whole bloody thing is hard to imagine.

DUNN: IT'S MANSLAUGHTER

Day thirteen
Friday 22 October 2004

BOTH MATTHEW and Samantha are in the front pew to hear their father's QC sum up his defence. Matthew is in a T-shirt and jeans and Samantha wears a singlet top, black pants and sneakers, with a finely woven green jumper slung diagonally over one shoulder. Gilda Pekin sits beside Matthew and a woman from the court's witness support service chats brightly about her own children to Samantha, who converses politely in return. Jane Ashton and her father sit at the other end of the same pew.

'We are almost at the end of the line,' Dunn promises the jury.

Dunn begins by attacking Leckie's suggestions about the rope and the sexual attack. Suddenly he is roaring, a great wave of sound that fills the room like a sonic boom: 'This is a cunning prosecutor's trick!' It is a trick to get them to ignore the crucial sequence of events that led to this 'unfortunate tragedy'. 'What happened here was that Mrs Ramage left her husband unexpectedly. Whatever the rights and wrongs of the marriage were, she left her husband while he was away. He'd been married for 23 years and he came home and his house is missing his wife and daughter. He went to four counsellors, he rang everybody from the cleaning lady to the builder. He rang and he talked and he asked and he'd booked in for meditation. And his wife had a plan and the plan was to let him down gently – in other words, to lie to him. And she lied to him and her friends lied to him: "Yes, there is a chance." This man has had a catastrophic blow . . . As my grandmother would say, "Time does heal things." But this is five weeks old, this is *fresh*.

'What happened, on 15 July they went to not one but to two counsellors, and Mrs Ramage, who no doubt you might think was used to lying to her husband, because in 1997 and 1998 she'd conducted an affair with a family friend, a married man – no doubt that meant lying to her husband and to her children and everybody else – she conducted an affair with another married man in 2002 and 2003, went out for dinner with him the night she separated from her husband, and her friend, Mrs Pekin, they all sat down and had, perhaps, a lovely dinner. She was used to lying to her husband about where she was going and what she was doing. As Mrs Pekin said to you, she would tell her husband she was going riding on Wednesdays when she was going out with her *lover*.' The word rolls around in his mouth and is spat out.

She told her sister and others that she was in love with Mr Webb. 'This is *nine days* after she's first gone out with him,' Dunn roars indignantly. 'She's *in love* with him!'

Between 15 July, when the Ramages saw Tom Paterson, and 21 July, when Julie went around to see the renovations, something changed: Julie realised she was in love with Laurence. 'And she went round there to give [Jamie] the message. And when she gave him the message, do you think she gave it to him so he'd understand it? Do you think she really gave it to him in a way that there was going to be no misunderstanding? Because what did she want to do? What was she doing on Monday 21 July but booking tickets to go to Noosa with Webb and arranging on the telephone with Annette Luckman to have a poetry reading . . . with Mr Webb, her lover, her perfect match, with whom she was on Cloud Nine.'

Dunn argues that the crime was clearly not premeditated because Jamie had told the builder that Julie was coming around, and because he did such a poor job of covering it up. 'Who's the obvious person that's then going to be the subject of attention? You don't have to be Sherlock Holmes to work this out. All signs pointed to him.' His dinner with Matt was a father's farewell, Dunn argues: 'What this man did after the killing of his wife is he bought himself a few hours.'

I look over at Jane's family. Ray Garrett's face is unreadable. Jane is chewing furiously on nicotine gum.

This man has just killed his wife, says Dunn: 'What a profound, traumatic, unpleasant thing that would be. His life, whatever else you might think, is going down the toilet rapidly . . . He is not thinking, you might think, at his most rational. Proof positive that this is sort of all a spur-of-the-moment loss of control is his erratic behaviour afterwards in laying a trail that points only to him.'

Dunn seizes upon the way Jamie had been preoccupied about whether Samantha did not want to see him any more. 'His thinking is so disordered that after having killed his wife he's kind of focusing on, "I've killed my wife but will my daughter still come and see me?" You might think that's logical or you might think it shows that this man was seriously rattled, that he's not functioning in a rational way. "I'm going to get caught. I'm going to go and see the police, but will my daughter still come and visit me?"'

Leckie's associate is trying to contain a cynical smile. Gilda Pekin is shaking her head, either in disagreement or sheer disbelief.

There are other possible explanations. Jamie could be waving his devotion to Samantha about as part of his defence as the fine family man. If genuine, Jamie's preoccupation with Samantha could have been sheer selfishness; another form of self-pity, another example of a selfish, domineering man putting himself first. Would Samantha still be there to serve his emotional needs now that Julie would not?

Dunn is on a roll now. His argument builds up into peaks like waves crashing upon the beach; as each one spends itself on the shore, the next one is building. Without ever moving from his place, Dunn is passionately persuasive, alternately cajoling and insistent. Surely, you can see this? And this? And this?

He conjures the playing card of family values – family values, on behalf of the man who strangled his wife – and waves it before the jury. 'You and I know that for most of us our wife, our family, our grandparents, these are all very big parts of our life; these are the cornerstones of our existence, our children, our family. These are things that we love and we cherish. And to be told that ... [for] the last ten years "I'm over you" ... that meant all those walks, those talks, those cuddles, those kisses, those nice moments, were all a sham. This man was *gutted* by the conversation that took place.'

The Crown had said Julie was frightened of being caught out having an affair: 'Well, she shouldn't have had the affair in the first place, you might think. But she wasn't so frightened that she didn't have more than one affair behind her children's back and behind her husband's back.' And Julie Ramage didn't mind 'exaggerating things and telling stories in a dramatic way': 'She told Laurence Webb that her husband knew about the nature of their relationship because he'd seen [details] of their going away on a calendar ... The calendar was looked at by the police, the diary was looked at by the police. There is no reference to Mr Webb going away on a holiday with Mrs Ramage. So was she someone who would make a little drama up or tell stories? Who knows?'

Dunn contrasts Julie's behaviour with Jamie's: he went on a self-improvement binge to try to save his marriage and his family. 'He wrote lists, he went to the counsellors, he tried to work on his spiritual side, which somebody told him about ... He enrolled in meditation, he made up CDs which he sent to his wife, he sent her flowers, he wrote her letters. He was focused on this, said Matt, it was all he was thinking about. He said he was useless at work and he would hear him crying and day after day his father would talk to him.'

Samantha's eyes are closed.

Dunn moves on to his dearly beloved counsellors. He repeats again his key words: anxious, emotionally fragile, vulnerable. 'In a state of anxiety your ability to cope is reduced . . . You can get to the state of mind where Mr Ramage is clinging like a drowning man to that life raft that says "hope", while there's stormy seas around him.' Dunn bellows his next sentence at the jury: '*He's in that situation because he's been lied to . . . as part of Mrs Ramage's strategy!* So the provocation that the defence relies upon isn't just 21 July. It is the weeks of conduct leading up to 21 July. He is lied to and he's lied to!'

Dunn thunders to get his point across, to have the jury understand not just rationally but on a gut level. It's as if he whips up anxiety in his listeners – how can you not feel a surge of adrenalin when you are being roared at? – and then gives them a peg on which to hang their emotional arousal, so that he can channel it to his own ends. Here, the peg is outrage: 'He's on an emotional seesaw! He's all over the place *because*' – and Dunn slams the bench in front of him with each word, *thump thump thump*, like a remorseless drumbeat – '*he's not being told the truth*!'

Dunn is like an old-time general rallying his troops for battle. 'The jury man' – it's not just in the rhetoric, it's in the delivery. And Dunn sure knows how to deliver.

NOT FOR the first time, I wonder what the outcome would have been if Jamie had not been 'let down gently'. He was such a one for certainty, for action, for instantly developing plans to fix any problem. Maybe it would have been a short, sharp shock that allowed him to face the truth and 'move on'. He could have plunged into plans for dealing with the end of the marriage rather than clinging to fantasies of saving it.

Or would he just have killed Julie that much sooner?

DUNN CONTRASTS Jamie's misery with Julie's heartless happiness. 'She felt like a teenager. She's single again, she's free, she's got money in the bank, she's got a job, she's able to come and go, she can go horse-riding all night if she wants to. She can go out and come home. She can go to the Botanical Hotel and meet Simon, the businessman from Sydney, or whatever. She's a free agent. She doesn't have to answer to her husband or have the meal on the table or indeed have the anxiety of looking after her son, doing Year 12 . . . By all reports she is empowered and she has no doubt been empowered by having these affairs.' For Julie, the world was 'a place where she was in control, as she was in control when she had the affairs. *She's the one who's calling the tune, you might think*'.

Jamie hears from De Young that the marriage is over, but from the session with Paterson he takes away the conviction that there is hope. Dunn is again almost shouting: 'What happens? *How sinister is this?* How sinister is this to this man's mental state? He's told it's off, virtually, and then there's a meeting an hour or two later and it's on. The fish comes out, the fish goes in, the fish goes out . . . Mrs Ramage says to him, "*I'm not going anywhere*!"'

On the Friday before her death, Laurence tells Julie that the relationship is serious and that he will ask his wife for a divorce. That night, Julie tells Matthew that there was still a chance of reconciliation. On the Saturday, after the football game, Samantha gets into bed to comfort her weeping father who has been told by Julie that she is seeing Laurence. On the Sunday night, Jane Ashton reassures Jamie that Julie's relationship with Laurence is not serious and that Julie is committed to counselling. Also on the Sunday night, Matthew asks his mother to tell his father the truth. And Jamie tells Jane, 'You know, deep down inside Julie likes me.' Says Dunn, 'This is a country mile away from the nonsense, may I suggest, that you heard yesterday, talking about possible sexual assaults, premeditated murder and rope.'

On that Monday, 'She went round there to do something that she wanted to make emphatic, and it was something that she wasn't going to do over the phone. This one was going to be face to face.

It wasn't going to be done by letter or email or phone. This one was going to be done face to face and what was she going to do, Mr Foreman, after she'd been talking about how she wanted her husband to know it was over, that she wanted her relationship with Laurence out in the open, that she was booking for her daughter and herself to go with Webb up to Noosa? She was going to end it, wasn't she? *She was going to end it!*'

The judge intervenes. It is time for the lunch break. A quick scan of the jurors suggests that Dunn has not won over the big woman with the soft heart. Perhaps it is because she has been looking over at Gilda Pekin, whose face is taut with unspilled grief.

AS THE court clears, I turn to the journalist sitting next to me. Peter Gregory, *The Age*'s Supreme Court reporter, has been watching parades of humanity through the legal system for more than twenty years. It has given him the unshockable air of a policeman.

'What does a woman leaving a violent man do?' I ask him. 'If she lets him down gently, she's lying to him. If she tells him the truth before he's ready to hear it, she's responsible for him lashing out. What does she do to keep herself safe?'

He looks back at me. He seems amused at my naivety but there is a glint of sympathy in those blue eyes that have seen it all. 'Run like buggery,' he says.

JULIE WENT to Marock Place that Monday for four reasons, Dunn tells the jury on its return. Firstly, she wanted her relationship with Webb out in the open; she was besotted and making big plans. 'Love is blind, love is foolish.' Secondly, she had to stop her husband: 'The husband is clinging to this hope . . . and he is no doubt an encumbrance to her new life. He is an anchor. What is she going to say to Laurence, her perfect match, the love of her life – "I've got to go to dinner with Jamie on Tuesday nights", or "I'm going to counselling this afternoon?"' Dunn is almost bellowing. 'She has to *get rid of her husband*!'

The third reason, he argues, is that Julie had been caught by her own lies. 'She's already told Laurence Webb that she's told Jamie about the full extent of their relationship . . . But she hadn't. She hadn't. You know that because Samantha asked her mother what she had told her father, and she told her daughter that she hadn't told Jamie Ramage the full details, the full story. You know from Matthew Ramage that the father hadn't been told the full story . . . What she's got to do is this: she's got to catch up with what she's already told Mr Webb . . . Is she going to say, "I'm sorry, my love, my soul mate, my perfect match; I've misled you," or is she going to go and give her husband the chop?'

And fourthly, Julie was going to tell Jamie the truth because Matthew had asked her to. 'Whatever these other friends and people say, you can rely upon Matthew and Samantha, the children, and they both told you she told them that she hadn't told the full picture.'

This tale is like a Greek tragedy, with its ghastly twists in a family setting.

JAMIE HAD told police that Julie was hurtful and belittling, Dunn says. Then he pauses briefly. He is not certain that his next card is the right one to play. He adopts a consultative manner, inviting the jurors to consider a point with him, much as he had invited me to join him in studying Julie's roll-neck jumper.

'Now, can I just stop and ask the women on the jury if you'd forgive me if I'm going in the wrong direction here, but this is the sort of thing that men sometimes think, and if I'm wrong, just throw it away, okay? Mrs Ramage was having her period, and you'll find in her handbag there were some tampons, and you know that Dr Lynch found a tampon. Now, it may be, you might think, that men tend to think that women get a bit scratchy at around that time – and if I'm wrong, dismiss it, okay? But Mrs Ramage went into that meeting, and according to Mr Ramage, what happened was that she said hurtful things. And this meeting, you understand, is the culmination of weeks of lies . . .'

He leaves it there. He knows he's in a minefield of gender politics but he also knows the make-up of the jury: probably only two women on it would be of menstruating age. The other women are older and, possibly, more conservative, and most of the jurors are male.

It is only one drop in the ocean of words Dunn will expend on his closing address but it is the point that will see him most savagely criticised after the trial. It is logically flawed: women who are scratchy 'at that time of the month' are irritable when they are *pre*-menstrual. Bleeding usually signals a change in hormone levels and a lift in mood. Even if Julie had been hormonally irritable, let's face it: who was it who was *really* having a bad day emotionally? Who was it who lost his temper in a murderous rage? Not the partner wearing a tampon. Any search for a chemical culprit would have to spotlight the role of testosterone in male aggression; Jamie's balls, not Julie's womb.

What is on trial here is not just Julie's sexual behaviour but female sexuality itself. The defence of sexual provocation is based upon the male notion of woman as Other. With it goes a whole package of beliefs, including the idea that a woman is more biologically determined than a man and that her unbridled sexuality is a danger to herself and others; that a wanton woman (a wanting woman?) is a moral evil in a way that a promiscuous man is not. What is being played out here, underneath the imposing formalities and the intellectual veneer, underneath the posturing about rationality and the façade of emotional distance, is an archetypal collision of the masculine with the feminine.

On a playing field that has never been level.

DUNN TAKES us line by line through Jamie's account of Julie's remarks to him. He unpacks each one of them carefully, repeating the line itself several times and then opening up its potential for hurt. 'Every issue of this man's life is being attacked: his children, his business, his love for her, his relationship with his children, his sexuality, his identity, his role as a man, his role as a husband, his role as a father.

And why? Because she wants to have a relationship out in the open with Laurence who she's known for *ten days*.' The hail of abuse was 'like the fly that lands on the bonnet of the car that's teetering on the edge of the cliff. And he lost it'.

Dunn returns again to his counsellors and to his particular favourite, Tom Paterson: 'He said it's important not to try to force a person to accept what they are not ready to accept because they are more likely to do something desperate.' This was particularly the case with Jamie Ramage 'because he was a businessman who was used to controlling his destiny and because of that, he's at greater risk, because it's harder [for him] . . . He was in a situation where, when confronted with this crisis, he was psychologically unable to deal with it. That is why the defence says to you, Yes, he killed his wife, but it is manslaughter.'

Dunn is doing brilliantly but not everyone who should be admiring him is doing so. Sitting in court with his elbows resting on his thighs and his hands clasped, Matthew Ramage looks the picture of misery.

Dunn suggests to the jury that there are things about that conversation with Julie that Jamie did not tell the police. Where did Jamie find 'Adam's' mobile telephone number, and why did he call him after killing Julie?

Then Dunn gives a lecture on the presumption of innocence. It means that the blackboard is clean. 'In other parts of the world, in Nazi Germany, what they did was they presumed people were guilty and they had to prove they were innocent. But in Australia, in our system, you're presumed innocent until you're proved guilty . . . In any contest between the citizen and the State, the State has great power and resources at its disposal. The State therefore . . . has to prove the guilt of the person. The accused man doesn't have to prove that he's innocent.'

He asks the jury to be on guard against prejudice: 'All I ask of you, ladies and gentlemen, is this: God forbid that anybody you know, connected with you – children, family – ever get involved in a criminal trial. But if they did, what you would want is the jury to apply the rule of law . . . If you have a reasonable doubt, you acquit.'

He tries to deal with any lingering doubts by pointing out that nobody has ever been found innocent in a court of law. 'Do you know why? Because there are only two verdicts a jury can bring in. The verdict is Guilty – that is, the case has been proved beyond reasonable doubt; or Not Guilty – the case has not been proved beyond reasonable doubt. We don't have a verdict of innocence.'

There is a short break. Then Dunn spends an hour arguing that it is clear that Jamie did not intend to injure Julie because her death was probably quick and she had no injuries such as fractures, which meant he had not used savage force. At the back of the courtroom, Jamie Ramage is doubled over, his head in his hands.

PROCEEDINGS ADJOURN until the following Monday and everyone escapes quickly. Five days in this courtroom produces a claustrophobic yearning for space and air. Back in the bustling street, the sun is hot but the chance to walk and stretch cramped limbs feels liberating.

My thoughts are not liberated, though. One of those silly songs that can echo inside your head for no reason is whirling like a merry-go-round in the back of my mind. I am halfway back to the office before I realise why I'm thinking of this song now. Twenty-odd years ago, as a tourist in London, I had seen a stage musical set in the 1930s called *Chicago* (now a film). There is a scene in which women prisoners who have killed their partners sing a rousing chorus about how they will claim provocation as their defence. They sing about how 'he' had it coming, but the version in my mind today has automatically replaced that with 'she'.

JANE ASHTON phones at the weekend. She has some telephone numbers for me and wants to talk about the case. Journalists like to think they are managing their contacts but the reverse is also true: contacts like to think they are managing the journalist. It is a relationship of uneasy interdependence. While Dunn has not seen me talking to Jane because she and I keep our distance in the courtroom, she has seen him chatting to me and she remarks sharply upon it.

Her greeting is cheerful but her voice drops when she talks about what happened to her sister, and her English vowels become shorter as she tries to hold in her anger over the way the trial is unfolding. She argues that in Jamie's own account of that last exchange, he was the one who initiated discussion of fractious subjects. 'Julie tried to change the subject and have lunch and he reintroduced them. Then she's finished her lunch and got up to leave. This wasn't some half-mad screaming woman taunting him. If this is provocation, what chance have we got?'

She tells me that she has been warned that often, in cases such as these, relatives are so distraught when the verdict comes in that they stop thinking clearly and lose the opportunity to punch home the need for legal change. During this call Jane says what she will say to reporters many times at the end of the Ramage trial: 'All women have the right to leave their partners. Provocation in domestic violence cases should be thrown out. It legalises honour killings.'

She talks about the impact of class as well as gender: 'This can happen to my sister. What if she was some little checkout chick in the western suburbs with four kids by different partners, then he kills her? What chance would she have if my sister has got no chance? I know eight people who say she told me that "If I leave him, he will kill me." Not one of those people has been allowed to say anything.'

It is not only the law that has appalled her. Jane is starting to feel bitter that many of the original mothers from Scotch College have decided not to come to Jamie's trial. She does not believe the excuse she has heard, that they are worried about looking like they were supporting Jamie; they could dispel this easily by coming up and saying hello to Julie's family. Jane suspects a deeper reluctance is at play. 'There were 1200 people at that church in Toorak [for Julie's funeral]; lovely children, lovely parents. But domestic violence is something that they don't want to acknowledge is going on in their suburb. They don't want to talk to their children, particularly their sons, about it. Julie spent hours cooking lasagne and soup and picking up their children for them. Where are these people now?'

We chat about the spectacle of the courtroom and Dunn's little jokes. She wonders whether she should start pelting him with tampons from the public gallery.

She talks about how she had fought for self-control to ensure she wouldn't become a spectacle herself. 'I *hate* losing it in public,' she says of her refusal to cry.

Jane rings off with a black joke. 'I've got to go now, *or my husband will kill me!*' Her laugh is not the kind you join in with; it is brittle, the kind of laugh that leaves you feeling sad and helpless.

PIETÀ

Day fourteen
Monday 25 October 2004

TODAY THERE is an end in sight. Surely Dunn must be finished soon. Then Justice Osborn will give his 'charge' to the jury, explaining to them how to apply the law in this case, and the jury will go out to decide its verdict. The familiar cast is in the side pews: in the rear, Jane Ashton with Gilda and Christine flanking her, and in the front, Ray Garrett with a friend, and Matthew, in jeans and a black T-shirt.

Dunn begins by going over his main points again, the way a TV serial recaps the highlights of the previous episode to jog the viewer's memory. But he has no need for succinctness. He repeats his performance at length. Along the way he adds a few sharp derogatory touches, such as, 'You remember Mr Webb, *with the tan?*'

He hints that Julie was a gold-digger and Jamie altruistic: '[Jamie] wasn't being critical of her. He didn't say, "Hang on, you've just pushed our debt up by $125,000!" He said, "What changes can I make that will make me better for you?"' Dunn repeats again his claims about the unsteadiness of Julie's female state: 'She's in love and her hormones were such, as you know, you will find tampons in her handbag and Dr Lynch said at that time she was menstruating.'

Dunn says, '[Jamie's] reaction to what he was told, combined with the weeks of what had happened before, was, as he told the police, to lose it. "I lost it." He struck her. He struck her. That would guarantee that he'd never have anything to do with her again, wouldn't it? That would guarantee that he would never have anything to do with his wife again. It was what she wanted.'

So now, Jamie hitting Julie is giving her 'what she wanted' because it would have brought finality to the relationship.

DUNN PLAYS up the intensity of the emotional hurt to Jamie and plays down the physical injuries that killed Julie. 'Remember, there are no broken bones,' he warns the jury. 'There's not a fracture to the nose, there's no broken teeth, there's no broken jaw, there's no broken *anything*.'

He ends his address with a lulling tone, an avuncular air and an invitation to the jury to consider how anyone, pushed far enough, could 'lose it'. 'This isn't the movies and it is not a Patricia Cornwell novel. This is real life, and human beings, however much we like to think of ourselves as masters of our destiny, we all have a fragility. All of us are capable of losing it in various ways. None of us, probably, has been put to the test like this. But this is a tragedy. There are absolutely no winners.'

In the end, the jury would have to accept that there are reasonable doubts about what Jamie intended with those punches, and that there is a lawful excuse. 'It is just a great tragedy that there wasn't some honesty at the outset of this situation and that there wasn't a little bit of time. And then, hopefully, none of us would have been here and life would have gone on, Matthew could have done his VCE and Mr and Mrs Ramage would have learnt to live with their situation and the sun would have gone up tomorrow.' Dunn thanks the jury for their attention and takes his seat.

By Dunn's account, Jamie Ramage was a fine, upstanding family man devoted to his wife and children who was tipped over the edge by weeks of lies.

JULIE'S MOTHER, Patricia Garrett, enters the courtroom for the first time. I had not expected to see her at all. Her emotional health has been fragile since she lost her daughter – she has had a stay in a private hospital, the Melbourne Clinic – and her family had feared she was not strong enough to face the trauma of the trial. She turns out to be a small woman with a pageboy haircut and a sweet face. She has dressed in a peach linen over-shirt, a white top and beige pants, her only jewellery a fine gold chain. Her face is tired and drawn, the skin softly wrinkled, but she has been a pretty woman; it is clear her daughters got their blue-eyed good looks from her. Her husband leads her gently around the courtroom by the hand. She looks lost, like a child at a new school, and gazes around the room vaguely as if not sure what to make of what she sees.

Her presence will have a big impact on at least one of the jurors. When they arrive back in court, one of them – an older woman with grey hair and metal-rimmed glasses – will spend a lot of time with her eyes fastened upon Pat Garrett.

WHEN OSBORN arrives, he begins his charge to the jury in a steady, dispassionate tone. As he points out that there were two stages to Jamie's attack – the punching and the throttling – Jane and her father gaze with concern at Patricia Garrett. When Osborn talks about 'neck compression', Julie's mother closes her eyes as if in pain. When the judge tells the jury that they must not conclude that Jamie is guilty of murder simply because he has previously been violent, it is as if a Mexican wave of grief passes from Patricia Garrett to her husband and daughter and back again: their faces register the emotion one after the other, as if some invisible current connects the three of them. Talk of the marks on Julie's neck causes her mother to blink hard. When the judge moves on to how Julie's body was dragged, Patricia Garrett wipes her eyes with a handkerchief.

By the time Osborn reaches his carefully prepared passage about how to judge whether the ordinary person could have lost self-control, Pat Garrett's head is resting on her husband's shoulder, her face pale, her mouth working, and her eyes closed as if she can bear no more.

There is something strangely familiar about the scene. This kind of anguish has been portrayed in many paintings and sculptures over the centuries, in the sorrowful faces and drooping postures of many different female figures. Patricia Garrett looks like a grieving Mary holding the body of her crucified child.

THE JURY GOES OUT

Day fifteen
Tuesday 26 October 2004

JUSTICE OSBORN spends the day reading his charge. He summarises each witness's evidence, the cases argued by the prosecution and the defence, and the legal principles that must be applied.

At 3.20 pm, the jurors rise to consider their verdict.

Part Four

BEHIND CLOSED DOORS

WHAT THE JURORS DIDN'T KNOW

IN THE 1940s, Hollywood stars Ingrid Bergman and Charles Boyer starred in a black-and-white film called *Gaslight*. The movie was billed 'the strange drama of a captive sweetheart'. It starts off as a romance: the two fall in love but Bergman thinks it too soon to marry a man she hardly knows. She leaves for a holiday on her own but as she steps off the train at her destination she is greeted by the charming, attentive Boyer, who says he could not bear to be parted from her even for a week. They marry quickly. When they return to Bergman's home in London, the film spirals into a film noir, a shadowy tale in which it is hard to know what is really going on and whether Boyer is the hero or the villain. Ingrid Bergman fears she is going mad: her loving, protective husband tells her that she is losing belongings, stealing possessions and imagining conversations that never occurred. And he tells her she is imagining the footsteps in the attic and the lowering of the gaslights when she is alone at night. He increases her fear, paranoia and self-doubt by isolating her from the outside world, at first by telling her he wants to prolong their honeymoon together, and later by warning that her madness – inherited from her mother, he claims, as if it is a peculiarly female fragility – makes her 'far from well enough' to go out.

It is only with the entrance of Joseph Cotten, who plays a Scotland Yard detective, that Bergman learns the truth. Cotten tells her, 'You're not going out of your mind. You're slowly and systematically *being driven* out of your mind.' Boyer is a jewel thief who had married his wife to access a fortune in gems hidden in her house and who wanted to get rid of Bergman by committing her to a psychiatric hospital. The melodrama was so popular with American women in the 1940s that it led to a new slang term, 'gaslighting': the manipulation of a woman's mind to try to make her doubt her own sense of reality. 'Are you gaslighting me?' became an expression of disbelief.

The character played by Boyer was a classic example of the psychologically abusive and controlling husband: he moved quickly to make the relationship permanent, he controlled the money and the social calendar, he isolated his wife from anyone who might help her or offer her a reality check, he put her down constantly and he suggested to her and to others that she was unstable. Those who work with such couples find that today's abusive husband is also likely to resist moves his partner might make towards study, which he fears would make her more independent of him, and is at best ambivalent about her work; he might tolerate her job as long as he can control the money it brings to the household. He might use the children and their needs to convince her she must stay. Sex with his partner is at best usage and at worst abusive, because he believes it is his wife's responsibility to service his sexual needs.

If he is physically violent as well as emotionally controlling, he might intimidate his partner by punching walls or smashing household objects. He might say afterwards that he 'lost it' but men's counsellors report that, even in the most frenzied temper tantrum, it is always her belongings that he smashes. Between attacks he can be so affectionate that she begins to believe that she must have been wrong about how bad it was, or that he has changed now.

Like the Charles Boyer character in *Gaslight*, the abusive man's actions are the means to a single end: control of his 'captive sweetheart'.

IN 1982, when Ray and Patricia Garrett visited Julie and Jamie in Australia, the marriage seemed fine. The Ramages took the Garretts around to different tourist spots – Lorne, the Gold Coast – and both couples enjoyed each other's company.

When the Garretts returned to England, they applied to migrate to Australia. Jane would have come too but she had just met her future husband, Howard. The Garretts arrived in August 1983 and stayed with Julie and Jamie for about five weeks. The Garretts each found jobs and bought cars within weeks and began hunting for their own home. But things became difficult: they found Jamie overbearing. Pat Garrett told police, 'Although we were all adults and working, we had to wait on Jamie ... He didn't seem to be concerned about anyone else.'

They became suspicious of Jamie's control over Julie, her mother says. 'We found a house, and as a thank you we wanted to buy Julie a new washing machine. She was very excited at the prospect. The next day she asked us to give her the money instead of the washing machine. She told us it was for kitchen improvements. My husband refused, and we bought her the washing machine. We knew that Jamie had influenced her to change her mind.'

One night the Garretts heard Jamie shouting at Julie. The next morning they found Jamie had punched a hole in the living-room plaster. 'Julie tended to laugh it off and said that Jamie didn't know his own strength.' The Garretts had also begun to worry about Jamie's drinking: there was too much of it, they thought, and it made him aggressive. Even when sober, Jamie was domineering, Ray Garrett told police: 'He seemed to want to be in control and if he was in a situation which he couldn't control, he would grab Julie and leave.'

A year later, in 1984, Julie rang her mother and asked her to get the spare bed ready. She said she couldn't live with Jamie any more. Gilda Pekin says that some time in the early eighties, Julie and Jamie had a fight in which he knocked her to the ground; perhaps this was it. In any case, she moved in with her parents for a few weeks and then into rented accommodation. Her mother says, 'We went to Queensland on holiday and Julie became ill with flu. Jamie came around with Lucozade and flowers. Soon she moved back.'

According to research, abused women try to leave an average of eight times before they finally succeed in breaking free of the relationship. Jane Ashton gave a bleak laugh when I told her this statistic. 'Like trying to give up smoking,' she said.

They are both deadly habits.

AFTER JULIE and Jamie reconciled, there was still plenty to worry the Garretts. Julie's mother noticed a picture was missing. 'The painting was painted by Ray's brother, John, of Northaw church where Jamie and Julie were married. It was a gift from John. Julie told me that Jamie had destroyed it. I found this odd. In fact John painted another picture of the village and the church which Julie left with us. She didn't want to take it home. She also had some Limoges china which was a gift from a town in France where she stayed as an eleven-year-old. Many times I tried to give it to her but she wouldn't take it. I now know why: I think that Jamie would have smashed it during their next argument.'

After that first separation, simmering problems between Jamie and Ray intensified. 'Jamie had a problem with Ray,' Pat Garrett says. 'Politically, they were opposites. Meals with drink would always develop into arguments over various topics. Jamie got more abusive as he drank. He would sneer at everything we held dear. I believe that Jamie thought that Ray knew about some of the violence in the relationship. At the time, we were unaware of the violence.'

Pat Garrett also told police that Jamie had bragged of a motoring offence when he and Julie were separated: 'I think it was for drink driving. He told us how he had not pulled over and drove home, ran inside and swigged whisky. It was something like that. When it went to court he had a good lawyer who picked holes in the two policemen's statements. Julie went to court and pleaded for him. She was heavily pregnant with Matthew. His licence was suspended for about four months. When Julie went into labour with Matthew, she had to drive herself to hospital because Jamie didn't have a licence.'

Police investigating Julie's killing searched for and failed to find any record of this brush with the law, but it occurred in the days before such offences were filed on a computer database, and those records are often difficult to access now.

A labouring Julie driving herself to hospital for the birth of her first child – so much for her promise to her parents on her eighteenth birthday that she now had someone who would look after her.

BOTH JULIE and Jamie had slept with other partners during their separation, which lasted several months. Years later, Julie told a startled Kate Clark that 'We both bonked everyone in sight.' When they reunited, Julie left her other relationships behind but Jamie continued one affair right into Matthew's pregnancy, according to Jane Ashton and Gilda Pekin. Gilda says, 'Julie told me that they'd had an almighty row when she was pregnant with Matthew. And she had stood there and screamed at him and said, "You can't touch me, I'm pregnant. *And you will stop this affair!*"' Gilda says it was the one time Julie felt able to really stand up to Jamie because she was shielded by her pregnant belly.

This makes a misunderstanding on Samantha's part all the more intriguing. In her statement to police after her mother's death, Samantha said, 'Mum told me that when she first had Matt and was pregnant with me that Dad had hit her and that he had broken her nose. She was going to leave him then but didn't because she couldn't afford to, basically.'

In fact, the broken nose happened in 1991, when Samantha was three or four years old. Did Julie try to win Samantha's support by embroidering the story to make her unborn daughter the target of the attack too? Or has Samantha's memory played a trick on her, unconsciously rewriting history because of her loyalty to her mother or her own emotional response to the story – any attack on my mother is an attack on me?

WHEN THE children were young, the Garretts were at first allowed to be close to them. They would take Samantha and Matthew down to their caravan on the coast at Inverloch for holidays. 'Fishing, ball games, great relationship,' their grandfather remembers. But there was one odd thing even then: when they returned the children to Julie, says Pat Garrett, 'if there were friends of Jamie and Julie [there], they were surprised to see her family. It was as if we weren't spoken about. Their friends would even ask if we were over on holiday'.

The arguments between Jamie and Ray worsened yet again. It is hard to know the full truth of this, as the police statements are taken from Julie's family and so represent their side of the story only. It is also hard to tell from the statements quite what the order of events was. For Pat Garrett, the serious trouble started at a dinner in the Ramages' first Balwyn house in about 1993, which began with Jamie sneering at her family. The Garretts left early, and afterwards 'Jamie told Julie that we weren't to see the children at Christmas. I begged her to let the children see us. Julie agreed to bring the children to see me on condition that Ray was not there.'

For the next three or four years, the Garretts saw their grandchildren only when Jamie and Julie wanted a babysitter. Jamie told Julie that she could only stay for twenty minutes when she dropped off or picked up the children. If she was any longer, he would ring her wanting to know where she was.

Once, the Garretts actually went inside the Ramages' new house at Marock Place when they were picking up the children. Ray told police that later, 'we were sitting at home having dinner around the table with Matt and Sam. The phone rang and I put it on speaker phone. It was Jamie. He abused me, telling me not to come into "his fucking house"; that the condition that Julie was allowed to live in Balwyn was if Pat and I didn't come into the house.'

Jane, too, found herself on the outer. She says now that she and Julie had a seesawing relationship. When Julie was close to Jamie, she rarely saw her sister. When the marriage was openly troubled, Jane was the first person Julie turned to. Overall, the tendency was clear: 'Slowly, over the years, Jamie pulled Julie away from the family.'

Jane believes Julie would parrot Jamie's attitudes in what she dubbed 'Jamie-speak': 'At certain stages, when she'd go back to him for a while, she'd talk and it wasn't her words, it was his words. It was like talking to him. She would justify where they were living, the children's schools. She would justify how she didn't see us very often. She would justify his behaviour... Like in *1984*, she was absolutely brainwashed.'

Christine Howgate, too, believes that Jamie dominated Julie's thinking: 'She didn't tell many people how bad it was because... he told her it was normal. He told her everyone behaved like this.'

One New Year's Eve, Jamie became aggressive with Jane. He was drunk, she says, and he asked her what his New Year's resolution should be. Jane suggested he try to be more compassionate and understanding towards other people. 'He became very aggressive; he was swearing at me. Howard and I went to leave. Julie got between him and us and he struck out at her, pushing her away. She told us to go and she would calm him down. He was in a rage.'

For reasons that were unclear to the Garretts, the situation with them and Jamie improved gradually over time. Pat Garrett says, 'We were allowed to go to school plays or watch Matthew play football. Although when we went, Jamie ignored us completely. He would only nod at us. We were always seated behind the family. Although we weren't comfortable, we always went if Julie invited us.'

In 2001, things changed again. Jamie and Julie argued in bed. He pushed her out of bed and on to the floor – because she refused to have sex, according to Jane Ashton. Julie told Gilda a more detailed story: Julie and Jamie argued about whether she should be 'allowed' free time or whether he had the right to know where she was every minute. Perhaps he suspected an affair. As often happened after a row, Jamie then wanted sex. 'Julie refused, so he threw her out of the bed.' Julie left Jamie briefly, staying overnight with Jane. When she returned, she insisted that she would stay only if Jamie mended fences with her family. Says Pat Garrett, 'As soon as she returned, Jamie rang us. He asked to speak to Ray. He invited us to Scotch College that evening because Matt was being presented with an award. We went and were greeted by Jamie and Julie. We were seated next to his mother and made to feel part of the family. The following Sunday we joined Julie, Jamie and Samantha at Howqua, Lauriston's boarding-school campus. He again was friendly and charming. He had made a complete turnaround towards us.' But she noticed that Julie was very cool towards Jamie.

Ray Garrett would not have called the turnaround 'complete'. He told police that even after relations improved in 2001, 'Jamie still wouldn't really acknowledge me. He wouldn't even look at me, very peculiar. He had even told Julie that his ambition in life was to outlive me. I found this very odd, considering that I am now 70.'

According to Philip Dunn, what had started all the trouble and made Jamie so unforgiving was a remark by Ray Garrett about Jamie's father, who died young from a smoking-related disease. It was along the lines of 'Well, maybe he shouldn't have smoked then'.

Everyone had a different piece of the puzzle that was Julie Ramage's complicated, compartmentalised life. Her family knew about Jamie's argumentativeness, controlling behaviour and attempts to cut her off from her relatives. But it was only late in the course of events that they heard about physical abuse. Julie had told Jane about the 1991 head-butt in which her nose was broken, but only some years afterwards. It was partly because they saw so little of Julie for so long that her family had only a hazy sense of her problems. It was her best friend, Gilda Pekin, who held the pieces of Julie's life marked 'bruised and battered'.

Over the years, Gilda noticed damage to Julie's face several times. The first two times were when their children were in kindergarten. Julie had bruises, a black eye and a mark on the side of her face. That first time, Julie told Gilda that she had walked into the door of a kitchen cupboard. The second time, she again said she had walked into an awkwardly placed kitchen-cupboard door. 'Julie, you've got to renovate that kitchen,' said Gilda.

The third time was in 1991 when Gilda went around to Julie's to mind the children while Julie went to university. (Julie was hoping to get a degree in home economics that would enable her to teach.) Gilda found Julie with two black eyes and a broken nose – it was the head-butt, though Gilda did not know it then.

Gilda tried to draw the truth out of her. 'This time, when the whole face was yellowed and the eyes were black, I said to her, "Julie, don't tell me it was that fucking cupboard again! You need to do something about this." And I remember she had on a skirt, and when someone gets terribly nervous, they move so quickly that the skirt flies out, and you are just taken aback by their action and you feel dismissed by it. Physically, she was flighty, really would not talk about it. And she didn't tell me that first time I saw her like that. It wasn't until a day or two later that she said, "Actually, my nose was broken and I have to go see a plastic surgeon."' Julie again said she had walked into a door but she seemed to feel ashamed and wanted no one to see her. Gilda did her kinder and school drop-offs because Julie did not want to leave the house.

It was another week before Julie admitted that Jamie had head-butted her during an argument, and even then she 'confessed' only when pressured. Gilda says, 'I found a nice quiet time and I confronted her about it. I said, "Julie, it can't go on like this," and she said, "It'll be OK. I will make the most of it. He's promised he won't do it again."'

Says Gilda now, 'What can you do? You feel ineffectual, helpless, hopeless. But the fact is that unless the person changes what they want and they come to ask you for help to achieve what they want, you really can't do anything at all.'

In fact, the plain-speaking Gilda did do something, and she believes Jamie Ramage never forgave her for it. 'He didn't like me after 1991. The broken nose. He knew I knew the truth of it, because I said to him, "Jamie, you can't do this to people." In a very intimidating way, he told me to mind my "*fucking* business".'

Even worse, Julie was angry about Gilda intervening. 'It was awful. She said, "You don't know what will happen to me. You can't say anything!" Because I didn't check first. I had four brothers and a dad and I came from a very upfront, straight-talking family, where the first rule about a family is love and the second is respect . . . But Julie ticked me off severely for it.' The friendship 'went quiet' for a while afterwards but resumed eventually around the everyday contact they had over their children.

Some years later, Julie told her sister Jane that Jamie had once broken her arm. Gilda Pekin remembers seeing Julie with a bandaged arm. Julie told her it was a greenstick fracture. 'She never told me how it came about,' Gilda says. 'It was several years after the broken nose, but still when the kids were in primary school . . . She said she didn't quite know how it happened. It was one of those mystery things.' They were both so busy, says Gilda, who had work and kids and study, that it was easy to let such apparently minor mishaps slip by. 'If she had an injury like that and gave me a plausible explanation, I would have said to her, "God, Julie, you're accident-prone. Stop being so clumsy."'

There was also a black eye that three horse-riding friends had seen and commented upon in the last few months of 2002. Julie told the horse-riding friends that she got it by walking into a cupboard but she told Gilda Pekin she got it horse-riding. She took the truth about this, along with the truth of so many other things, with her when she died.

GILDA PEKIN sheds light on another aspect of Julie's life. She says Jamie didn't like Julie studying. Jamie wouldn't allow her to spend money on babysitters, so she and Gilda would babysit for each other. When Julie began at university, she often missed classes.

'Jamie made it difficult,' says Gilda. 'He wouldn't turn up when he was supposed to look after the children.' He would be home early every other night of the week but somehow could never manage it on Wednesdays, Julie's night for classes. She found it hard, with Matthew in primary school and Samantha in kindergarten. 'After about a year of study, she decided to discontinue.' Julie's second attempt to get herself an education ended like the first: foiled by the man in her life.

Gilda was also the friend who noticed most about Jamie's day-to-day control of Julie. At dinner parties, Gilda says, Jamie would sit at the head of the table – even when he was at someone else's table. When he was ready to leave, he would sit with arms folded and say, 'Ju-*lie*!', as if he were snapping his fingers or whistling for a dog. Julie would race around picking up her dishes and packing up her children, ready to load the family into the car quickly.

Jane Ashton told police, 'He was trying to create a *Home Beautiful* wife.'

GILDA WASN'T the only person to sense that things were not right. Jane Ashton and Christine Howgate knew about Jamie's financial control of Julie. When Samantha was desperate for a pony, Jane had to buy it for her and offer free agistment. Julie had to pay the money back secretly over several months. Jane told police, 'Jamie wouldn't pay the money for the pony, even though it appeared that money wasn't an issue for them. He was controlling Julie through financial restriction. Therefore Julie had to hide money from him just so the kids could have things and she could live a reasonable life.'

Christine Howgate knew how Julie managed to salt money away into hollow logs of which Jamie knew nothing. 'Because she was the financial controller for Eco-d, she used to pay herself most of her money in the cheque that he knew about and then pay herself some money in cash. This was also to pay the cleaning lady extra, because he wouldn't pay the cleaning lady more than $12.50 an hour, and she wanted to pay her $15; I don't remember the numbers, but what he wanted was unfair and not enough. So she would pay her the balance in cash and leave it in a place where the cleaning lady knew about it.'

Jamie had to have a hand in every household purchase. Julie was required to produce receipts for everything she bought. His interest ranged from Samantha's choice of shoes (according to Kate Clark, who found it odd that the fifteen-year-old was not just given a budget and told to buy them herself) to quilt covers and his wife's haircuts. Says Christine, 'She'd never chosen her own doona cover. How many men care? She and I used to use the same hairdresser. She went to Libby, and Libby told me that he would stand behind her and tell her how to cut her hair. *Weird* stuff.'

Christine has always understood the point of the overt control. She was confused, though, by another habit of Jamie's that made no sense to her. She describes it this way: 'On the few occasions we would see them together socially as couples, he would say things to my husband like, "There's something not quite right about Julie" – undermining her. And he would know that that would get back to me.'

She looks at me, puzzled. 'Why would he do that?'

Christine has never seen *Gaslight*.

JAMIE ALSO used the children to try to manipulate Julie. According to Christine, in the past he had told Julie that if she left him, the business partnership would have to be dissolved, there would be no money and the children would have to be pulled out of private school.

During the separation, Kate Clark says she was disturbed to notice the depth of his 'non-emotional, non-loving' attachment to Julie. 'He said with some – not pride, but with some satisfaction – that he thought that if Matt refused to see Julie for the breakfasts that he'd been having with her, that that would be a good way to make her see reason.'

Kate told him, 'Jamie, you can't do that!'

'Really?'

'Yes! Call Matt off! You can't use Matt as leverage to get her to come back. You can't threaten her with the withdrawal of Matt's affection. That won't work!'

'Oh. Okay. Well, I'll tell Matt about that.'

He didn't really understand why it was a problem, Clark says, but he did give her the impression he would take her advice on it.

SOMETIMES JAMIE vented his anger on people other than Julie. Jane Ashton claims he once punched a business associate after stewing for three days over an argument. Rhonda McMurtrie told police that when Matthew was fifteen – and a tall fifteen – Jamie 'stated very confidently that he hit Matt as part of his discipline'. The McMurtries were shocked.

Samantha, too, had copped it more than once. She said in her statement to police, 'Dad has unnecessarily physically punished me more than I would consider was what a normal father would do. The last time that I can recall Dad hitting me would have been last summer, I can't remember why, but it would have been for something stupid I had said or done. Dad gave me a black eye once; that was last year. We were in the car driving home from a friend's place. Can't remember why it happened, but he hit or slapped me the wrong way across the face and it caused a bit of a bruise, redness and a lump. It wasn't like the worst time Dad had hit me.

'Dad had a temper but I never thought he would kill Mum. I thought that he would get angry about the separation at some stage, but I thought he may do something to the house or something like that.'

Only one part of this chilling passage made it into evidence at the trial. It was Samantha's softening remark: 'I don't think that Mum was scared of Dad. When they had arguments, Mum would speak her mind, but would eventually give up.'

ACCORDING TO Samiro Douglas from the Women's Information and Referral Exchange (WIRE), sexual abuse is the kind women talk about last, and least. Like rape victims, abused partners feel ashamed and somehow responsible for having caused it. It was only from 1997, when Julie confided in Gilda Pekin about her affair with a father at the primary school, that her best friend began gleaning information about this side of Julie's life. Julie told several friends and her lover Laurence Webb that Jamie Ramage insisted upon a particular sexual practice that she found repugnant. Pekin says, 'From Julie's description of their sex life, it was on command, the kind of stuff that he wanted; in her words, "Not the sort of thing that you expect between a loving couple who've been married for twenty years." The kind of stuff that he wanted was really ugly, pornographic, not a warm loving relationship at all.'

Christine Howgate had received hints of this, too, and is upset that she did not understand at the time why Julie wanted to raise it. 'She tried to talk to me once when we were walking about [that sexual practice]. And I went, "No, don't go there!" The question was something like, "What would you do if your husband suggested it?" She was trying to talk, she was trying to find out if it was normal behaviour, and my reaction was shutdown. The only other thing I said to her on another occasion, when she talked about how often he wanted sex, and how aggressive he was, was that "You don't have to do anything you don't want to do, ever."'

Jane Ashton told police, 'Julie confided in me that she didn't find Jamie sexually attractive any more. She told me that he would force her to have sex with him via emotionally controlling her by questioning her love for him. She told me she had to be sexually compliant due to threat of violence or anger.'

By the time she left her marriage, Julie was also confiding in workmates about this side of her life. Tarsha Warren told police, 'She also mentioned to me that Jamie was highly sexual. She wasn't as interested as he was. She told me that he would roll over every morning and tap her on the shoulder and she felt like a piece of meat. She said that it felt like rape. She was upset when she talked about it. It was unusual for her to show emotion, because she was very professional and kept her personal feelings aside so it didn't interfere with work.' Julie told a similar story to Laurence Webb:

'The relationship had broken down to the point where sex was a matter of rape, against her will, in a very unpleasant manner.'

Could Jamie have been utterly unaware of how Julie experienced sex with him? When questioned by police about the last time he had had sex with Julie, Jamie had said only that 'it was normal sex for us'. Dunn had said in court that Jamie had absolutely no idea that Julie felt like this about their sexual encounters, and he suggested that Julie had told such stories because they were self-serving, justifying her infidelity.

She did use those stories to justify leaving her husband. Even her boss got to hear about it. The week before Julie left Marock Place, Felicity Holding told Julie she disapproved of her leaving the marriage while Matthew was doing VCE. Holding later told police, 'The following Monday, I came in and spoke with Julie and said I understood her decision. She told me that I had no idea what it's like, that Jamie demanded sex every day from her, whether it was a quickie in the morning or whatever. It was totally for him rather than her. It was like he had to do it every day as a control thing. I had accepted that she was going and this made me really accept it.'

Which is more sickening – what Julie said she experienced, or the fact that she had to reveal her humiliation to outsiders to justify leaving a bad marriage? Like Gulliver tied down by hundreds of tiny ropes in Lilliput, the middle-class wife and mother has to struggle against all the things that bind her to a bad relationship: her children's welfare, their private schooling, the nice house, financial security, and fear of the condemnation of those who will disapprove of her 'selfishness' and 'disloyalty' – or envy her new-found freedom.

Gulliver had it easy compared to Julie Ramage. Tied to the ground, he merely lost the freedom to move about. Julie Ramage, tied to the marital bed, felt she had lost sovereignty over her own body.

IT WAS in the marital bed, on the night of Thursday 5 June 2003, that Julie Ramage made the fateful decision to leave.

That evening she had gone out to a farewell for a work colleague. When she got home, she found Jamie furious and Samantha upset. Samantha had gone somewhere after school and arrived home two hours late. Jamie had gone through his daughter's diary while she was out and was enraged by what he had read. Jamie abused Samantha to Julie and Julie defended her, saying he couldn't talk like that about his own daughter and that she was a good kid. According to Julie, who told both a workmate and Gilda Pekin about it the next day, Jamie then said to Julie that it was hard to raise Samantha as a lady *'when she has a slut for a mother'*.

Her workmate Joanne McLean told police, 'That was the thing that made her think, "I'm out of here". She told me that after this he demanded sex. She said that she just lay there and didn't move. She had made up her mind that she was leaving.'

Julie Ramage was not going to lie back and take it any more.

ACCORDING TO her sister, Julie told family lawyer Caroline Counsel that she didn't want a lot of money. She didn't want to ruin Jamie or his business, which would be their children's future, and only wanted enough to buy herself a small home. Gilda Pekin helped Julie work out how much money to take when she left: enough to cover Samantha's schooling (Matt's was paid up), two years' rent, and $60,000 for legal fees for a Family Court battle with Jamie over assets.

Gilda gave her one more piece of advice. She grins, remembering: 'I said, "Before you leave, you should make sure you have a full house of decent underwear." She just looked at me like I was crazy, but I said, "Your standard of living is going to plummet when you leave, and his will go up. Your health will improve, but his will fail."' It's the classic scenario, borne out by research: women's emotional well-being is low before they leave a difficult marriage and picks up once they start their new lives, but men are on a downhill track for some time afterwards. In this sense, the Ramages were like any other couple in which the woman was the partner who pulled the plug.

They were unlike most others in that Julie talked to several people about taking out a restraining order. According to Jane Ashton, her lawyer advised her to do it, but Julie felt that Jamie's response to her leaving in the past had always been to be charming and try to woo her back. Julie told Christine Howgate that she would not take Counsel's advice about the restraining order because she feared it would set Jamie off, and she wanted to still be able to do things like celebrate the children's birthdays together: 'She thought that was important for the kids.' She told her horse-riding friend Annette Luckman she doubted that her application for one would be successful. 'Who would ever believe me?' she said, throwing her arms out in a gesture of helplessness.

But she did promise her anxious mother that she would never, ever see Jamie alone. 'I'm not silly,' she told her. Two days before she died.

JAMIE TOLD his side of the story to a family friend who cannot be named here. She is protective about her identity because she has been so open about the rest of her life in our interview. 'Helen', as she wishes to be called, was a friend to both Julie and Jamie and was the only one who challenged him about whether Julie had left him because of violence. Like the other characters in this drama, she lives in a comfortable house in a desirable suburb. Family pictures are scattered throughout her home; the family dog has the run of the place and is absent-mindedly petted whenever it passes her. Helen is an open woman with a kind and chatty manner.

Jamie called to see Helen one night during the separation. He told her that he thought that she and Julie were very alike and that he wanted her advice on how to get Julie back. They opened a bottle of wine and sat and talked until 2 am.

He did not know how alike they were. Helen also has a history of domestic violence earlier in her marriage. So, when they had canvassed every other possible reason why Julie would have left him, Helen asked Jamie bluntly if he had ever hit Julie. There was a long and heavy silence. Guardedly, Jamie admitted that he had.

Says Helen, 'It makes my blood boil now. He said, "Yes I have, but it amounted to nothing more than pushing and shoving." I didn't for one minute believe that. Nup. Call it instinct, call it intuition.'

Helen's husband asked him how often there was aggression in the relationship. Jamie replied that it was 'no more than in a normal marriage'. Asked what triggered the aggression, Jamie told Helen 'that Julie didn't communicate effectively and didn't make clear what her intentions were'. That got Helen's blood up again: 'If you are in fear or intimidated by somebody, you will step around them,' she says. Jamie complained that Julie could not move on and too often referred to events back in the past. Helen told him, 'Of course she would; having been there myself, the reason you still bring it into the forefront is because the issues are not resolved.' Jamie, seeking sympathy and advice, got a bucketful of home truths. To his credit, he stayed and listened to them.

But Helen doubted he took much on board. 'He never gave anything away. He would ask you a question, he would request you answer that, you had to give him an answer, he wouldn't let it lie. But he would never respond to an answer, so you never had feedback from him. You didn't know if he was listening, if he'd already made his mind up; he was just so single-minded, you could have been way off the mark.'

Helen's husband became increasingly uncomfortable at the turn the conversation had taken and left. Jamie told Helen that he had no male friends in Australia who would understand how he was feeling. He was angry that Julie would not come and see the renovated kitchen she had designed, and he was confused that she wanted to go to some social engagements with him but didn't want to come home. He said, 'She can't have it both ways.' He argued that her place was with the family; Helen told him that Julie needed space away from him because she was feeling stifled. 'Then there was more about him and what this was doing to him. I counteracted that by putting the writing on the wall: "James, she has gone for good reason, and my support would be with Julie."'

Jamie smelled danger. 'He said, "I don't want you talking to Julie."'

Jamie saw parallels in Helen's marriage and his own and acknowledged that Julie had left because of his aggression. But, in a stunning act of hubris, *he told Helen that he thought her marital problems were worse than his*. 'He said, "What's wrong with Julie and I is nothing compared to all of our friends." He'd made up his mind that everyone else was in a far more dire position; he just said, "Julie and I, our problems are fixable. They'll be fixed."' He even offered to speak to Helen's husband about her marital difficulties on her behalf. A bemused Helen declined the offer.

Jamie also told Helen that he was not going to let all this drag on for too long. He was drawing a line in the sand: 'Another couple of weeks was all he was willing to put up with.'

He killed Julie two weeks later, to the day.

IT SEEMS extraordinary that Jamie Ramage listened to Helen talk until two in the morning about how a woman feels when she is hit by a man, and yet he killed his wife soon afterwards in what started as a flurry of punches. Helen looks at me sadly and nods with the helplessness of one who knows her heart-felt efforts have come to nought. 'Mmm. That's why I believe he never listened to anything anyone said to him.'

In his conversation with Helen, Jamie Ramage used the classic deflector shields of the abusive man to avoid owning the truth about himself: he denied much of what he had done, he minimised the seriousness of the behaviour he did admit to, and he blamed his partner for triggering his anger.

HELEN HAS a quick sympathy for Julie's affairs, although she knew nothing of them at the time. 'I can relate to that. I did it too.' She looks at me almost beseechingly, as if there is an urgent need for me to understand, not so that I will 'forgive' – she feels no need for that – but so that I will grasp the depth of pain behind the flight into pleasure. 'When you are being abused, physically and mentally, over such a long period of time, you are left feeling absolutely worthless. Julie had affairs because when nothing you say is respected, when nothing you can do is right, you are left feeling like you're nothing but an orifice. And that just leaves you so empty.

'Julie was not a bad person. She was not the person painted in court. Julie's life was her children, the home; to me, she was everything good and wholesome. She didn't go out to seek an affair. It's affection. You need to be loved. It's to find some self-worth, to know that you're normal and to understand that you're not mental, you're not ill, you're not sick. You're just a human being trying to get through life expecting what everybody expects.' She sighs and shakes her head. 'Nobody claims to be perfect. Julie certainly didn't, and I certainly don't. But you can't be wrong all the time.'

For friends such as Helen, no verdict and no sentence could compensate for Julie's death. But they did hope for a result that would make up for the law's silencing of Julie's voice.

Part Five

COURT IN THE CROSSFIRE

VERDICT

Day sixteen
Thursday 28 October 2004

WHEN A jury goes out, no one knows what to expect. It could be gone half an hour or a month. This is the point at which lawyers and judges, for all their robes and power within the system, are as much reduced to the sidelines as the friends and relatives watching the case. It is like a vigil for a birth or a death: prolonged and helpless waiting, in a vacuum of unknowingness, ends suddenly in a surge of activity and emotion. For the lawyer who is to lose, the longer the jury is out, the more honourable the verdict upon his performance: at least he mounted a good enough case to make them think and argue.

The Ramage jurors told their tipstaff that they had a verdict just before 3 pm. They had been out for two days. The calls went out to lawyers, family and journalists. It was a mild, grey afternoon. I raced up the two and a half city blocks to the court. It is hard to follow a story this closely and not be swept up in its drama. Others, too, had this sense of anticipation about the moment of truth; in court, the public gallery began filling with strangers to the case, court-watchers who float about the precinct watching trials for entertainment. The best theatre is often provided by the verdict.

Julie's parents and sister are here already in the side pews. They have come into town from the outer suburbs each day and simply waited. Her mother blinks hard trying not to cry and her father stares straight ahead. Jane tries to break the tension by cracking a joke and her mother smiles for just a moment. It transforms her face out of the mask of grief. But her expression quickly collapses again; like a bridge whose pylons have crumbled, her trembling mouth has not the strength to hold up a smile. Leckie arrives and then Dunn. They greet each other quietly, conscious either of the gravity of the moment or the sea of spectators, and begin to shuffle their papers.

Jamie Ramage arrives last. He would have spent the past two days sitting on a hard bench in one of those small, green, noisome cells, waiting to hear his fate. There would have been nothing to do but read and think. Or brood. Now he sits forward on the edge of his allotted pew, his mouth working nervously as he fingers the middle button on the open jacket of his navy suit. Then he draws a deep breath and sits up ramrod straight. He brings his forefinger to his thumb in a circular gesture and slowly begins flicking imaginary pieces of fluff from the sleeve of his jacket. Hard. If you were close enough, you would hear the forceful snap of his fingers. It is as if each flick rids him of an untidy emotion that he doesn't want hanging from him today. The exercise seems to have the desired effect. By the time he has finished, he has himself under control. He resumes his usual unreadable demeanour.

The judge arrives to a room tense with expectation. The court regulars go through the ritual of rising, bowing and sitting again. The jury files in, all eyes upon them. The woman with the steel-rimmed glasses, who has taken to sitting next to the foreman, fastens her eyes upon Patricia Garrett, who is sitting opposite her. Only one of the jurors looks over at Jamie, the older woman I have always thought of as the retired teacher. The others look at the judge or stare into space. If the old line about juries is true – 'If they can't look you in the eye, it's because they have convicted you' – then Jamie Ramage has lost.

Jamie is asked to stand. He scrambles to his feet. The grey-haired foreman stands too and gives the verdict in a steady voice.

Not guilty of murder. Guilty of manslaughter.

There is a moment of shock while his words sink in. No one moves or speaks. Then I swing round and stare at Jamie Ramage. His faint, dusty eyebrows shoot up into his forehead with surprise at the unexpected scrutiny. His eyes are like brown beads in his head, hard and glassy. We gaze at each other for a long moment in what feels like mutual incomprehension. Shaken, and embarrassed at my own impulsiveness, I swing back to face the front. Patricia Garrett has drawn a long breath and lets it out in a quiet sob. Ray Garrett is shaking his white head in disbelief, looking down at the floor. Jane's face is hard with anger. The judge thanks the jurors and they rise to leave, the grey-haired woman – feeling sad? sorry? curious? – still watching Patricia Garrett. Julie's mother has been struggling to hold back her tears and now, as the twelve people on whom she had pinned the pitiful last of her hopes turn to leave, the sobs break out in ragged bursts. Her shoulders heave with the force of it.

It is as if she is weeping behind glass. The proceedings continue around her. Jamie Ramage is asked whether he has anything to say or any reason that judgement should not be passed upon him. His voice is low. 'No.'

Dunn rises to his feet, as smooth and confident as ever despite the distress in the pews only a couple of metres from him. He begins talking about a delay with a psychiatric report into Jamie's mental state; it might not be possible to have it ready until December. Jane, her face now twisted with fury, jumps to her feet. She stalks out of the courtroom with her head high and her stiff back radiating contempt. The Garretts rise to follow her. Ray leads his sobbing wife by the hand. As they pass Jamie's pew, Patricia Garrett lunges towards him and glares at him, hissing, *'Bastard!'*

Jamie's head is bowed. He makes no reply.

THE GARRETTS' exit triggers an exodus as reporters scramble to follow them. We needn't have rushed. No one will get a quote right now. We all halt as we enter the stone-tiled waiting area outside the courtroom, with its large wooden table and benches. This is as far as Patricia Garrett has managed to stagger. She is sitting on the nearest bench. Her upper body is slumped on to the table in an ungainly sprawl, with no regard for her carefully ironed over-shirt. Her soft old face is on the unyielding wood. She is crying hard, her small body shuddering with pain. Her wails are not loud but something about their quality makes them ring out through the echoey space. She pays no mind. Like anyone in extremis, she is beyond shame.

The reporters are not. We turn our eyes away to give her privacy and retreat to corners. Rivals consult in murmurs over how best to proceed. No one can afford to miss a comment by the Garretts but no one wants to breach the terrible force-field of her grief. Its primal rawness – from an elderly, conservative Englishwoman, born of the nation that invented the stiff upper lip – is a shocking contrast to the robed formality of the proceedings on the other side of the wall. It is a reminder of the brutal truths at the heart of this story; the human loss and suffering that tugs like an undertow below the erudite legal argument.

All those lawyerly words seem empty now. Even the journalists – those compulsive score-keepers of public events, trained to analyse everything glibly in terms of wins and losses – realise that this is not a game, and that no one has won.

MOST OF the media pack follows Jane Ashton out to the front steps of the Supreme Court. A couple of us wait inside for the Garretts, who have disappeared. When they return, Julie's mother is composed but leans on her husband as if she has trouble holding herself up. I catch her eye and she returns my gaze. We follow them out to one of the small courtyards and my companion asks her the useful but classically trite reporter's question in the face of epic catastrophe: How does she feel?

She leans against a stone wall, her face bloodless. She has a quiet voice and has not lost her English accent. 'I'm just devastated. The law's an ass, that's all I can say.'

Does she feel justice has been done? Her voice is still soft but it begins to shake with the intensity of her fury. 'No, definitely not. *My gentle daughter*' – the three words come out like a moan – 'she would not have provoked him because she was frightened of him. She was frightened he was going to kill her horse. So she never would have provoked him, never in a million years would she have put herself in that situation, *never*!'

Did she share her fears with you? 'Constantly. But we weren't allowed to say what she told us. That's hearsay. He can say anything he likes and that's allowed. If that's justice . . .' She slumps further and closes her eyes. Ray Garrett, holding his wife and trying to offer the jury the benefit of a doubt, suggests that they made their decision based on the fact that Jamie has two children. But, he says, 'They're not children. And one thing we fear is his control – he had great influence on everything that the children were doing and everything that happened. He's the most controlling, methodical person; highly intelligent but very, very dangerous. It's sad that they are not going to put him away for many years because it would give a chance for the kids to grow up and try to lead a normal life.'

The other reporter asks why the children were not here today. Patricia looks away and says sadly, 'We don't know.' Ray says, 'There's been a lot of pressure put on them. Basically, this all happened because of the children. Julie stayed with him for years and years because of the children.'

'And she's paid for it with her life,' says her mother bitterly.

They talk a little more about how Julie had promised them never to be alone with Jamie, and how they are convinced she would never have gone to the house that day if she thought the builder wouldn't be there. Then Patricia Garrett gives the warning she wants to go out to the world: 'Any woman that's in a relationship where she feels threatened, I tell her not to stay for the sake of the children.

To get out. My daughter stayed for the children and she's paid the ultimate price. They've got no mother now, and I'm just devastated.'

She nods a dismissal and we stand back. Grief has a dignity and authority all of its own. The Garretts walk heavily through the courtyards of the court complex, picking up a couple of women friends along the way. They put their arms around Pat Garrett as she walks out the glass doors and down the worn stone steps to the waiting cameras and the forest of microphone booms. She holds herself together enough to repeat what she has told us, with one extra: she demands that the legal defence of provocation be abolished.

JANE ASHTON rings me at the office when she has finished her interviews with the other media. She is still furious but she has gone to some trouble to organise her thoughts to get her message across effectively. She claims not to be surprised at the verdict, having seen it coming, but still expresses disappointment in the jury system and the 'ordinary man' test: 'I hoped that the "ordinary man" would have been able to help us. I don't see how the ordinary man could have done this.'

The fact that provocation can be used as a defence to murder means that women do not have a legal right to leave their partners in a safe and civilised way, she says, reading from a prepared statement. 'The claim that my sister provoked him allows him to exonerate himself and blame her for his loss of control. Provocation carries with it the assumption that a man has a right to punish his wife if she defies him . . . Females can have their characters blackened and their struggles as victims trivialised, whereas an abuser's testimony as to how he was provoked and his emotional state prior is sanctioned by the law. The burden shouldn't be placed on the dead woman to vindicate herself and her conduct.'

Jane Ashton is a full-time housewife and mother who lives in the outer suburbs. She has a university education and had worked as a volunteer in a women's refuge while she was a student, but since she had children her main preoccupations have been them and her horse-riding. Now, like Christine Howgate, she has found herself politicised the hard way. She declares that the case demonstrates the way the law is imbued with the patriarchal belief that women are the chattels of men.

Jane would say this again and again. Blonde, pretty, composed and articulate – and the living image of her dead sister – she would be welcomed on prime-time current affairs television shows and by Melbourne's radio talk-back kings. Newspapers ran big feature stories on the case and editorialised against the defence of provocation. The letters pages ran hot; the Ramage case had everyone talking. Colleagues fell out in the workplace over it, as did husbands and wives in their homes. Lawyers on different sides of the debate critiqued each other sharply in public and slagged off at each other savagely in private. Not always, but often, the argument divided along gender lines, with members of each sex dumbfounded at the attitudes held by the other.

Round and round it went, the analysis of men and women, love and marriage, sex and deceit, male aggression and privilege, female gold-digging and passivity . . . Had the law got it wrong? How had all those therapists missed what was looming? And what is it with men like Jamie Ramage, anyway? *What on earth had gone on in his head?*

THE CASE FOR CHANGE

JENNY MORGAN is small, cheerful and quick. She has close-cropped hair and funky glasses, a sharp intellect and a droll sense of humour. She is not a practising lawyer, but she talked about legal issues with the blunt, blokey vigour of a barrister. She is a professor of law at Melbourne University. Several years ago, the law department left the traditional sandstone cloisters of the old university campus and moved into a flash multi-storey tower in nearby Carlton. Morgan now has a modern office with sweeping views and a curved white desk loaded with books and papers.

Jenny Morgan has featured in a previous book about men and women and the politics of gender. She is the academic whom writer Helen Garner called 'Dr M' in the book *The First Stone*. That book was about a legal case in which two female students had accused the master of a residential college at Melbourne University of groping them. A critical Garner, horrified 'that feminism had come to this', questioned whether the students should have personally confronted the master rather than taken him to court for assault, and explored the master's claims of a feminist conspiracy backing the girls. Morgan talks about the book with a blithe lack of ill-will and jokes that at least she got a PhD out of it (Garner's pseudonym for her implied that she had a doctorate). At the time, Morgan told a national ABC audience that the line Garner took in *The First Stone* effectively said that young women should not challenge powerful men who harass them.

Morgan's feminist credentials and her background in criminal and discrimination law have seen her invited on to bodies as varied as the Victorian Law Reform Commission's committee on defences to homicide, which was looking at provocation, and the Australian Football League's working group on violence against women; she's helping write the fair-play rules for lawyers and for footy players. As someone who has written often about provocation – mostly calling for its abolition – she has been watching the Ramage case closely. I tell her the tampon story, expecting outrage, but she looks at me with wry sympathy. She has heard it all before. She has *taught* it all before.

Morgan is tired tonight – it's the end of a long day, and she has more work to do after I leave – but she rallies to trot out the arguments against provocation. She thinks the defence is unsalvageable. 'The traditional provocation case is like this one, a sexual jealousy case. Case after case after case, when I teach the law, is of a man killing a woman in a case of sexual jealousy. Women hardly ever, if at all, kill in those circumstances. They kill their partners in response to violence. Men kill their partners because they've left them, they taunt them, they're doing it with somebody else, or they might be doing it with somebody else. And that's long been accepted.'

The fact that a woman has left a man should not reduce the verdict in any way, she says crossly. Her next sentence comes with a full point in between each word, as if she is punching them out. '*Marriages break up all the time.* And even if she does say "Your prick's too small, I prefer him, I've never liked you" – why is sexual jealousy something we should recognise in law? Why is sexual jealousy seen as something we can all understand and forgive?' Given the fact that nearly all such cases involve men killing women, 'It's not a concession to human frailty. It's a concession to *male* frailty.' What's more, she adds tartly, her research suggests that provocation is much more likely to be led if the defence emphasises the woman's sexual behaviour. 'I speculate that if the defence lawyers don't "sexualise" her behaviour, if they don't emphasise the sex bit, the judge is less likely to leave [the question of] provocation to the jury.' The title of one of Morgan's papers, which looks at the stories lawyers create about women killed by their partners, is *Dead women tell no tales: Tales are told about them.*

Reading this paper before the interview, it struck me that it went to the heart of some of the issues in the Ramage case. Morgan quotes an American academic, Martha Mahoney, who has identified something she calls 'separation assault' – an attack in which a woman's partner is trying to prevent her from leaving, punish her for leaving, or force her to return. Mahoney sees it as an attempt to regain power in a relationship. In many 'confessions of adultery' homicides, the victim has either said she is going to leave or has already left. Mahoney says these cases might be failed attempts at control rather than 'about adultery', but if only the final, deadly assault is examined, the fact that it was an attack on separation rather than a response to adultery might remain hidden.

In Jamie Ramage's record of interview, he did accuse Julie of taunting him. But he said it was *when she got up to leave* that he lost control.

I LEAVE Morgan's office with a bundle of papers about provocation. It makes depressing reading. There is case after case where the man has claimed the woman insulted him sexually. In 1989 (*R v Gardner*), a man broke into a house with a knife to confront his ex-partner, whom he had several times threatened to kill. He claimed later that she taunted him about having had sex with a friend, who was sleeping in a separate room. He killed both his ex-partner and her friend. Even in this extreme case – the killer broke in, and he arrived armed with a knife – an appeal decided that the killer should have been allowed provocation.

An Italian man named Moffa who killed his Australian wife claimed she had told him 'I've been enjoying myself screwing with everybody in the street!' A judge drily remarked that in Moffa's description of his marriage, he 'featured as the industrious, generous and forgiving spouse, and his wife as his inconstant, ungrateful and spendthrift partner'. How do we know that his wife said what he claimed? How do we know it was not just his paranoid fantasy, his own fears of her infidelity being turned into words he put into her mouth?

To the law, that doesn't necessarily matter. In a 1990 case, the Victorian Court of Appeal ruled that 'if the applicant was provoked into killing his wife by conduct on her part which he *believed* to have taken place, the question of whether the crime might have been reduced to manslaughter by such provocation should have been left to the jury, *even though the applicant's belief was wholly the product of delusion.*' (My italics). So, a man could claim provocation even if he *falsely imagines* his wife to be unfaithful to him.

There is one more fact I have scribbled down. Manslaughter attracts a maximum sentence of twenty years, with a median sentence of six years. Murder attracts a maximum sentence of life and has a median sentence of seventeen years. Jamie Ramage could be out of prison in six years. And Julie Ramage is dead.

A VINDICATION OF THE RIGHTS OF WOMAN

SOMEONE ONCE explained change to me as being like a chemistry experiment in which the scientist is trying to make a test-tube of liquid crystallise. To the liquid is added another substance, drop by drop. Nothing changes. More drops. Nothing changes. Then suddenly, with one last drop, the liquid solidifies. The point of the story is that big change, even when it seems sudden, is always incremental. So it is here, too. With the crystallising of public revulsion about the defence of provocation, Jamie Ramage was merely that last, crucial drop.

It is a warm grey day after the verdict but before the sentencing in the Ramage case. The State Government is holding a genteel morning tea at Parliament House to launch proposed changes to homicide laws. A table loaded with scones and jam and cream sits up the back of a grand room with thick carpet of a hideous historic green. The 100-odd people assembled here for what might be a momentous occasion include Laurence Webb, a black-clad Jane Ashton and Professor Jenny Morgan. The media would seize upon this day as part of the backwash of the Ramage case. In fact this review was promised three years ago by the State's Attorney-General, Rob Hulls, when the government refused a mercy plea for Heather Osland, an abused woman who had killed her husband. But the public outrage about the Ramage case does mean that political follow-through on any proposed changes is far more likely.

Rob Hulls is a former lawyer and a big man with broad shoulders and blunt features. When he stands at the lectern, he easily dominates the room. He says the defences of provocation and self-defence were developed piecemeal by the courts 'in an era in which assumptions about male and female behaviour were steeped in misogyny'. Provocation went back to the 16th and 17th centuries, when drunken brawls and fights arising from breaches of honour were commonplace. Also reminiscent of that era 'are the propertied concepts of gender that allowed provocation to persist. These are the days when man-made law – and it was made by men – treated women as chattels. It's time, then, to bring the law into the 21st century . . . For too long, the law has failed women in many ways . . . It's excused the Ugly Australians of male behaviour or shifted the blame for such violence on to its victims.'

I hope the wounded ghost of Julie Ramage is somewhere in the room.

WHEN HULLS finishes, there is a sweet scene. The big man bends over and grabs a wooden box and puts it behind the lectern. On to it steps an older woman who is short and finely boned, built like a fragile piece of porcelain. This is Marcia Neave, long a senior legal figure and currently the chairwoman of the Victorian Law Reform Commission. Her first words are to Hulls: 'Thank you for moving the box so that I can be seen.'

The simple exchange seems deeply symbolic of men and women and the law. Women *can* take their rightful place in the boys' club, if only men use their power to make room for them.

Neave tells the audience that about one-third of homicides involve a person killing their sexual partner, their former partner, or a sexual rival. Of that third, 75 per cent involve men killing women. The commissioners have recommended that the partial excuse of provocation be abolished. They had debated whether to modify it but decided it was unworkable. 'We don't believe that it is any longer appropriate for our community to recognise rage as a partial excuse in an intentional killing. It shouldn't be an excuse for a killing that a person wants to leave a relationship or has left, that a person has had an affair, or that a person has been said to have "looked at" or "spoken to" or spat at the accused.'

The commission's decision was complicated by the fact that there are cases in which it is possible to empathise with a killer who had been provoked, for example, in the case of a parent who kills someone they believe has sexually abused their child. The commission has recommended that the law of self-defence be changed to allow for such cases, and to allow a defence for abused women who kill their partners. 'We think that a person should be able to argue self-defence if they believe it is inevitable that they will be harmed, even if the harm might not occur immediately. That would cover the case of a woman who is told by her husband, "Just wait and I'll bash you"; he goes to sleep, and she kills him.'

And there are to be changes to the laws of evidence. If the victim of a killing had told others of a history of violence, then those others should be able to testify about it. Juries should hear expert evidence on the dynamics of family violence to help them understand how victims and perpetrators typically behave, and why it is that women don't leave. Provocation will remain in the law as a factor that judges can consider during sentencing, but it will never go to a jury or affect a verdict again.

Almost every problem that arose in the trial of Jamie Ramage has been addressed. Every proposed change is an implicit condemnation of the way the legal system has been operating until now. Every proposed change is an implicit apology to Julie Ramage and to all the other dead women whose spirits have been humiliated in the dock.

Better late than never. As it was, the bruised Patricia Garrett would later tell reporters, the changes 'might help others, but it's all too late for us'.

THE CASE AGAINST CHANGE

A BARRISTER named Douglas Potter was one of the first lawyers to protest publicly about the proposed changes to the law. His letter to *The Age* claimed that the law was moving towards making great allowances for women and over-penalising men. He pointed to a recent case in which a young mother with severe post-natal depression had drowned her five-week-old baby and escaped jail. He wrote: 'I assume that the decision to sentence Leanne Azzopardi to an 18-month community-based order after she pleaded guilty to infanticide will not raise any ire in the community – despite the fact there are several reasons why it should, given recent hysteria about other court decisions.

'This case should be compared with the case of James Ramage . . . Both cases concern a person in a position of power over the victim. Both cases concern a situation where, but for the law, they would be convicted of murder. Both cases concern lies told to cover the truth – a consciousness of guilt. Both cases highlight human frailty . . . Azzopardi (apparently) was a poor, fragile woman who cracked under pressure and killed her child. Ramage is portrayed by some as a calculating killer who has been a beneficiary of a system that protects killers. Surely we can't live in a society that allows women (the nurturers, protectors and carers) to kill defenceless babies but says that men are allowed no weaknesses.'

Potter's office is small, hot and windowless, with two computers on one desk. There is a barrister's white jabot on a bookshelf, a can opener on the floor and piles of books on a chair. Potter is middle-aged and tanned with a grey goatee, a shaved head and an air of impassive toughness. It turns out that he was a policeman for eighteen years before he became a lawyer (he practises mainly in the Family Court).

Potter believes that the changes would over-compensate for injustices against women in the past. He agrees that the debate is dividing the legal community along the lines of sex, with mostly women defending the changes and mostly men criticising them. His own line on provocation seems ambivalent. At first, he argues this way, his arms folded across his chest: 'If the jury accepts that a man can use the defence of provocation because a woman has said something hurtful to him, if the jury accepts that's okay in society, then that's society's voice. I don't know why change should be thrust upon society just because people are sitting back not liking what they're hearing from juries.' The reality, he says, 'is that women use words to hurt men, and *men use fists to hurt women because they don't cope with the emotional torment that some women subject them to*'. The savagery of words versus the savagery of blows.

Later, he modifies his stance. As a society, he acknowledges, we have got to say that men killing women over issues of jealousy or verbal taunting is unacceptable. He suggests that the defence of provocation could be forbidden in those cases rather than abolished altogether. It should be left available to abused women who kill violent partners and to men in some situations where they kill other men. A wider defence of diminished responsibility should be introduced to cover situations in which stressed people lose self-control, such as the depressed, sleepless new *father* who is driven to kill his baby.

Then Potter comes back again to what he sees as the woman's contribution to domestic violence: 'We've also got to say to women, "You've got to consider men's emotions and don't use hurtful words to men." *Women provoke men. They know how to wind them up.* Particularly ones who have a partner who they know can be fired up. He may not be violent, but he tends to punch holes in walls and be explosive, and they know how to push the buttons. We've got all these laws to protect women with crimes of family violence . . . If you're going to make men more accountable, you've got to make women more accountable.'

Potter says women should also take responsibility by leaving bad relationships. I ask him about the fact that leaving is the time a woman is most likely to be killed or beaten. He makes a dismissive gesture with one hand. 'During every year, there are 40,000-odd intervention orders taken out in Victoria. The majority of those involve relationships, obviously; some are under the stalking provisions but that makes up a very small number. Most men will comply with those orders, including ones who it has been suggested are violent.' He is also worried that changing the law to allow easier defences for women who kill violent partners is giving such women too much licence: 'Why don't women pick up the phone and ring the police? If they can pick up an axe and kill their husband, why can't they pick up the phone and prevent a murder?'

THEY KNOW *how to wind them up* – ugly though it is, there is a hard kernel of truth in this. Walking back to the office after our interview, I remember a woman who once told me that her husband hit her. He was in counselling to deal with his violence, she said. Then she looked at me sideways, smiling, her eyes bright with malice. 'It's my fault, you know,' she said lightly. 'I push him and push him until he loses it.' She spoke as if it were a little game where she was in control, pulling his strings; a game she enjoyed playing. As if *her* anger, too, was somehow released when he hit her and melted into a puddle of remorse – as he inevitably did. Words are weapons too, and women are often more adept with them. And this woman knew full well that she was ducking responsibility for her end of the problem.

But there still remains the question of commensurate force, of the disparity between a taunt and a backhander. And the question of what it is that makes male feelings so privileged that they must be protected from hurt or challenge.

BARRISTER DAVID Neal is another legal figure who weighed into the Ramage controversy; in his case, with a large opinion piece in *The Age* defending provocation. Like Potter, he challenges the Government's proposal that post-natal depression should be the only mental condition that 'excuses' murder. Provocation does not involve a recognised mental illness, although it is sometimes referred to as covering cases of 'temporary insanity'. But men who kill their partners do have mental problems: 'You get some idea of the extent of psychological breakdown in domestic killings from the fact that one in five of the killers commit suicide at the time of the killing or soon after.'

Neal is a tall, pale man with blue eyes and bushy stand-up hair cut short. When he talks, he leans back in his chair with his long legs stretched out and his hands clasped behind his head in the commanding male pose so rarely used by women. Neal has never been part of a murder trial. His practice is based largely on health and occupational safety cases. But Neal used to teach law at the University of New South Wales and produced a 1991 report on defences to homicide for the Victorian Law Reform Commission. He says we need provocation because there is a big difference between the contract assassin who is part of a gangland killing spree and the person like Jamie Ramage whose 'choice' about whether to kill is heavily conditioned by external forces. He believes there should also be a defence of 'diminished responsibility' (in which a person's extreme mental or emotional state, short of insanity, is a mitigating factor). Neal is 'allergic' to the idea that sentences in murder trials should be used to send a message to the community about what is acceptable behaviour: 'I very much adhere to the view that you don't use people as a means to an end.'

But he acknowledges that provocation is a 'blame the victim' defence that is unnecessarily hurtful to the family and friends of the victim.

What, then, is to be done with the controlling man who kills his partner because she is leaving or has had an affair? Should he be allowed to claim provocation? 'My solution is to leave it to juries to sort the good cases from the bad ones. We ask juries to make decisions about what is essentially unknowable, what's going on in people's heads. I don't see how we can do anything better than that.'

I ask about the effect of different compositions in juries and describe the make-up in the Ramage case. Neal believes a lot of bull is talked about the importance of this. The argument that older men would have disapproved of Julie Ramage can be countered with the argument that it's more likely they would have taken the traditional, chivalrous approach common to their generation: that a man should protect a woman and that it's cowardly for a man to hit his wife. He points to an Australian study that found that jurors were a representative cross-section of the community, and an American poll of judges that found that in 90 per cent of cases, judges thought their juries had either got it right or had made a reasonable call.

But should we, as a community, accept the principle that a man's claim that a woman made him angry by leaving him or having an affair should be able to soften his verdict and his sentence for having killed her?

'I don't like the way the question's put, really. I think the question has to be: Are there circumstances in which people can be overwhelmed by circumstances such that their crime is manslaughter rather than murder? And my answer to that is yes.' Neal talks about a case in which a woman had shot dead her husband when she saw him talking to two other women. The husband had previously threatened to take his sexual conquests back to the family home. 'I think the degree of humiliation of that woman in that case was absolute and overwhelming ... And when the worm turns, I'm not surprised, because there comes a point where the level of humiliation is so destructive that you expect that someone will either just psychologically collapse altogether or they'll finally say, in an outburst of rage, *"You're not going to obliterate me like this!"*'

'OBLITERATE'. THE word resonates. Neal has put his finger on something here. Maybe this is part of what Jamie Ramage had experienced. If Julie did hit him with a barrage of home truths, did it leave him feeling that she was utterly wiping him not just now, but in terms of their whole history together? Is that why he wiped her – a sense of threat to his *emotional* survival?

JULIE'S LAWYER

TO INTERVIEW Julie's family lawyer, Caroline Counsel, I wear my daggiest suit: grey, tailored, boring, but useful in conservative environments. When I see her, I laugh and remark upon my foolishness. Counsel has arrived in the small consulting room at her offices in a swish of ruffled skirts and a top that buttons asymmetrically in front and reveals glimpses of midriff as she moves. She sits down, crosses one beautifully shod foot over the other and laughs with me. Counsel is tall, with a womanly shape, short black curly hair and brown almond-eyes. She is like her clothes: stylish, self-assured and extroverted. She says she languished for years as a young lawyer in 'take-me-seriously' black suits, her only concession to femininity her signature large earrings. Those were the days when an older male judge who disapproved of a female lawyer's attire – a trouser suit, for example – could simply tell her from the bench, 'I cannot hear you.' Eventually, Counsel and her female colleagues just said 'To hell with it.'

Counsel has been practising family law for twenty years; about half of her clients are men and the other half women. Her most famous client is now Julie Ramage. Counsel cannot discuss Julie's details because of lawyer–client privilege, so we must dance around the principles involved by talking about hypothetical situations. I want to know whether there was anything that Julie Ramage could have done to avoid her fate. 'Let's talk about a *theoretical* woman who has a husband who is controlling and possibly emotionally abusive but who hasn't actually struck her in years. How do you advise a woman like this? If this theoretical woman is also middle-class, I imagine taking out an intervention order would be a red rag to a bull?'

Counsel nods. 'It would be the least desirable course of action for her to take. Of course, it would be the advice we would have to give her because under the law, at first blush, that is the only protection we could afford her. So you would say to the theoretical woman, "Look, I hear what you're saying that this hasn't happened in years, but there is clearly a history of violence. You are about to drop a bombshell on this bloke; you're about to say, 'I'm out of here.' He is not going to like that at all, and we should talk about the practical aspects of extrication. And we should talk about non-legal means of self-protection."' Counsel says women often refuse an intervention order because they fear it will inflame their partners further and because they feel it is useless in terms of real protection. 'If he wants to kill me, he will' and 'How does a piece of paper stop a man taking a punch?' are common responses.

But Counsel's advice would not end there. She tells such women to make sure they have physical protection. They must try to move to a place where a father or a brother or some other male will watch out for them; they must try never to be on their own. 'Then, make sure that you start a process – rather than Will I/Won't I, commit to the process of separation because then you break the chain of control; you break the opportunity for manipulation. The theoretical woman might say, "But I want to stay in touch with him to appease him, to make sure he's okay, to work out where he's coming from . . ."' She makes a sweeping gesture with her arms. 'Forget it! You've left him. No longer your concern.'

The woman's leaving must be perfectly planned, and she must take with her whatever personal belongings she values. 'We have a day-of-departure plan. An abusive person will work out the other person's Achilles heel. If they can't get to them physically, they will then work around some other way. First it will be the kids, and if the kids can't be influenced, then what they do is destroy things. I've had a whole household of furniture destroyed by a bloke who was pissed off with a wife leaving; burnt all the family photos of the kids growing up, burnt all her memorabilia. So you say, "Anything that is precious to you, get out."'

No, Counsel says firmly, she is most definitely not party to the 'let him down gently' school of thought. Separation needs to be sudden and complete, but with safety, and the man must not be told where she is. The next step is to start the court process as quickly as possible. 'Because then the reality of what's happened is drummed home; not by you, you're not putting your neck on the chopping block every time you have to deal with him. You've got the lawyers, the court, saying, "It's over. We're moving you on."'

The theoretical woman still has two children who are dependent. How can she move to an address he doesn't know when they are sharing the children?

It is possible to have a moratorium on contact for an initial period, Counsel says, which requires the husband to request the court for contact. The difficulty once contact is established is silencing the children so that they do not tell their father their mother's new address. It's not so easy when the abuse is subtle, she admits. Her vivacity fades for a moment and she draws a weary breath. This work must take its toll even on the ebullient Counsel. 'I've had situations where women have ended up with broken bones, internal bleeding, in hospital; where the husband has entered the front door of the hospital and the woman has had to be exited out the back to another hospital so that he can't get to her. It's pretty obvious what his agenda is there because he's dumb. But the more subtle it is, the worse it is. It's harder to get people convinced about it. Where you have, in the theoretical woman's realm, a bit of violence but dated, it's much harder to say, "This is what you should do." Whereas if it's bleedingly obvious, you can warn her, "Don't see him, don't let the kids see him."'

And taking Counsel's advice might not have done the ghost of Julie Ramage any good either. What would a defence lawyer have made of her seeking an intervention order, or hiding her address? It might just have bolstered his argument that she provoked Jamie. The woman who dies while trying to leave a violent man is like the medieval woman thrown into a pond to see if she is a witch. Her attempts to save her own life can be used against her.

COUNSEL – APT name for a lawyer – drops any attempt at professional neutrality when asked about Jamie Ramage's trial. This she *can* comment on. She folds her arms sternly in front of her and her voice, which has been calm and measured, sharpens with disgust. 'I will not be rational. I won't be like a lawyer because I can't. And I've stopped trying to say' – here she puts on the deep plummy tones of a pontificating upper-class man – '"Oh, yes, the law of provocation, it needed a bit of dusting off." I just say that's *bullshit*; that somebody can take a life, murder someone, and then from the moment he sits down with the police, he's got it all worked out where he's heading. He knew how to play the law because he had access; it's like any person that has the means, the connections and the money.'

Counsel goes on to describe herself as a feminist, and her business card is in the colours adopted by the British suffragettes: purple, green and white. She at first responds with feminist prickliness to Potter's claim that women 'shouldn't wind men up'.

'Oh, so now it's all our fault!' she snaps. But then, as we continue to talk, it turns out that she, too, has spent time wondering about how women contribute to abusive marriages. She had one client who used to taunt her husband to 'hit me, hit me here!' 'That was all she knew. It was worse than that; it was almost like the fact that he would actually take the trouble to hit her was an affirmation of his love for her. They had no other form of dialogue.' The Family

Court decided that, although there had been violence, his behaviour was mitigated by hers.

I tell her the story of the woman I knew who bragged about taunting her husband until he hit her. Counsel grasps it instantly. She says she sometimes lectures women – usually upper-middle-class women – about preserving asset bases. 'I cover it from a property perspective, but the analogy holds true [for domestic violence]. Men who ultimately take out guarantees over assets and go deeper into debt – I don't think they wake up one morning in a happy marriage and say' – she rubs her hands together in mock glee – '"Well, hon, today I'm going to bankrupt us!" And I get somewhat impatient with the women who sit back and say, "How in the hell did that happen?" *You* were there too. *You* took no responsibility.'

A woman shouldn't almost wilfully create a situation where she is a victim and then demand special treatment on the basis of it?

'That's right. It's very hard to say this, I must say, to the feminists. It's also hard for feminists to swallow the unpleasant fact that there are some women who go out and get intervention orders simply because they want to shove it up their exes and be able to manipulate things such as contact in the short term. And what happens is that through the gaps of each gender's mistrust of the other, the real victims fall. That's what worries me about the women who cry wolf. What about the women who actually need the intervention order? What about those situations where they are blameless?'

Counsel knows that for women in such marriages, what began as love only slowly turns to domination. 'I say to my clients, "I do not want you to give yourself a moment of grief about the fact that you have been part of this process – which you clearly have been. Because water torture doesn't hurt. The first drop never hurts."'

WE TALK, as women do, about relationships. I wonder whether Counsel's job has given her a jaundiced view of marriage. She laughs and nods. We toss around the question of whether it is ever possible for one person to be close to another without losing some of their power and independence; whether all relationships end up with one partner sacrificing more of themselves to the wants and needs of the other. And whether that person is more likely to be the woman. One American marriage researcher famously concluded that 'A woman *dwindles* into a wife'. Counsel says, 'I think the individual has to work really hard at it. On a daily basis, you have to be eyes up: "What's happening? What does this signify? Am I prepared to give way on this?"'

Suddenly, she brightens. It's as if she has decided we have had enough of this gloom. She has a theory, she says merrily. Would I like to hear it? Counsel joked with her husband recently that women should be in the houses with children and men should be out on the plains, in nature. Men should be together in groups but segregated from women. 'And so, when you have a window-sash problem, you go to the edge of the plains, and you say' – she cups her hands around her mouth and calls hollowly, as if from a great distance, '"Window-sash repair man!" And the window-sash repair man comes in and says, "Oh yes, I can fix that for you, not a problem." And if you like the look of him, and if you feel like procreating with him, you do.'

You want a matriarchy?

'Yes. I do.' She begins to laugh. 'And my husband said to me, "What are we all doing on the plains?" And I said, "Like I care!"'

Part Six

READING THE ENTRAILS

TO HAVE AND TO HOLD

LAWYERS DO not have the Ramage debacle all to themselves. Before he ever reached the legal system, Jamie Ramage took himself – and in two cases, his wife – to a total of five different counsellors. One of them was a meditation instructor, but to the other four he described his marriage and his feelings more fully. The law is the ambulance at the bottom of the cliff; what had happened to the safety fence at the top of it? How could experienced professionals *not* have seen what was coming? What does this case say about the effectiveness of that modern pursuit, therapy?

Rosemary De Young was the only counsellor who declined to be interviewed for this book. Her explanation was that she is 'a private person'. The others agreed on the basis that they could talk about the generalities of cases such as this one but, because of client confidentiality, could not discuss Julie and Jamie Ramage specifically.

I wanted to know about the dynamics of abusive marriages. I also wanted to know what creates men like James Ramage and what goes on inside them in the build-up to violence and in the terrible moment of its release. In the end, the clearest answer to that last question came from someone who had never met the man.

TOM PATERSON does not so much sit down and stand up as fold and unfold his great length. For such a tall man, he works in quite a small room: a bland ground-floor office in a laneway of industrial buildings on the Ramages' side of town. It is furnished like a bachelor pad, minimally. His desk is against one wall. His chair sits facing a pair that are strategically placed to face him but which are also slightly turned towards each other. The occupants would be free to look at each other or not, as they chose. Mostly he sees more than one client at a time because he is a couples and family therapist. I take one of the two chairs and wonder if it was Jamie's or Julie's.

There is no need to warm Tom Paterson up with small talk. He has something he wants me to know first-off. He says he was deputy director of the State's Marriage Guidance Council in the late 1970s and 1980s. He clears his throat. 'In that time, we had a couple of homicides in the agency. They weren't my clients. And they bore some similarities [to the Ramages] in that, in both of these cases, too, there wasn't obvious current violence and intimidation going on.' These are 'the ones that get under your guard'.

Where there *is* current violence, the therapist is much more alert and takes precautions: 'You are particularly much more ready to warn the woman, "For God's sake, don't do anything which might provoke him in any way!"'

Paterson's gaze is steady but his voice has an unexpected quaver in it. Even in court it had been clear that, as a clinician who prided himself on his skills, he was shocked to have let this one through. His anecdote suggests that no one could have seen this one coming. He points out that Jamie seemed utterly contrite about his controlling behaviour; that neither of them mentioned violence as a recent issue; and that Julie had not told any of the therapists she was in a new relationship. There was no clear indication that the situation could be explosive.

I ask him what else counts as a 'clear indication'.

'Where there are threats. And I've had a number of cases where the man has said that he's scared that he'll kill her. And also where there is ongoing violence. The typical case is where a woman is very trapped in a relationship, where the only way to avoid violence in the short term is to be extremely compliant, not to put a foot wrong.

'The tragic thing about these kinds of situations is that it's almost always when the woman makes the move to leave that her life is in serious danger. People often say, "Why doesn't she leave, why does she stay with the guy?" It's often very unsafe to leave. It becomes increasingly unsafe to stay, as well, because the situation escalates. What happens is the man becomes more and more isolated in the family. People lock him out more and more, which creates a situation where he becomes more paranoid, more vigilant, and he feels cut off, he feels an outsider.'

How might this actually play out in a family? 'The whole process is circular. If you end up being an isolated person in the family, you get angry. A typical scenario is the woman and her children are all having great fun at home and they're all chatting and carrying on in the kitchen while she's cooking the meal. He walks into the house; suddenly, silence falls. He gets a tinny out of the fridge and goes into the lounge room and sits and watches the telly. After a while, the conversation starts again in the kitchen and he's totally removed from it. He feels bloody angry. They're all having fun without him. And the smallest thing will trigger a huge angry outburst on his part because it's a paranoid world that he lives in; a world where they talk about him, they insult him behind his back and all that sort of thing, *but no one ever levels with him*. People who live by intimidation of others are invariably incredibly lonely people because all they have is hangers-on. They don't have anybody who tells them the truth.'

I THINK of Samantha's years of hiding her mother's secrets from her father; of Matthew, begging his mother to tell his father the truth about Laurence. Of all the friends who knew Julie wasn't coming back who didn't feel able to tell him so. Yes, Jamie Ramage was isolated in that way. But lonely? It's hard to say. He felt that he had no close friends but during the separation Jamie talked endlessly to so many people. And they were *decent* people. If there is one thing that stands out about this crime, it is the relative goodness of the people in the circle from which it sprang. Jamie's killing of Julie was not the result of a surrounding moral vacuum or a subculture of malice, selfishness or brutality. The people he called upon – Kate Clark, Rob Moodie, 'Helen' – were thoughtful and informed. They listened patiently. They cared about him and tried to help. Even those who disliked him – the Garretts, Jane Ashton, Gilda Pekin – agreed to talk to him. *Everyone* gave him the time of day. But kindness was not enough.

PATERSON SAYS that angry, controlling men often only recognise their loneliness when they lose their one 'friend', their partner. When she leaves, or threatens to, his terror of losing her forever can flip into dangerous rage. 'My experience is that the only solution that works, the most safe solution, is not to force the man to accept that the marriage is absolutely over. To say, "Look, we need some time to pass" – a long process where there's still a bit of dialogue, it's not 100 per cent clear that she's left forever.'

So Julie Ramage's let-him-down-gently strategy . . . ?

He says firmly, 'Was a *sensible* strategy.' Paterson was setting Jamie up with many appointments in the future so that he would have time to adjust. 'And the more that he did that, the safer it would have become.'

Paterson says wife-battering begins when, early in the relationship, 'The woman doesn't stand up to her husband and, in a way, *capitulates* to his attempts to try and control her. And the pattern gets set up, and then it intensifies over time.'

What creates angry, controlling men?

He says there are insecure, anxious people – women as well as men – who cannot feel calm unless everything around them is precisely organised the way they want it. Add to this the fact that men are bigger and stronger than women and have higher social status, and then add traditional views of marriage – Paterson becomes irate and adopts the tone of an evangelist condemning a dangerous heresy. 'There is an idea that, in a way, marriage gives you the right to *possess* somebody. Even in the marriage vows, in the past at least, the vow was "To have and to hold from this day forward". "To have" – it easily implies ownership. You have no rights to control another person, even if that person's your partner. They're free to be whoever they want to be and live in whatever way they want to. You've got choices and they've got choices. I think it is part of growing through a marriage to be able to let your partner go, let them be who they want to be.'

He says that domestic violence is just as common in middle-class families as it is in working-class families. It is related most closely not to the *class* of a family but to its *structure*; the traditional family is its traditional home. 'The whole idea about the man being the breadwinner, the woman being the little woman who supports this – it breeds a kind of separation and alienation between men and women, and it creates a power imbalance. If we really wanted to have families that were stable and wanted to reduce the divorce rate, we'd try to set it up so that men and women could participate more or less equally in the home and more or less equally in the workforce.' Sharing the nurturance of children is a unifying force, he says.

Paterson is not a young man. He must be in his sixties. It is startling to hear such iconoclastic ideas coming from this greybeard. Modern marital theory – no wonder Jamie Ramage, with his idea of counselling as a fast-track way to get Julie back into his arms, had gone from therapist to therapist. No one was going to tell him what he wanted to hear.

I ASK Paterson why it is that women who are hit often blame themselves for it, as women who are raped can do. He says, 'Even people who are assaulted by a stranger in the street often blame themselves. I think it's tied up with our need for control; if we did cause it, then the world's a less horrendously unpredictable place than it really is. "Maybe I should have done this, maybe I should have done that . . . " [In a violent marriage], a woman keeps thinking that if only she hadn't spoken up, if only she hadn't set him off by going and visiting someone and being home late, well, then, it wouldn't have happened. So then she stops visiting people, and her life becomes more closed and cut off from others.'

Trying to see Jamie's side of the story, I ask Paterson about the claims Jamie had made to 'Helen': that he was angry with Julie for not speaking up about what she wanted and telling him what she thought. Was this part of Julie's contribution to their problems? Paterson says sternly, 'How could she tell him what she wanted? She wouldn't dare. That is exactly what happens in a relationship with intimidation. The person who is in the one-down position learns to be extremely careful and to tell him what he wants to hear rather than what she thinks.'

So, how does love turn into this? Or was it never love in the first place? And what are the characteristics of *happy* couples? Again, Paterson says, it ties up with letting go of the idea of possession. 'If you deeply love another person, or anything at all – nature's the same, if you love the bush you don't bloody try and change it, you enjoy it the way it is. And there is quite a bit of research saying one of the key factors in success in couples therapy is helping the partners stop trying to change each other. And when they can actually accept each other, as they are, they're each more free to go in the directions they want to grow in. But the desire to want the other person to fit into a particular mould and to use any means at your disposal to make that person be who you want them to be is the cardinal mistake that people make in all relationships. To love another person is to allow them to be who they are, live out their own potentialities, dreams and hopes.'

Even though that might take them away from you?

'Exactly. But, curiously enough, if you actually allow that to happen, people often value that relationship so much that they will organise their lives so they will maintain that relationship. It becomes one of their important values.'

So the New Age bumper sticker has it right: *If you love something, set it free.* If only Jamie had been able to bear Julie's family, and her horse-riding, and her longing to study and make something of herself . . .

THIS STORY is littered with 'If onlys'. Paterson is tormented by them too. This business has been devastating for him as a therapist, he says, traumatising. He raises his chin and glares at me defensively from behind his glasses, as if daring me to criticise him for what he is about to tell me. 'I was *extremely* upset about it. I sought help myself from a colleague.' His mouth snaps shut. That is as much as he wants to say about that.

But it has been a big admission. The Ramage affair has sent the therapist into therapy. Jamie did indeed unleash a tsunami of survivor guilt.

THERE IS another question about this saga: Can you ever really know anyone? Jamie apparently had no idea about Julie's affairs. And despite all she knew about Jamie, Julie did go to Marock Place on that last day. She must have walked into that house thinking she would be safe with him. And she was wrong.

This, too, is familiar ground for Paterson. 'You can never be 100 per cent sure of another person. One of the common problems in relationships is that we start to think we actually know the other person. "Really," people say, "I can read him like a book, he's fairly predictable." We need to accept that in a relationship, the Other is always mysterious. There are always things that we haven't yet understood and, of course, the other person is always changing. But in this situation, he'd given her a great deal of reason to be more secure with him. For a long time, he was taking the blame, taking responsibility, saying, "Yes, I need to change this and that," and he hadn't done anything to her horses when she left and so on.

So she had a false sense of security. And that's why a whole bevy of professionals didn't see it either.'

There is also something buried in this tangled tale about communication, about whether anyone can truly *hear* anyone else. Jamie and Julie each came away from encounters with counsellors with an entirely different perspective on what had been said in the room, and the therapists' perspectives were different again. How could this be?

Paterson deals with this point so airily that I feel the question was naïve. 'Oh, everybody does that. People hear what they want to hear. Memory is not like a record on tape-recording. Memory is much more like the reinvention of a story. Memory is notoriously unreliable.'

What does Paterson's disbelief in the power of memory say about the truth of all the stories I have collected from others for this book? Maybe my sources, in all good faith, are sometimes unconsciously 'reinventing' as they go. I have picked it up a few times when they contradict themselves over a detail, or others contradict them. Once or twice I have detected deliberate fudges. Those, I have simply left out of the story. But other than that, how would you ever know? The best I can do to compensate for the possibility is to attribute claims to sources wherever possible.

THE WAY Paterson talks about one aspect of marriage makes me laugh. He points out that since about the 14th century, couples have lived together for an average of only 15 to 20 years, but now divorce has replaced death as the main reason marriages end. 'Prior to that, people got relief from marriage by their partner dying.' He is startled when I grin and point out that he has made marriage sound like an ailment; something that one needs 'relief' from, like a migraine or a bout of flu. 'From bad marriages, anyway,' he concedes, smiling.

But what he is leading up to is a scathing denunciation of how the law dealt with Jamie's killing of Julie. He is still burning over the way his evidence was used. 'For separation to be treated as a provocation seems to me to be totally crazy. In our society, a normal, ordinary person has got to be able to cope with that because it's going to happen to about half of us. To think that someone saying, "Look, it's over, mate" is a provocation worthy of changing murder to manslaughter is *absolutely, totally wrong*! Men have to learn to cope with these things because it's a normal life event in a world where people now live for very long periods.'

For all Paterson's convictions about the defence of provocation, he still holds fast to the view that Julie was unwise to have pursued a new relationship with Laurence Webb; at the very least, she should not have let Jamie know about it.

Men and women are different about sex, he says. For a woman, the pathway to sex is through an intimate emotional connection, whereas for men, it's sex that provides the intimacy. 'If it's the man who's having the affair, the female partner is much more likely to be worried about the intimacy between him and this other woman and the sense of emotional abandonment because he's emotionally involved with somebody else. If it's the woman having an affair, her male partner will be incredibly preoccupied with the sex. He'll be absolutely torn apart by the idea of her having sex with someone else.'

With the Ramages, added to this was Jamie's terror that the relationship might be over, and the need to shield him from the truth until he was ready to accept it. 'Sometimes it takes one or two years, but it's worth it.'

I digest the implications of this. 'Does this mean that the woman leaving an abusive relationship can't have another sexual relationship for one or two years?'

'Well, you need to keep it a very good secret. It's very dangerous. You can see that that's what led to her death. He killed her when she was in this new relationship. If she had not done anything to force him to recognise it was over, she might have survived.' He can see the alarm in my eyes. He says hurriedly that he knows that this is absolutely not fair because it means the woman can't have her own life. 'But if your life's at stake . . .'

We are both quiet for a moment. Then I ask, 'So, in a way, Jamie *did* own Julie, didn't he?'

He looks back at me gravely. The man who believes so passionately in the importance of freedom in a relationship doesn't flinch from what he must say.

'He did own her. Oh, very much so.'

LOVE, HONOUR – AND OBEY

SHARON MARCUS, like Paterson, is willing to be interviewed about family violence but because of professional confidentiality she will not be able to talk about Ramages. She invites me to her home for our interview.

Marcus lives in a solid, comfortable art-deco house decorated, like her, with an air of prosperity. Her lounge room has original oil paintings on the wall, thick rugs on the floor and a scented-oil burner on the wide coffee table, which has a glass top and curly ironwork legs. Marcus is in jeans and slip-on shoes. Her long, wavy dark hair is frosted with streaks and she wears a big cluster-diamond ring on her wedding finger. Her fingernails and her toenails have the thick white edging of the modern manicure. She is warm and welcoming, delighted to be able to help, and curls her lithe body up on the cream sofa like a schoolgirl.

Her precise, lightly accented English turns out to be the product of South Africa, but it was in Australia that she trained as a psychologist and family therapist. She works with 'system theory', the idea that a family forms a system in which the behaviour of each member of the family helps maintain the status quo. According to system theory, the woman in a violent relationship acts in a way that helps the man maintain his control.

Marcus explains it this way, and it does seem to fit the Julie and Jamie Ramage story. 'Let's say that very early in the relationship, the man says, "You're not allowed to go out with your mates." And she phones up her mates and says, "I'm sorry, I'm not allowed to, my husband won't hear of it." What happens there is that she's immediately maintaining his behaviour. She's not challenging it. She's not saying, "What about me?" She's saying, "I'll help you." She's contributing to that dynamic because she's fearful of his reaction, she doesn't want to hurt him, she doesn't want to come home from being out with her friends and find him in a bad mood. She doesn't want to have a fight because it's just not worth it. But all of those are *maintaining behaviours*.

'Right in the beginning of the relationship, what if she had stood up and said, "What makes you feel angry about me going out? Is that really necessary? I feel that I deserve to have time with my friends. And can we agree that I will have my time on a Monday, and you will have your time with the boys on a Saturday, and we can both enjoy our time then and our time together?"'

Julie Ramage did insist on her horse-riding but the price she paid, by all accounts, was Jamie's eternal sulking. According to her sister Jane, Julie came home one day exhilarated from a ride and told him she felt glowing. Jamie told her the outdoor life was giving her dry, wrinkled skin, and he poked at her eyes disapprovingly, puncturing her happiness with every prod. I tell Marcus this story, and ask her what the woman is to do if the man pays her back for every small effort she makes to hold on to herself?

Marcus says that is the point at which the woman should ask her partner to go to counselling because many couples do not have the 'language' needed to be able to talk their problems through.

Jamie Ramage had told therapists that he would not have gone to counselling if Julie had asked him six months earlier. It took the separation to make him realise it was necessary. For them, this was the pattern over and over. Jamie crossed the line, Julie left him, sometimes only briefly, and only then did he offer to compromise. She kept trying to stand up for herself but he kept wearing her down. She was like a moon caught in the gravitational pull of a larger planet. She never managed to get him to change his orbit.

MARCUS SAYS she has not seen much in the way of explicit violence in middle-class families even though her practice, in an outer eastern suburb, is solidly middle-class. What she does see is controlling behaviour. She says there are women whose husbands force them to ask each morning for the money they need that day, and who are grilled each night about how they spent it. There are women who comply with their husband's control because otherwise he will deliberately cause an upset with the children. 'On the extreme side is control with feeding, where the man feels the need to keep his wife fat and unattractive. He buys a lot of food and makes sure she eats a lot because he's worried that if she becomes attractive, he will lose her to someone else. Another one is that if the wife works, he will not allow her to travel for work on her own. He will go with her. She's not allowed to leave without him, and if he has to come back for a meeting for his own work, she has to come back with him.'

Behind the need for control is a terrible insecurity in the man. Marcus sees part of her job as helping him find out the source of it: 'He wasn't born like that.' Just condemning the aggressor, without seeking to understand him, goes nowhere towards fixing the problem, she says.

Before the Ramage case, Marcus had never had a client kill or be killed. Hearing about Julie and Jamie was a huge shock: 'Just its impact on me in terms of this is what human beings are capable of. And how can people avoid getting into this situation?' Marcus has a colleague who has researched the topic. Her conclusion was that dangerousness is almost impossible for counsellors to predict. 'The complexities of thought mean that to predict dangerousness, the therapist would have to know many different variables that you can't possibly know. And those elements are transient; they can be here today and not tomorrow.'

So, therapists must work without a safety net? No, she says firmly, it's not like that at all. Her basic premise is that her clients are responsible for what they do. The bubbly Marcus will not carry any of Jamie Ramage's guilt for him.

I ASK her the question that has been troubling me ever since I saw the counsellors – Dunn's 'bleeding hearts' – give evidence at the trial. 'Do therapists believe in wickedness, or are they so focused on understanding without judging that morality gets suspended?'

She throws her head back and laughs. 'That is an *excellent* question.' And her answer? 'You are not God. It is not for you to judge people on who they are. "Wickedness" is an interpretation. In therapy, that is not what our role is.' She decides to check the term in a dictionary. She lays the big book on her lap and reads: '*Wickedness*: Wicked. Sinful. *Iniquitous*.' The word rolls off her tongue. 'Given to or involving immorality. Spiteful. Ill-tempered. Intending to give pain. Playfully malicious. *Foul* . . . !' She delivers the archaic word so drolly that we both laugh. She looks back at me in amusement. 'Which interpretation should we put on your question?'

DO WE have a language of morality today for what the Jamies do to the Julies – not just in terms of bashing and killing, but in terms of the suffocating daily control, the slow self-aggrandisement of one human being at the expense of the other? Violence counsellors say the most common cry of women leaving an abusive marriage is not grief over their physical injuries but despair over the way they feel emotionally crushed, emptied out: 'I'm nothing. I'm a nothing. He's taken everything from me.'

Shouldn't this theft of the spirit be named as a wrong?

THE DANCE OF ANGER

WHEN I visited Vienna more than twenty years ago, I bought a postcard with a picture of Freud's couch. It is plumped high with pillows at one end so that anyone lying on it would have been half sitting-up. Thrown over the couch and the pillows is an exotic Iranian rug lushly patterned in rust and black. Upon it, I presumed, had lain Freud's famous patients, such as the Wolf Man. That couch had always captured my imagination. It had heard people's deepest, darkest thoughts and feelings, their childhood terrors, their adult lusts and loathings. From the outpourings it had borne came a new understanding of what it is to be human. One of Freud's early psychoanalytic colleagues was the Swiss psychiatrist Carl Jung. After Jung and Freud parted ways, Jung founded a separate school of psychotherapy that also relied on the importance of dreams and on the idea of the unconscious mind as a seat of truth. He created many of the concepts we take for granted today, such as 'introvert', 'extrovert', 'complex', 'archetype' and that New-Age favourite, 'synchronicity' (the idea that coincidences can be meaningful).

Peter Fullerton is a Jungian analyst. The journalist in me wanted a depth-psychologist's take on the Ramage dynamic. The voyeur in me longed to see his couch, a place where Melbourne people lie to bare their souls to the analytic gaze. Fullerton works in an unpretentious 1940s yellow-brick-veneer building that used to be a home. It is opposite a railway station in an obscure north-eastern suburb of Melbourne, the kind of suburb that is known only to the people who live in it or around it. But it's a suburb that was handy for Jamie Ramage as it is only a twenty-minute drive from Balwyn. Jamie actually passed through it on his way to the bush grave, bearing in the boot the woman who had been the focus of his previous visits to Fullerton. Synchronicity?

Fullerton's consulting room is large and airy with a window looking out on to the street. Up against the far wall is his couch, a single bed covered with a dark tapestry rug. On one end of the bed, the end near Fullerton's armchair, is a beige bedroom pillow with a pink blanket tucked neatly underneath it. It all looks too pragmatic by half, almost disappointing in its ordinariness. But this room does see drama and distress; Fullerton has two man-size boxes of tissues at the ready.

About 20 per cent of Fullerton's practice is couples. He explains his work this way: Those couples who make their way to him are usually gripped by a profound unconscious issue. He tries to interpret what they are both doing *to the marriage*. Take the typical warring couple, who arrive arguing and expecting him to take one or other side. Instead, he will try to analyse the language they are using to identify what is unconsciously shared between them. He gives an example of what he says is the classic situation; he does not remark upon it, but it is one that mirrors the Ramages. The classic couple is one where he appears to be controlling and she appears over-emotional. Fullerton tries to point out the ways in which each of them, in fact, is controlling *and* 'feelingful'. 'The "feeling" woman has to recognise that a lot of what she's doing is quite controlling, a control expressed in her unconscious conviction that this division (in which the man is seen as the aggressive partner) is the only safe way to proceed in the relationship.'

Fullerton will ask the woman about her father. She will often say he was a controlling figure too: '"I left him. That's it. He's out of my life, gone, finished, and he's not going to have that influence on me any more."' And Fullerton will tell her, 'But you've chosen someone who's giving you exactly what you thought you were getting away from. What you're doing, in choosing someone like your partner, is engaging with this whole issue of control and your own version of being controlling.'

Fullerton believes that everyone – even analysts, who have been analysed themselves – unconsciously chooses a partner who presents them with exactly the emotional problems they failed to resolve while growing up in their original family. In itself, this is not what defines a marriage as troubled because having such problems is universal for married people. The real difficulties arise only when a couple cannot create the conditions necessary to work those problems out together. For the woman complaining of a domineering man, the more specific question becomes: Why has she given over her authority to her partner?

By this point I am wriggling in my chair. What he is saying seems to come uncomfortably close to the idea that the woman *is* contributing to the man's violence. That in some unconscious way, she *is* asking for it? But I keep my peace for now. I want to see where this goes. I ask him where such a man gets his assumptions about his entitlements.

Fullerton's explanation goes like this: The domineering man has a defensive state of mind. He feels anxious and vulnerable, and he hides that from himself and others by taking authority. Often such a man has been crushed by a powerfully controlling mother or father who has failed to teach him about negotiation. One day, as a growing son, he learns that he is physically strong now and doesn't have to cop their dictatorial behaviour any more. Then he flips, himself becoming the kind of controlling figure he so resented. But while he might be 'defended' emotionally – that is, unaware of his anxious, vulnerable feelings – he is unlikely to be happy: 'He invests in the fantasy that he's happy because to become aware of his unhappiness is so anxiety-provoking that he's not sure he can hold himself together, or that he will survive. He fears falling to pieces.'

Fullerton says the woman is also likely to be defending herself against anxieties and aggressive feelings of her own. The woman's aggression might play itself out in secret affairs. Fullerton's question for her then becomes: 'Can you see that this affair is actually quite controlling of your marriage? You are taking parts of yourself and investing them elsewhere. That's depriving the relationship. Is that not an aggressive act?'

The stories Julie told about Jamie flood my mind. What if, I ask tentatively, she's having affairs because he is sexually controlling to a point that she experiences sex as rape?

He accepts this proposition matter-of-factly, nodding briefly. As a medic of the mind, he has probably seen the worst people can do to each other. In the same cool voice he says, 'When couples are hurt and wounded they often respond very aggressively because that's human nature. Affairs are also powerful litmuses. They draw attention to something. And if it's possible for the partner who's having the affair to come in and say, "Look, we need to talk, because I had an affair. I had it because of this and this and this going on in our relationship. And you and I have to look at it" – well, that's very different from this affair kept secret followed by this affair kept secret followed by this affair kept secret. With the latter, there's no learning, it's just round and round the merry-go-round. It's not just creating distance. It's *breaking the marital container*.'

So, maybe from the viewpoint of psychology, Jamie and Julie had emotional problems that were of equal 'size', if you like. 'But there is also a moral dimension to a relationship,' I protest. 'The man who hits and abuses and controls his wife, and the woman whose rescue fantasy, or fear of being alone, or fear of standing up for herself ties her to him, probably in the therapists' hierarchy are equally neurotic and equal contributors to the problem. But the woman who tries to be nice is surely on sounder *moral* ground than the man who hits her? Surely?'

'While they become more conscious of those states of mind that terrify them,' he acknowledges briefly. But he points out again that part of the problem is that the woman is disowning her own aggression. He talks about 'projection'. This is a psychological defence that allows us to disown something bad in ourselves by 'projecting' it on to someone else. We see the flaw in them instead of us. In marriage, the woman can project her own aggression on to the man.

I remember something one of Julie's friends had told me. Julie had told Jamie during the separation that she had been listening *in the bath* to the CD of songs he had given to her. It had struck me as a surprisingly seductive thing for Julie to say. It didn't make sense that she was torturing the obsessive Jamie with images of her listening, naked and wet and soapy, to the love songs he had collected for her. Did it leave him sitting in that cold, empty house, imagining her with one shapely leg out of the suds, her toes curled around a tap? Did Julie make that remark artlessly? Or could it have been a verbal stiletto – did some angry, hostile part of her actually enjoy dicking him about?

But I still come back to: How does the passive aggression of Julie's infidelity weigh up against the nose-breaking aggression of Jamie's Liverpool kiss?

I ASK Fullerton that question I have been sitting on: 'You have to suspend judgement of your patient if you are to help them. Does that mean that in the world of psychology there is no good and evil?'

Absolutely not, he says with vigour. He talks about a child development researcher called Winnicott, who argued that the human baby comes into the world with an inherent capacity to know the difference between right and wrong. It is the parent's job to wait for the right moment to reinforce the child's recognition of that difference.

Take the two-year-old who hits another child in the eye with a toy brick and looks confused when the hurt child bursts into tears. Fullerton says that to help the child learn empathy for another's hurt, the parent would ask,

'"Why are you puzzled?"'

'The child might say, "Why is she crying?"'

'"Why do you think she's crying?"'

'"Um, I hit her with a brick."'

'"Quite right. Does that hurt?"'

'"Yes."'

'"Is that a good thing?"'

'And then the child characteristically cries themselves because what they then feel is their *own* sense that they have done something wrong. For some kids that experience is wiped out by the Victorian idea that parents know what is right and wrong. When parents say, "Don't do that *because I say so*!" they wipe out the child's empathy with the parent's own sense of what's right and wrong.'

Driving home, I think about Jamie Ramage hitting his fifteen-year-old son as a form of discipline. Little Jamie must not have had the Winnicottian experience.

THERE IS a lot more to come from Peter Fullerton, but we are halfway through a second interview before it appears. I had been wondering at the way Fullerton seemed less distressed than Tom Paterson by his link with the Ramages. He heard about the killing on the radio news driving home. He remarks upon what a tragedy it was, what a waste of Julie's life, what a grief to the children. But he does this with the same detached air he has when he talks about psychodynamic theory. Maybe, I thought, it's because he saw Jamie alone and never met Julie. The real answer is quite unexpected. He's been here before.

I've thrown him a pop-psych question about Jungian 'anima' figures. Jamie had been very cut off from the feminine side of himself, his 'anima'. In killing Julie, was he trying to kill off his own more tender feelings?

There is a long pause, and when Fullerton speaks again his voice is quieter. 'I worked in marriage guidance years ago. And one of the first quite painful experiences as a new professional in that territory was with a young couple where the husband shot the wife and then shot himself. And one of the thoughts my supervisor offered to me was a question: "Why did they need to kill the parent of the opposite sex? What's being re-enacted, literally, that perhaps in all of us has a status imaginally?"'

'Everyone wants to kill their mother and father at some point?'

'Absolutely. And in these cases, there's something about that that becomes *concretised*, for one reason or another.'

It must have been devastating as a young therapist to have a couple die in such a shooting, I venture. 'Well, yes,' he says shortly. 'But it's just fundamentally tragic. It's young people at the early stages of their life, with a deeply troubled element that was probably shared between the two of them. But really, for me, it was the universe saying, "Okay, if you're going to work in this area of marital relationships, learn about this stuff, *because this is what everyone faces*. Every relationship faces this kind of impulse." In the vast majority of relationships, the people understand that the impulses are symbolic: symbolic of an impulse to psychologically separate from the parents, or of a longing to bring a childlike dependent state of mind to an end.'

As a more experienced therapist, looking back, was there anything with that young couple that should have alerted him?

'Yes,' he says instantly. 'The husband had been trained in the army, and the husband mentioned firearms a number of times. And to any couple mentioning firearms, after that experience, I now say quite directly, "What do you do with them? Where are they? Be very careful with firearms, firearms are far too easy."'

He comes back again to the message he had so earnestly been delivering in our last interview: with this young couple who died, 'what was going on in that situation was actually something that involved both parties'.

I'm struggling again. '*He* killed her and killed himself, didn't he? So, in terms of who lost it to the point of murder it didn't involve both parties . . .'

He does not answer me. His eyes are cast down to the floor. The silence lengthens. I persevere uncertainly: 'Unless she lay down and consented to being shot . . . ?'

That draws a reply. 'I doubt it. No one knows. What I want to say is tricky, because you're trying to explore an actual event and what I'm speaking about has validity in the actual event, I believe, but the essence of its validity is . . . the psychological *precursors* to the event. I've worked with a lot of couples in the Tavistock Institute [in London] where violence was an issue. The vast majority of them came to us with both the husband and wife identifying the flaw in the husband. "The husband has trouble with violence and we need you to help us so that he can control his violence." The attempts to resolve the situation from just tackling the husband failed each time. The only time that it started to work, when it had any impact, was to actually say to them, "There is something here that is shared between the two of you, and what we need to explore is the meaning of the violence for both of you."'

Can he give me an example of what the woman is bringing to the equation that helps the violence to continue? Because that general thesis, I warn him, will make every feminist in Australia go bananas.

He nods. 'That's why I paused. Helen Garner got into real trouble when she was trying to do something not dissimilar in the book of hers, *The First Stone*.'

'She talked about how the girls had power as well?'

'Exactly. And that's what I'm talking about. I'm talking about something that is constellated between two individuals.'

He offers the example of another couple he saw in London. The woman had grown up in a small authoritarian Christian sect that was closed to outsiders. She had no sense of what Fullerton calls 'her own authority'. When she married a man with low self-esteem who became controlling, she reacted as she had to the sect: she pushed him away. This made him want to lock everything down –

in relation to his wife, literally. He would put her in a room and lock the door. When the therapists told her that she had an active part in this, she hit the roof. 'But I'm the victim!'

But if she tries to stand up for herself, doesn't his violence and control increase in response? So how is it possible for her to grow and change safely?

The *system* escalates the violence, Fullerton says. 'We had to do a lot of work with the man about his own sense of shame. He had no way of feeling his own sense of shame. He would beat his wife and then feel terrible. She would come in bruised; he would come in crumpled emotionally because he was so ashamed. But all he did was move from being split off from his shame to being completely overwhelmed by it. He failed to go down the pathway where his shame would have warned him that what he was about to do was wrong in his own terms.' The man kept telling the therapists he needed his wife to tell him when he was doing the wrong thing. The therapists pointed out that he needed to be able to do this for himself or the abuse would continue. 'Because you can't hear what she's saying when you're doing wrong. And anyway, you two can't rely on her knowing when you're doing wrong because there's a bit of her involved in keeping the wrongdoing going.'

In the end, the man had a dream that made it clear to him. He was aware of himself while simultaneously floating above himself, looking down at himself as he dreamt. The therapists seized upon it. 'What that gave us the chance to talk about was, "Look, you *can* look down and see what's happening, and from that position you *can* define what's right for you and what's wrong for you. So you don't need the wife to tell you."'

I HAVE heard one story about Jamie Ramage's shame. It comes from his friend Rob Moodie. A couple of days after Julie's killing, Rob, one of Jamie's brothers and a friend went to visit Jamie in the cells underneath Melbourne's Magistrates Court. Rob Moodie wanted an explanation: 'Because I had seen him the day before [the killing], you see. What in hell went on? Why?'

Jamie could not tell him. Jamie could not even look at him. 'He was a wreck. He was bowed, completely ashamed.'

Rob sighs. 'He sort of said, "I don't know why, really. I don't know what happened."'

And therein lies my last question for Fullerton. As an analyst who has also worked in prisons, he must know what happens when a killer has the dreadful moment where he realises, at a gut level, what he has done; the moment when he goes down to the core of himself and faces what was unleashed. By most accounts, Jamie Ramage, who remembers the killing in a dissociated way – as if he is watching a film, an observer rather than a participant – has yet to experience it.

Fullerton says this moment of understanding is a point at which killers can often become suicidal. Getting in touch with their destructive impulses leaves them tempted to turn those impulses against themselves – both to erase the pain, and to contain those destructive impulses forever.

LATER, I wonder uneasily about what all this says about women. Are we inherently weaker than men on a psychological level? Why are we so commonly bullied? Why do wives still 'surrender their authority' to their husbands? Surely it can't *all* be due to what happens in a woman's original family. The idea that it can be attributed to innate traits of female temperament is equally dispiriting.

I remember a feature story I wrote some years earlier on a related topic and call it up on the paper's computer system. The story was pegged to the case of a Victorian woman called Heather Osland, who had killed her partner after years of abuse and was making an unsuccessful appeal to the High Court against her murder conviction. She was later refused a mercy plea by the Victorian Government. I had begun the story with a quote from the poem 'Daddy' by the tortured, suicidal poet Sylvia Plath that declared every woman loves a fascist brute.

With that story I was really trying to ask: Is Plath right? Do women ask for it?

The story described the dynamics of abusive relationships. Research suggests that abusive men blame others for their problems, deal poorly with stress and believe that wives and children are there to serve them. Both partners tend to come from families with similar emotional dynamics but there is a gender split in their response to it, with men growing up to batter and women growing up to be battered. In the story I quoted Dr Jon Kear-Colwell, then senior lecturer in forensic psychology at Charles Sturt University in Bathurst, who pointed out that all male mammals are more aggressive than females. These innate differences are then reinforced by child-rearing practices: 'Often when boys are punished by their parents, they are given a smack on the leg; it's the behaviour that's dealt with. When girls are naughty, guilt is used to make them feel responsible.'

So, while abused women might not love the fascist boot, they do tend to feel responsible for having somehow provoked the kick. They also tend to feel responsible for 'healing' the emotional wounds of the man who delivers it. There must be something to the theory that abused women have a particular kind of emotional make-up because research also suggests there is a tendency for women who leave one violent relationship to gravitate towards another one.

This kind of psychologising exasperates women's activists. They analyse the issue politically and see battering as an extreme outcome of the power imbalance between men and women in society. The battered woman is not psychologically defective; she is having a normal human reaction to extraordinary stresses. This theory, too, has credence. There is evidence that an abusive environment can reduce *anyone* to psychic rubble.

In what has become a famous social experiment, in 1973 a Californian psychology professor, Philip Zimbardo, recruited intelligent middle-class university students – all men – to live in a mock prison for two weeks. The men were screened to ensure they were psychologically stable, and randomly assigned the role of guard or prisoner. One could not argue that they were conditioned to subservience by traditional sex roles, or that they had unconsciously 'selected' their fate because of unresolved emotional issues from their childhoods.

The 'guards' in the experiment quickly turned sadistic. The abuse they meted out to the 'prisoners' triggered in their captives symptoms including extreme depression, disorganised thinking, uncontrollable crying and fits of rage – classic responses of the battered woman. The experiment had to be aborted after only six days.

Zimbardo later wrote that a perverted symbiotic relationship had developed: 'As the guards became more aggressive, prisoners became more passive; assertion by the guards led to dependency in the prisoners; self-aggrandisement was met with self-deprecation, authority with helplessness, and the counterpart of the guards' sense of mastery and control was the depression and hopelessness [of] the prisoners.'

Zimbardo speculated that this might also happen in the everyday social 'jails' of racism, sexism – and bad marriages.

FULLERTON RECOMMENDED a book to help answer my queries about what happens inside a killer's head. It is by a British forensic psychoanalyst called Arthur Hyatt-Williams, who worked with violent criminals in and out of prison for many years, and is called *Cruelty, Violence and Murder: Understanding the Criminal Mind*. Every time I dip into it, I find another template that can be placed over Jamie Ramage to test for size.

The fascist personality? Fanatically pursues experiences that will boost his ego. Feels arrogance and scorn for most other people. Shame predominates over guilt, his pride is brittle and he is narcissistic. He is tyrannical in relationships.

The paranoid man? Is dour, unforgiving and vengeful. Minimises good experiences, maximises any affront or grievance. Anger and a sense of persecution can increase over time after an affront until, after a period of false calm, it erupts into violence.

The chronically cruel man? Has a cruel conscience that persecutes him for qualities he hates in himself. So he projects these qualities on to his victim and punishes the victim to avoid his own emotional pain.

Hyatt-Williams found it striking that *all* the murderous patients he studied were bogged down in a state of mind in which 'persecutory anxiety' predominated over 'depressive anxiety'. With depressive anxiety, the main feeling is self-blame. The person asks himself what he has not done, or has done badly, to bring his troubles upon himself: 'How can I put things right and make amends for my shortcomings?' Depressive anxiety sounds like the state that Jamie brought to the five therapists.

But an individual can tolerate only a certain amount of blame. If this amount is exceeded, the feeling of responsibility associated with depressive anxiety is replaced by a paranoid feeling of being 'got at'. Then the person regresses into 'persecutory anxiety'. Hyatt-Williams says this is 'a primitive response to threat, internal or external, actual or supposed. It is a state of mind in which aggrievement is rampant and responsibility muted. Action to silence, quell, obliterate or annihilate supposed persecution is felt to be totally justifiable. The victim or other people are felt to bear responsibility for the persecution'.

Is this what happened to the meek, contrite Jamie who could not do enough to fix his marriage? Did he flip into seeing Julie as an attacker, Julie as the persecutor to be annihilated?

Maybe this whole complicated story boils down to one simple fact: Jamie killed Julie because he stopped blaming himself for the breakdown of the marriage and started blaming her.

MEN'S BUSINESS

THE ODDEST thing happens when Denise Roberts takes a breath to speak. The two men at the table with her fall silent, even if one of them had been about to say something himself. It is almost as if she has first right to hold the floor. This is part of what these three people do for a living: they model, for abusive men, respectful interactions between men and women.

Denise Roberts works with women fleeing domestic violence. She is a slender woman in her forties with red hair cut in a feathered pageboy and fine creamy skin. She used to call the partners of the women she worked with 'perps' – an epithet that can't help but come out of the mouth like a spit – short for 'perpetrators of violence'. She doesn't do that any more, not since she began working at night with men seeking help for their violent behaviour. 'I was totally shocked. I heard men saying that they felt ashamed, that they couldn't believe that their family was still with them; they would talk about the violence quite directly, without trying to fob it off as so many do. To hear them talk about the pain they inflict upon their families, and how they were in pain as well – that just blew me away.'

The two men with Denise are Danny Blay, a wiry, energetic young man who is the manager of No to Violence, Victoria's male family violence prevention association, and Christopher Grace, an older, quieter man who is a psychologist working with violent men. We have all come together in Blay's headquarters, a nondescript office above an inner-suburban shopping plaza; its only noteworthy feature is a security button that allows the staff to buzz people in and out. Those involved in the politics of the family have a healthy respect for the possibility that it will spill over into violence against them.

We talk about what can be done. Roberts believes the State should take out intervention orders against violent men instead of leaving it to their partners to do this, but Blay points out that this does not guarantee safety for the woman because the violence is likely to intensify. They talk about how doctors in general practice should do more than send women away with anti-depressants and advice about parenting courses. 'Or they might be referred to couple counselling, which we think is *extremely* dangerous,' says Blay. He says many men refuse to go to counselling unless the woman comes with them, but there could be terrible repercussions later for a woman who discloses the full truth to a therapist in front of her partner. 'There is also potential for a therapist who isn't trained to a high level in family violence issues to take sides inappropriately, to collude with the man who is saying, "But you don't do X, Y and Z"; participating in blaming the woman. That happens daily.'

The men who do choose to come to men's programs are aged from their twenties to their sixties but are, on average, in their thirties. Their partners have either walked out or threatened to, and they come because they do not want to face the consequences of a marital breakdown – for themselves, their children, their home and, often, their business. The first struggle is to get them to realise that they *never* 'just lose it' – the phrase Jamie Ramage used in his interview with police – even if their loss of temper seems to happen quickly. Says Grace, 'The business of "losing it" is a whole series of thought-stacking: "Here you are, on the bloody phone, talking to your best mate or your mother." That's the build-up. Then it's: "She's married to her mother, she's married to her friend, and where are the kids, the place is a mess . . ."'

He says such a man gets tense in discussions with his partner because what she sees as raising issues, he experiences as criticism. 'And so what you often see is that men then flex their muscle, they regain the power by getting physical or yelling or slamming doors.' Such men also have trouble understanding their own feelings: they often label as anger more subtle emotions such as jealousy, disappointment, embarrassment or hurt.

What about the argument that women are more verbally adept than men and shouldn't wind them up? The three say, almost in unison, that men have got to be able to bear being provoked. And they can, argues Blay: 'You ask those men, why are they violent? "She winds me up, she stresses me . . . "

'Change the scenario to their boss. What kind of job do you have? Under pressure? What if the boss says, "No, you're not going home tonight, you're finishing this report and I don't care if you're here till seven o'clock in the morning doing it." Are you going to get up and belt your boss?

'If a policeman pulls you over and says you went through a red light and you say no it was yellow, do you jump out and belt the copper? No? Why? Different power imbalance. Different sets of consequences. You get fired; you get locked up in jail. And men know that they can get away with violence against women. Men do get away with it all the time.'

He cocks his head to one side and says firmly, 'Men are violent towards women because it works, and because they can.'

Denise Roberts has seen in shelters women who have been married to doctors, lawyers and psychologists. 'It's not just the unemployed, it's not something that just happens in the lower classes of society.' The only difference is that middle-class people are able to hide it better: 'The women collude with the men to hide it. The women don't want the world to know this is happening to them. They feel ashamed. She doesn't want her friends to know, or the people she has contact with at dinner parties. She doesn't want to lose face. And when you've got wealth and that kind of class structure, the man makes sure that she's not marked. He doesn't hit her in the face or anywhere that shows.' She says women stay 'because they can't leave yet, they don't want to lose the relationship, they're not strong enough, they don't want to take the kids away from their dad, they can't afford it, where are they going to live – and he's going to track her down anyway, he won't leave her alone.'

IT IS Christopher Grace who explains most clearly what must have happened inside Jamie Ramage. He uses everyday language to describe what Hyatt-Williams defined so scientifically: the potentially deadly flip from regret to blame. Counsellors *must* recognise that a separated man with a history of violence is a dangerous man, Grace says. Safety is an issue for both the man, who is at risk of suicide, and his partner, who is at risk of being beaten or killed. Grace begins to talk about one of his clients who was thrown out of the family home a few weeks earlier after belting up his wife. He could easily be talking about Jamie Ramage.

'He's an absolute mess; not sleeping, and therefore more dangerous. As long as he's remorseful, safety is less of a concern. But when he moves out of remorse and gets into this total isolation, this tunnel-type thinking pattern, where he thinks, *"I'm the victim here, and she's conspired for this, and I've lost all my family"* – then he can be very impulsive. He's *very* dangerous. A lot of my work is to educate him that this is a possibility.' Grace keeps his voice low but its tone becomes stern and challenging, and he gives me the direct, unflinching gaze he uses with it when talking man to man. His quiet strength of purpose is almost intimidating: '"How are you going to protect yourself if this happens? How are you going to protect the safety of your family?"'

So what are the strategies? 'He's got to get some sleep, he's got to avoid spending too much time by himself, he needs to talk to Men's Referral Service telephone counsellors.' Adds Roberts, 'He needs not to drink too much. He needs *not* to get in a car and drive around the streets looking for his partner.'

The three of them seem to have an instinctive understanding of what had happened inside Jamie Ramage's head. This man whose obsessive, controlling behaviour was such a puzzle to everyone around him is a familiar character to them. They say he represents one kind of man they see. An awful truth is dawning for me. Perhaps men like Jamie Ramage are not a rarity.

I check it back with them. So, what Jamie went through is actually very common? Separated men often get like this?

Yes, says each of them. Yes. Yes.

And even cases that don't end in death can do dreadful damage, says Grace. 'There are a lot of women who don't die, but their suffering is incredible. They get bashed, they get abused, they're scared witless, they suffer post-traumatic stress disorder. They may be separated from their men and they may be feeling safer but the pain has come out and they don't trust men. Their lives are shattered.'

Grace says that in any one week, there are 450 men enrolled in group programs in Victoria to help them change their violent behaviour. Demand far outstrips supply, as does demand for emergency housing for women and children fleeing violent and abusive men.

The courses must make a difference to many families. But it's like trying to empty the ocean with a teacup.

I HAD started this book looking for some answers; among them, what should Julie Ramage have done? Is there any way she could have avoided her fate?

Now, I have Caroline Counsel emphatic that a woman in an abusive relationship should leave, cut off all contact and allow the legal system to bring home to the man the finality of her move. I have Tom Paterson insisting that the safest strategy is to let him down gently, even if it takes years. Peter Fullerton is unequivocal that therapy works only when both partners engage in it, while

Danny Blay warns it is dangerous for a woman to go to couples counselling with a violent man.

No wonder abused women are frightened and confused. Not only is there no consensus on the safe way to go; there is not even consensus on the safe way to stay.

Part Seven

THE SCALES AND THE SWORD

THE PLEA

Day seventeen
Wednesday 1 December 2004

THE JUDGES must hot-bunk. We are in a different court today, Court Two. It is like a mirror-image of the one in which the trial was held. The jury box is on the right rather than the left, and the lawyers have also switched sides: Dunn is on the left, and Leckie is on the right. Julie's family are not to be seen; perhaps some of them are in the visitors gallery upstairs. Jamie Ramage's place is still at the back of the room but this time he is in a traditional dock, a pulpit-like box that leaves only his head and neck visible. He looks caged. He has been jailed now for 499 days.

His family are here, too, carefully placed in the front row of the downstairs pews like chess pieces on Philip Dunn's board. For the first time Jamie's mother is in court. She looks so much like him there can be no doubt. Now 80, she is a stocky woman with a broad face and brown eyes and her son's features, fattened and wrinkled. Her short, thick grey hair is swept up from her forehead and she is dressed in a lavender suit. In Victorian times lavender, like grey, was one of the transitional mourning colours gentlewomen moved into when they had done their time in black. What is it like for her to be here, an old woman witnessing her son's shame? At least she is flanked by her grandchildren. Samantha is wearing a white cardigan with a lacy weave. Her black hair is up and back, wound into a bun on the top of her head. Matthew is on his grandmother's other side, in a charcoal-grey top with long sleeves. They are both carrying themselves with their familiar courtroom self-possession.

Leckie begins by tendering victim impact statements to the judge. They are from Ray and Pat Garrett, Jane Ashton, Laurence Webb and Gilda Pekin.

Dunn launches into why Jamie Ramage deserves a light sentence. He begins with a sketch of Jamie's life in prison. His first job was taking care of intellectually disabled prisoners. Now he is a gardener, 'which is a trusted position because, unlike nearly all other prisoners, he has access to tools, which can be quite dangerous'. Dunn keeps the best for last. Jamie Ramage has become a Good Samaritan: 'He is one of eight people within the prison system of 750 who has done a series of courses, who are what's called "listeners". Within the prison system they have a program called SASH. That stands for Suicide and Apprehended Serious Harm. A very small number of prisoners have been chosen by the prison administrators to be counsellors to listen to people, to explain to them and just listen to their problems. Since the implementation of the SASH program, suicide and apprehended harm, I am instructed, has decreased by two-thirds.'

The man with little insight, the man who was unable to soothe his own anxieties and called in a platoon of others to support him, the man who could not understand his wife's unhappiness or tolerate her desire to be separate from him – the man who bashed and strangled to death the wife he is supposed to have loved – is counselling others on their emotional troubles. It gives one pause. If he was one of the top eight candidates in a field of 750 men, the others must have been seriously unpromising. Perhaps his middle-class smoothness had recommended him to the prison authorities. The job has serious implications for him and how he sees himself. It is a role he had previously fancied himself in: he offered to counsel 'Helen's' husband for her because he believed her marital problems were worse than his. His new prison role might only reinforce his belief in his own superiority and his conviction that there is nothing innately wrong with him, and that killing Julie was just the result of 'losing it' under pressure.

Is no part of the system going to make Jamie Ramage face himself?

DUNN'S VOICE is slow and pleasant; today his delivery has none of the pyrotechnics of his jury address. At this stage it is Justice Osborn he must win over, and judges, who pride themselves on their logic and intellect, tend to turn a withering eye on theatrics. Dunn moulds the facts so gently that it is easy to give over and be massaged into acceptance. He says the judge should take into consideration that Jamie had turned himself in and pleaded guilty to manslaughter; that when he committed the crime, he was emotionally fragile and suffering an adjustment disorder; and that the crime was not premeditated. The judge points out, quietly but incisively, that if the jury let Jamie off on provocation, it was because they believed he had intent to kill but had been provoked. 'Provocation manslaughter should be regarded as serious precisely because it *does* involve a deliberate killing.'

I knew from having spoken to Jane Ashton that she was longing to write her victim impact statement; to have, at last, some way of explaining to this impassive legal system what the killing had meant for her. But now Dunn takes aim at the victim impact statements. He argues that many of them contain inadmissible material that is aimed at unduly affecting the judge in his sentencing. He quotes from another judge who had warned that sentencing should not be corrupted by whether or not the victim wanted to extend mercy: 'The victim of a crime is the worst possible judge.'

Jamie's mother is mopping her eyes. A court helper bends over her with a cup of water.

It becomes clear that there had been angry claims in some of the statements, and questions about why Jamie had not paid school fees and about why he has never apologised to Julie's family. Dunn objects to most of Jane's victim impact statement and great swathes of Gilda Pekin's and Laurence Webb's.

Attacks on Jamie Ramage over money are unfair and unfounded, he tells the judge; Jamie has signed all his assets over to the children. Because the Office of Public Prosecutions had frozen his assets, he has been relying on family and friends to support his children and pay his legal fees. He says that Jamie wanted to write to his wife's family last year to express his regret but was strongly advised by his lawyers not to do so. He still can't understand what happened: 'He describes it as like watching a movie or looking at somebody else's life. It is, to him, incomprehensible that he behaved the way that he did and, as you have seen in a bundle of reports that have been handed to you, he did contemplate suicide as the easiest way out to spare everybody the embarrassment [of the trial], but it was the thought of his children that obviously kept him going.'

There was another way he could have spared everybody the embarrassment of a trial. He could have pleaded guilty to murder.

THE QC next turns to Jamie's background. 'He is a man, obviously, whose character has been moulded because of the way he was brought up.' Jamie's mother is still dabbing her eyes. Dunn turns and gestures towards her as if she is an exhibit and tells the judge that she is mobile despite her age; she has daily contact with Matthew and Samantha and catches a tram and a train to see her son in prison. Jamie is also visited by his brothers and by his children: 'The choice they have had to make is obviously difficult because their father has killed their mother . . . and they have had to rationalise, I suppose . . .' He trails away, as if recognising he has drifted on to an unhelpful path.

He tenders reports from people who have had dealings with Jamie since he was imprisoned: psychiatrist Dr Lester Walton, psychologist Tim Watson-Munro, Anglican Archdeacon Philip

Newman, a Salvation Army major, a prison counsellor, a fellow inmate, and a Catholic nun. Justice Osborn takes up the psychiatric reports. He says Watson-Munro suggests that Jamie had a 'catathymic crisis', which goes much further than the evidence given at the trial. But Dr Walton's report is consistent with Tom Paterson's evidence that Jamie had a psychological vulnerability, 'and that because of his underlying obsessional personality traits he's not a man who could easily adjust to changed circumstances'. Walton's report said this is a well-recognised scenario in people with obsessional personalities: once they finally do lose self-control, the loss of self-control is often extreme.

But Osborn has a twist: he says that if he decides that Julie was killed with murderous intent, 'Dr Walton's evidence provides a framework within which that might be understood.' Jamie Ramage has been impaled by part of his own medical evidence.

AFTERWARDS, I tried to look up 'catathymic crisis'. It wasn't in a dictionary of psychology or even a dictionary of psychoanalysis. A medical dictionary on the internet described it as 'an isolated, non-repetitive act of violence that develops as a result of intolerable tension'. Well, yes.

There was a fuller description in Hyatt-Williams' book, *Cruelty, Violence and Murder*. He writes that a potential killer can have dangerous forces 'in limbo' inside his mind for years. The person can be 'split off' from sensing or understanding those violent impulses and continues to be run by the part of himself that keeps the murderous feelings locked away. Then, one day, he or she 'short-circuits'. Something happens inside the person that allows the murderousness to break loose, 'so that the whole of the energies of the individual became devoted to enacting the murderous deed'. In a catathymic crisis, the person experiences the violent act as the only solution to a deep emotional conflict. And here's the rub: the person might be aware of the external pressures upon him but he does not at all understand the true trigger, that crucial inner conflict.

Its real nature, says Hyatt-Williams, 'lies below the threshold of the person's consciousness'.

Applied to Jamie Ramage, this theory raises more questions than it answers. It does not tell us in any detail what went on in his mind before and during the killing of his wife; it indicates he probably doesn't know himself. But catathymic theory does suggest this: a propensity for deadly violence lurked in Jamie Ramage's unconscious long before he actually did the deed.

THE JUDGE is giving Dunn a hard time today. He's cynical about Jamie's alleged remorse. The way he bundled up her body 'doesn't bespeak remorse to me'. As for Jamie's police interview – the judge says Jamie is palpably suppressing emotion, and it is difficult to interpret that, but any regret seems to be regret for what he's done and nothing that involves 'real identification' with his wife.

Dunn redoubles his efforts. He lays out his treasures: Archdeacon Newman on Jamie's tearfulness; the way Jamie told police he 'hated himself' after burying Julie; the prison counsellor who reported that sessions have often had to stop because of Jamie's weeping, and that Jamie has trouble sleeping and trouble repressing the memory of 'the incident'. The Catholic nun, Sister Mary O'Shannassy, says Jamie was distraught during his first few days in jail. She writes, 'Over the months since, we have had regular conversations. James is unable to make any sense of what happened, unable to understand his own behaviour . . . "I can't believe this has happened, how can I ever be forgiven, how can I fix this and make it better?"'

JULIAN LECKIE sweeps away all Dunn's assertions. He vehemently warns that one must not lose sight of the real victim, Julie Ramage. Her life can never be returned to her, and her husband 'has never, never shown any true remorse for what he has done to that woman'. Jamie Ramage had no choice but to plead guilty to manslaughter, so his plea shouldn't carry much weight. As for the comments of those who have met him in prison – the judge should bear in mind that prisoners can plan what they say to people who they know will be called upon to provide mitigating material in court. 'Particularly in light of the fact that he was a selfish, self-obsessed man and much of what he's done throughout has been to protect himself.'

The judge must decide – beyond reasonable doubt – whether the jury came to its verdict based on lack of intent, or on provocation. He and Leckie become absorbed in the details of the killing; again we hear how Jamie got down on the ground to strangle her, and how she fought for a bit but not for long. Leckie points out that Julie was much smaller and weaker than Jamie and lists her injuries from the 'ferocious' attack. That goes on, and on, before he moves into an equally detailed description of Jamie's disposal of Julie's body. Matthew stares blankly into the middle distance, his mouth a little open. Samantha distracts herself by rummaging in a large cloth shoulderbag with a bright tropical pattern. Its colours are vividly, defiantly young and alive.

How many times have they heard this now? It has been gone over at the committal, the trial, and now the plea hearing. Every ghastly detail of their mother's killing by their father must be permanently imprinted on their minds.

Leckie points out that the provocation, if it did happen, was not high, and that immediately after the outburst Jamie behaved as if he was very much under control. As for his 'adjustment disorder' – anyone going through the break-up of a long-term relationship would be depressed and have trouble coping. 'But we do!'

Regarding Dunn's claim that Jamie had signed everything over to the children: under the law, he had no claim on Julie's estate or on anything they had jointly owned from the moment he was convicted of her killing.

Justice Osborn intervenes with a hint for Leckie. Would the prosecutor like to make any points regarding 'general deterrence' – the idea that this sentence should send a message to the community that male violence against women will not be tolerated? An eager Leckie grabs the baton and runs with it. This sentence should be used to set an example about men taking out their anger and frustration on women, he says. It's a huge problem; one has only to look at the thousands of intervention orders going through the magistrates courts. Dunn replies that there is no point in general deterrence in cases where people have lost self-control.

As he listens, Osborn's face is severe and his lips are pursed. There has been no sign of his previous geniality today. Is it the difference between a trial and a plea hearing, or a consequence of the media frenzy around Jane Ashton and the defence of provocation? A lawyer tells me later that a former judge told him that while judges always deny being influenced by the media, they do read criticism about their cases. Community feeling is not something they can entirely ignore. It may be that in winning, Jamie Ramage has lost.

The judge announces that he will pass sentence in eight days. The tipstaff stands and makes the ritual call: 'This honourable court stands adjourned *sine die*. God save the Queen.'

THE SENTENCING

Day eighteen
Thursday 9 December 2004

IN THE two months since the trial began, Melbourne has moved from a wintry spring to the beginnings of summer. Today is hazy and warm with the promise of new beginnings; a day when officeworkers will be able to lunch under the plane trees in nearby gardens. In the waiting area outside Court Two a large crowd has gathered, buzzing with chat, for what they thought would be a 10 am start. The atmosphere is animated rather than sombre; it feels more like a theatre premiere than a wake, despite the sobering presence of a hefty contingent of security guards. The Garretts are here early, Pat in the familiar peach over-shirt and Ray in a blue chequered shirt and beige jacket. They are surrounded by friends from their retirement village and their Probus club. Christine Howgate and Rhonda McMurtrie are here, and Jamie's business partner, Anthony Brady. So is Caroline Counsel, Julie's lawyer. Counsel says that at a legal dinner the night before, the betting had been that

Jamie Ramage would get 'ten with seven'; a 'head sentence' of ten years, with a minimum of seven to be served before parole.

Seven years for a life.

At 10.25 am the tipstaff begins moving through the crowd to round up the journalists. He takes us through a side door directly into the three rows of pews assigned to media. The seating priority ensures that the media are not only offered access but are safely corralled so that the Garretts are not hard up against anyone who is studying them. It is the closest thing to privacy that a public court can provide.

The court is jammed, upstairs and downstairs, and despite the high ceiling the air is already stuffy. Laurence Webb sits in a prominent row and Gilda Pekin is nearby, dressed all in black. More distant comrades in grief have come to close ranks with the Garretts: a reporter says that George Halvagis is here – his daughter Mersina was murdered some years ago while praying at her grandmother's grave – and so is Noel McNamara, president of a victim support group and the father of a young woman killed by her partner. Jane and Howard Ashton arrive at the last minute and slip into a seat next to the Garretts. A cheerful Dunn arrives with his usual swift stride. He takes off his wig and plops it on the bar table to air his hot head, running his hand over his crown of flattened grey hair. This is like the final scene of a Hercule Poirot novel, in which the whole cast of characters touched by a killing gathers for the denouement.

In the media pews, a reporter remarks on the size of the crowd. The actual killing of Julie Ramage got no press coverage and the committal only a little. This huge public interest has built up gradually. Is it the Jaguar factor? Would there have been the same attention for a wife-killer in blue overalls who carted the body off in a ute?

It is only a few minutes but the wait seems to drag on. We are like a church congregation waiting for a bride or a coffin. The proceedings cannot begin without the presence of the key person around whom everything revolves. The reporters make desultory conversation. A photographer says he got a shot of Jamie Ramage as he left the prison van this morning. For the first time, he did not cover his head.

AT 10.32 am the tipstaff picks up a phone at his bench to call the cells. 'You can bring Mr Ramage down now.' Jamie arrives minutes later and takes his place in the dock quickly. He is in his usual dark suit with a white shirt and a navy tie with a small pattern. He is blinking rapidly and his mouth works nervously, his tongue pushing around the inside of his cheeks. He is pale and his mouth is turned down at the corners. He has lost his Easter Island air today. The wait for sentencing must have weighed on his mind; he looks as if he might burst into tears.

All stand as Justice Osborn arrives. He seats himself and moves straight into it, saying curtly, 'Mr Ramage, would you stand, please?' From then on, whenever the judge raises his eyes from the pages of judgement he is reading, he looks directly at the miserable man in the dock, as if this is just between the two of them. The judgement itself is written this way too. All the way through, Osborn refers to Jamie as 'you'.

Jamie clasps his hands in front of him and looks down at the carpet as the judge recites the history of the marriage. He purses his lips when Osborn says he accepts that Jamie found the marriage breakdown unexpected and emotionally destabilising. He raises his eyes when the judge acknowledges his obsessive ruminating and his attempts to recruit others to help. He drops his gaze at the mention of Laurence Webb. His mouth tightens at the mention of his attempts to finish the renovations.

The Garretts are holding hands. Ray Garrett's face is graven and his brow furrowed. Pat Garrett is leaning back with her eyes closed. She has the look of a medical patient in pain: helpless, resigned, hurting.

Jamie's chest heaves visibly as Osborn talks about how those close to him were reluctant to tell him the truth about Laurence: 'In hindsight, it can be seen that you got mixed messages about the situation.' Jamie looks up hopefully when the judge says he believes his account of that final exchange: 'I am prepared to accept that this account sets out the essential sequence of events. It is circumstantial and detailed and describes a spiralling confrontation in a manner which would not easily be invented.'

Jamie's mouth tightens as the judge repeats '"sex with you repulses me"'. As the judge begins yet another detailed description of the killing, Pat Garrett's eyes and mouth fly open with distress. She bites her trembling bottom lip with her top teeth. At the bar table, Philip Dunn sits with his back to her and to his client. The lawyer's face is impassive and his feet are placed neatly together on the floor. He is utterly still but for his pen moving smoothly over his notepad.

The judge tells Jamie, 'I am satisfied beyond reasonable doubt that you caused your wife's death with the intention of either killing her or causing her really serious injury. I am so satisfied by reason of the account given by you in your record of interview and by the medical evidence. It follows that I propose to sentence you on the basis that the jury has accepted that the Crown in this case failed to negative provocation.'

But then, unexpectedly, the judge distances himself from the law he is about to apply. He points out that the Crown did not oppose provocation going to the jury in this case and says, 'In my view, the Crown was correct to adopt this position as reflecting the current law, and I, of course, must apply the current law – *whatever view I might hold of the desirability of change to it.*'

In this case, at least, Justice Robert Osborn does not want to pick up the dead rat that is the defence of provocation. But he will, as so many other judges and lawyers have before him.

THE JUDGE says he is satisfied that Julie was not in any immediate fear of violence from Jamie or she would not have travelled alone with him to Geelong two days before her death, told him about Laurence Webb or come to see him alone on that last day. He accepts that the killing was not premeditated and that in the final argument, 'in which both parties said a series of hurtful things to each other, that you were unambiguously told what you feared most was true, namely that the marriage was over and that your wife had found a new lover'.

Jamie's mouth becomes a thin line. As the judge details his burial and cover-up after the killing, Jamie stares back at him, his eyes narrowing. The judge says he must accept the jury's decision that the provocation was enough to have provoked a loss of self-control in an ordinary person. But the attack was carried out with murderous intent, was a brutal and continuing assault and had been triggered by provocation that was, objectively, 'far from extreme. It was rather of a character which many members of the community must confront during the course of the breakdown of a relationship'. Jamie's mouth curves down at the sides in an upturned 'U' as the judge points out, 'You have effectively destroyed the life that you had built up for yourself.'

The judge accepts the evidence that Jamie had personality problems that made it difficult to adjust to emotionally challenging changes in his life, and he accepts Dr Lester Walton's opinion that it is unlikely he will reoffend. But he also says, 'I must record some underlying concern as to your capacity to function in a non-violent manner within a marital relationship, should you re-establish one. I say this because it seems apparent that your offence was the product of core aspects of your personality, and it seems to me that these will not easily change.'

Dunn's concept of a normal man driven to the edge has finally been punctured. But it is like a balloon drifting unnoticed to the floor, its air leaking out without so much as a hiss. Can this one quiet sentence, delivered as an aside, counterbalance Dunn's cataract of words?

OSBORN DOES not believe Jamie has shown true remorse. 'I accept that, as Archdeacon Newman states in one of those letters, you have had difficulty in understanding how you did what you did, and that you have felt almost as if someone else had killed Julie. Further, I accept that you have felt a deep sense of personal failure.

But it does not seem to me that either the Archdeacon's letter or the evidence as a whole reflect a real compassion for Julie or an acceptance of the enormity of what you did to her ... I am not persuaded that this loss and regret has extended beyond your personal loss.' Jamie is to be unshriven.

The judge says he must also consider general deterrence. 'Domestic killings involve the cruel and brutal subjugation of one party to a relationship to the emotional inadequacy and violence of the other. The deliberate taking of another's life is an act of the utmost gravity and, in the domestic context, often carries with it not only the tragic and untimely loss of life of the victim but also severe consequential emotional trauma to all those who knew and loved that victim.

'The effect of provocation is not to justify or exculpate the accused with respect to the killing but simply to reduce the crime from murder to manslaughter. As de Jersey CJ of the Supreme Court of Queensland has recently said: " ... when personal relationships fracture, for whatever reason, the notion that one of the partners, perceiving himself or herself to be the injured party, [may] take the life of the other is an outrage which must be discouraged by strong judicial responses."

'... You have caused enormous grief and continuing emotional pain and suffering to your children, your wife's family and to a number of her friends.'

It is at this point that Jamie draws in a sharp breath. A young blonde woman in the downstairs pews – perhaps one of Julie's Eco-d friends – is now openly weeping. The judge reads on in his steady, cultured voice, his pale features unrelenting. He points out that the maximum penalty for manslaughter is twenty years' jail. There is no significant pause before what he says next. The end-point of these long and tortured proceedings is dropped into the courtroom with the matter-of-factness of all his previous remarks. 'I sentence you to eleven years' imprisonment for the manslaughter of Julie Ramage. I fix a non-parole period of eight years.'

Reporters with legal nous would later assess this to be the longest sentence that Osborn could have given without risking an appeal.

But given the time that he has served, and with good behaviour, the man in the dock will be out in six and a half years. Is he relieved? Appalled? He is the only one to know. His face is blank. The shutters are down again on Jamie Ramage.

IT'S OVER. After the long build-up it feels like an anti-climax. People do not turn to each other, there are no excited whispers. The big moment seems to have had a flattening rather than an uplifting effect. A kind of tiredness descends upon the room, as if people are thinking 'All that, for this?' Patricia Garrett and Jane Ashton watch the convicted man being taken away, his head down. Not Ray Garrett. He continues to stare straight ahead of him, as if he has vowed never to lay eyes on Jamie Ramage again.

Later, hugging a friend, Julie's mother looks dazed. She says, 'I don't know how I feel. I'm numb. I can't feel anything.'

Maybe that's what the dead feeling in the courtroom was: mass emotional exhaustion.

IN THE waiting area, the hubbub gradually builds as people find their voices again. I approach Laurence Webb but he is uneasy about commenting. 'Jane didn't want me to spread the media around,' he says. It appears that there is a media game plan, and individual interviews to individual reporters are not part of it. But he tells me he doesn't think the sentence reflects the degree of outcry there has been over the case. He would have expected between twelve and fifteen years. At least the judgement 'clearly shows the provocation law is outdated; it doesn't fit with what our society expects'.

The deep blue of Christine Howgate's eyes are red-rimmed, the only imperfection in her appearance. She has come dressed as to a formal occasion, one deserving of respect, in a cream dress and jacket. 'I think Julie suffered a lot more than he's going to,' she says with her usual directness. 'But it's never fair. White-collar crime – if it's a big enough amount of money, you can be sentenced to fifteen years. It just doesn't add up. Where's the perspective there?'

Rhonda McMurtrie is another friend of Julie's standing alone in the noisy crowd. She smiles a greeting but she is also in tears. 'I feel very flat. It's a very draining experience. No amount of years can make up for the loss of a beautiful human being. It's with great sadness that I have to say that justice isn't done. But I was lifted in confidence that this can be the start of something positive. To me, a lot of regard for Julie came from that judge, and regard for women generally, which gives me hope that society will no longer accept the actions of men like James.'

Then her uncertain smile vanishes, and she abandons the flowery language of hope for something earthier. 'James, from this point on, has got a bugger of a life to expect. He deserves it. He deserves every bit of that.'

REPORTERS APPROACH the Garretts. Julie's father is being philosophical. He says in a voice husky with age, 'I think the judge gave him the maximum he could within the law so there's not much we can do about that. We'd have liked something more, but that was it.' He hopes that their lives will be better from this point: 'It's been going on for eighteen months and it's not very pleasant. For anyone to lose a daughter – the impact is horrendous. It's not the natural way of life, is it?'

A young male reporter tells Ray Garrett, 'He'll be out in six and a half years, sir.'

Ray's tired blue eyes widen momentarily with shock. He is disbelieving. He says dismissively, 'I doubt it.' But his wife swings her head from side to side in distress, 'He will. He will. He'll be out!'

Ray protests helplessly, 'But – the loss of a life . . .'

Says his wife, in an anguished moan, 'A *beautiful* life . . .'

They cut short questions about their grief. Too painful to talk about, they say.

OUTSIDE, JULIE'S best friend Gilda Pekin is standing in the street, small and alone, her face blotched with crying. A few metres from her is the previously fearsome Felicity Holding, that stylish Boadicea of the witness box. She had seemed such a large figure in court; in fact, she is physically tiny. She, too, is standing in the busy street with red eyes and tears streaming unashamedly down her face. All these women who had publicly held themselves together so well during the trial are overflowing with grief now that it is over. Whatever else there might be in Jamie Ramage's downfall, joy clearly has no part in it.

Jane Ashton is holding her press conference on the steps of the Supreme Court. She is an experienced media performer now and talks to the dark blankness of camera lenses with confidence. The passion of the broader cause has given her something to cling to throughout this ordeal. I suspect there are times when her anger is the only thing keeping her upright and wonder how she will be when the grief it holds at bay finally hits with full force.

She praises the judge's comments – 'There was a very strong message here that women should be able to leave relationships safely' – and says the judicial system has been out of step with the rest of society for some time: 'The old boys' network and the patriarchal system . . . is on its way down.' She is still angry that Julie's voice was not heard because of the hearsay rules and that she was demonised in court. Expert witnesses and the victim's family and friends need to be able to tell her history. 'A man who has been an abuser for a number of years – this has to be taken into account. This wasn't a man who just lost it once. This was a man who lost it continually . . . when she was living with him.'

Jane deftly fields a question about why the Ramage children were not here for the sentencing. 'My sense is that there was nothing they could contribute today, and I think they've probably been through enough and just want to get on with their lives.' And she talks about how the sentence is not commensurate with the loss: 'Julie was 42 when she died. Our family lives forever, so she was going to have another 40 years of life, and she hasn't got that now.'

THAT NIGHT, Jane appears on a TV current affairs show. The show's staff have titled the segment *Loved to Death*.

Three weeks of court proceedings and dozens of interviews later, even the media that are sympathetic still don't get it. Love? That suffocating possessiveness and intimidating control, that infantile neediness, that blinkered focus on his feelings at the expense of hers – surely that wasn't love. Jamie Ramage had stolen Julie's life, appropriating it to himself, long before he killed her. *Love* had nothing to do with it.

THE ART OF THE ADVOCATE

PHILIP DUNN and I are to have lunch. He chooses a Japanese restaurant close to his office and mine, in a busy street near the courts and the cluster of table-top-dancing joints and sex shops that have sprung up at our end of town. The soft-speaking waitresses here wear kimonos, and the furniture has simple lines and dark wood. Dunn arrives ten minutes late with his mobile phone plastered to his ear. His gait is slightly stiff, something that is disguised when he is wearing his silk gown. Apologetic and genial, he is in a navy suit and his best feminine-side shirt: it is candy pink with a white collar and cuffs and snazzy gold cufflinks. Yes, he is happy for my tape-machine to be on. In three hours of talking, there will only be one sentence that he doesn't want recorded. He edits it out himself by putting his hand over the recorder's microphone while he speaks. More negotiations go on over the red wine than over what will be on the record. He orders a bento box, an apartment tower of food. When it arrives, he lays the lacquered containers contentedly around him and digs in.

It turns out to be a pleasurable interview. The man was made for dinner parties. Dunn is warm, chatty, witty and direct. He has a storehouse of tasty anecdotes. He tells me brutal things about the way he works but he does it with the shoulder-shrugging charm of an errant schoolboy. He is a formidable fencing companion and a man who hugely enjoys the thrust and parry of argument.

He has no qualms about slapping on to the table extraordinary claims about Jamie Ramage's side of the story that were never raised in court.

'After the committal, I had a number of phone calls, as did Steve Pica, from people – men and women – who in part were connected to Julie Ramage and men she'd had affairs with. Going right back into the 1980s. And so I said to Steve, "You'd better talk to these people and get some statements from them."'

I feel the journalist's urge to pin the generality down into details. 'So how many affairs were there, other than "Adam"?'

'I know of five.'

'*Five?*'

'Yes. A couple of these people said, "Oh God, we can't live with this knowledge. It might have an impact on the case." One bloke said, "I told my wife at the time that I wasn't, but now I'm divorced and now I can say, yes I was having an affair with Julie Ramage." A couple were just malicious about her, saying, "She's not all she's cracked up to be, mate. Go underneath that Miss Goody Two-Shoes exterior!"'

He registers my surprise with mild satisfaction and says gently, 'When you lift the carpet, you've really got no idea what you're going to find. And none of us can be too holier-than-thou.'

This takes some digesting. For Dunn, knowledge of those other affairs would have confirmed the rightness of his provocation defence. The news does say something about the swirling undercurrents of rage in this marriage, and it does leave Julie's wifely martyrdom wobbling on its plinth. But to those who do not believe in the justice of the sexual provocation defence, it changes nothing about the rights and wrongs of the legal case.

And it's never as simple as that, is it? There is *always* another side to the story.

I take Julie's affairs and raise him Jamie's alleged extracurricular activities. I tell Dunn that Julie told Christine Howgate and Gilda Pekin that Jamie had had an extramarital affair. That Jane Ashton claims that a business card from a brothel was found in Jamie's office desk after his arrest. That Julie had told Gilda she found what she thought were receipts for massage parlours when she was looking over documents before she left. Julie had also claimed to several people that she had found condoms in Jamie's washbag when he returned from overseas trips – and Julie had had her tubes tied and did not need to use contraceptives.

Dunn leans back and purses his lips. 'Mmm. He's a very closed book when you talk to him. But I wouldn't be surprised if he went to a brothel. Why not? Particularly if he's – once he's been estranged.'

'It sounds like their sex was pretty regular though.'

'That doesn't mean it was anything special.'

'If it's not anything special, is a brothel where you go?'

'[The psychologist] Watson-Munro reckoned that after the separation in the eighties he was always fearful of another one.' Dunn pauses for a mouthful of chicken. 'Which would make him more possessive. If he was demanding sex every morning, that would be beyond love or physical pleasure. That would be anxiety. Men are like that, you know. "If we're sleeping together, everything's OK." For the male, I think, it's, "I'm still allowed to go there." If she said no to sex, he would think he's being rejected, not just sexually but in other ways as well. So sex is the opposite of rejection; it's a confirmation that "We're all right."'

We chew in silence for a moment. Dunn's line would explain how Jamie's experience of their sex life could be *so* different to Julie's. On one level, the theory is comforting; at least it is possible Jamie was not knowingly forcing himself upon her (although Julie's claim that he threw her out of bed for refusing sex would challenge that). But even if Dunn's theory is accepted, it is still dismaying that such physical closeness between two people can be accompanied by such a yawning emotional gulf. Our own Germaine Greer long ago coined a term for what men are doing when they have intercourse with a woman without emotional intimacy. She calls it 'masturbation in the vagina'.

But I haven't got enough red in me to run that by Phil Dunn.

WE GET on to his Rational Alternative Theories (RATs). He had two in the Ramage case. RAT II was the 'Love, Actually' theorem. RAT I was simply that Julie had socked it to Jamie because she now had the confidence to get on with her life. When Dunn developed RAT I it was before the committal, and he did not realise then that Julie felt she had found her great love. 'I thought Laurence Webb was just someone she was boofin' out in the bloody boondocks.'

He returns to his beloved RAT as if he enjoys petting it. 'When she started to give it to James, something kind of got released in her . . . It went back to every bloody humiliation, every time he told her to change her dress because it wasn't right; it went back to every order he had ever given her. When he was on the receiving end, she got on a roll. She went for him. And I think that he actually lost it.'

He pauses ruminatively. 'And the thing I don't understand is that most people in that situation call the cops. To me, as I kind of sat there, conjuring it about in my mind, that was one bit I hadn't understood.'

I ASK Dunn about the crackling antagonism in court between him and Jane Ashton and Gilda Pekin. He says he wanted the jury to know he didn't trust their evidence. He chooses his words carefully. 'I think they're perceiving it, in a rational sense, from their own perspective. And I also portrayed that I thought Laurence Webb was a cad.'

'I suspect he's not.'

'It doesn't matter.' He chuckles. 'It doesn't matter in the big scheme of things. But he knew this woman had been separated for four to five weeks. He was going to move into her house.'

I'm getting cross now. 'He wasn't going to move into her house. I read this paragraph in the committal transcript where he said to you, "No, we were not going to move in together, we were going to share between the two houses."'

'That's not what he said at the trial.'

My voice is testy. 'It *is* what he said at the trial. It's not what *you* said at the trial.'

'Well, I tried my best,' he says good-naturedly. 'He should've eased off on her.'

Anyway, he says, his personal view is irrelevant: 'What I've got to try and work out is what the jury's going to gulp down.'

He says he had planned to 'belt' Gilda Pekin, the holder of so much of Julie's miserable history, if much of the evidence in her police statement had not been thrown out in the voir dire. 'Well, you know, the message and the messenger . . .'

I look back at him, puzzled. 'No. I'm lost.'

The chopsticks carry another morsel to his mouth. 'Well, you've gotta shoot the messenger sometimes. If you say to me, "The sun is shining," and that's not the information I want to hear, then I say "Karen Kissane's a liar!"'

He continues to chew. My mouth has dropped open. 'Oh my God, is it as remorseless as that? If you just don't like what they're saying, and you can't attack their evidence, then you attack their characters?'

'Well, you would look at it . . .'

I think of all the interviews I have had with grief-stricken women who loved Julie Ramage; of all the stories of illness and anxiety and depression linked to the stress of the trial.

In a response that highlights the way there are grey areas on all sides in a case like this, he talks about how he had intended to attack one witness over that witness's statement to police. The witness had denied knowing the full truth about Julie's relationship with 'Adam'. I say it seems an understandable fudge in the circumstances. I imagine the witness was being loyal to Julie and protective of the Ramage children and of 'Adam'.

The air between us has cooled. We move on.

'THERE'S A family theory that he dug the grave beforehand; that there wasn't time on the day to drive all that way and dig it then,' I tell him.

Dunn can understand the family thinking that. 'But when people are in a very heightened state, you'd be surprised what they're capable of; energy. Like rats in a cage, they can move hard and fast when they have to. I'll tell you why they're wrong. I have had some theoretical discussions with James Ramage about the illogicality of all this. And he's not an unintelligent man. Had he wanted to murder his wife because the marriage was over, inviting her to the house and killing her there, and telling people he was having her to lunch, and parking her car 800 metres away is the last thing a man of his intelligence and attention to detail would have done. In all my conversations with James Ramage, and I've spent many hours with him, he's as mystified as anybody as to why he did this. He sees it as illogical.'

What he is to tell me next comes out slowly and cautiously, like a small animal poking its nose out of a safe burrow. Dunn says that Jamie was stunned when he found out about the other affairs, 'the depth of them'. I nod absently, assuming he means Jamie was stunned when he found out about the affairs through Dunn's callers. But I will soon be disabused of that idea.

Dunn says, 'I think he suspected [the affairs], and that's why he had the morning sex thing. And what he said in his very earliest statement to his solicitor was *greater detail to the fatal conversation.*' He pauses to see if I get it. 'Greater detail. She mentioned "Adam" to him and she mentioned a few other things. And he said that when he was talking to the police, he didn't want the children to know about these things.'

Finally, I twig to what he means. 'So she mentioned the other five affairs *in that last row?*'

He gives me a solemn look that means assent. 'Oh God,' I say, startled yet again.

'That's what she said. "I haven't loved you for ten years, I've done this, I've done that." They were our earliest instructions. And we had a kind of ethical problem, because he has said something in the record of interview [with police], and he has from within a day of the record of interview given an expanded version of that, dated, fortunately, by the solicitor. But if we called him, the Crown would make mincemeat of him over the fact that he didn't say it to police. But that's why he rang Adam. Remember, at five o'clock he rang Adam?

'She told him about Adam, and she told him she had been talking to Adam that morning, and why she'd gone to Adam as opposed to having sex with him. He looked at her phone and saw this number, which was a number he had seen come up on her phone in the past. And he rang and asked, "Is that Adam?"'

I gather my wits enough to say, 'But Adam said he never got a call.'

Dunn opens his arms, palms towards me, and shrugs. 'Well, maybe Ramage is wrong. Take your pick. You might find it hard to believe he'd make all that up because it's checkable. She told him about others. And I said, "Why in the name of God didn't you tell the police this?" And he said, "Because I just assumed I'd be pleading guilty. And the children would never find out about their mother having the affairs."

'And, see, we stopped him pleading guilty.'

YOU'VE GOT no idea what you're going to find when you lift the carpet. If this story were a modern parable, what would be its lessons? That the veneer of bourgeois respectability can be paper thin. That you never really know anybody.

In that final row, did Julie lose her temper before Jamie lost his? Did she try to kill off the relationship in a way that ended with her being killed?

Yet there still remains the question of misogyny in the law. Should her affairs have justified softening her husband's crime from murder to manslaughter? Jamie did not *own* her. And why was it permissible for the court process to explore her affairs, but not for anyone to ask whether Jamie had been unfaithful too? Much of the power of Dunn's argument came from the contrast he made between Julie's fecklessness and infidelity and Jamie's obsessive clinging to the role of good husband and father. No one *ever* challenged Jamie's fidelity. I'd asked Dunn about the question of Jamie's sexual history in an earlier phone discussion. He dismissed it instantly, startled even to hear it raised. 'It wasn't relevant,' he said. Legally, I suppose he meant.

The law is a parallel universe.

I ASK Dunn about jury selection. Does gender matter, and what does he rely on when he is making his challenges? Instinct, he says. 'It's easier to get an acquittal in a rape with women than it is with men, as a rule of thumb. There was one very instructive case. When the complainant, the woman, was saying, "I'm under the West Gate Bridge in the back of a panel van, and he's pulling my pantyhose off," all the men are . . .' Dunn puts his head in his hands and looks down at the table, as if ashamed or embarrassed. 'And all the women are . . .' And he looks across at me in a puzzled, disbelieving way. 'I don't know what their thinking was – "What's she doing there?" perhaps – but I just used to notice that.'

For his first murder trial on his own, Dunn put that knowledge into practice. He was acting for a man who had stabbed his wife to death in a domestic, 'a nice old buffer'.

If he was such a nice old buffer, how did he come to kill his wife?

'His wife was an alcoholic and a first-class bitch. He'd had cancer of the voice-box and the neighbours heard her calling out to him, "Why don't you die of cancer, you dirty old bastard?" The defence team – I remember saying, "We're going for an all-female jury, gang." My junior [counsel] went, "Oh fuck! What are you doing?" And I said, "We are going to have an all-female jury." We got eleven-one: eleven women and one man.'

He looks over at me, hugely amused. 'And you know what those bloody women did? *They made the man the foreman!*'

HE WAS happy with the Ramage jury: 'Balanced, conservative, traditional values.' And delighted when they quickly elected a middle-aged man in a suit as foreman.

Was he pleased because he thought a conservative jury would deplore her extramarital affairs and the fact that she had left in her son's Year 12?

He nods. 'Year 12! Puh-leeze!' he says disapprovingly. Then he brightens, remembering another gem: 'And the Brazilian.'

'The Brazilian' was the photograph of Julie Ramage's pubis that I had glimpsed from a distance in court during the voir dire, which showed she had waxed her pubic hair into a narrow strip. Dunn has his secret women's business rather askew. A Brazilian is a full pubic wax. Julie seemed to have what beauticians tell me is called a XX or a XXX; *then* comes the Brazilian. But this is not the point I want to argue with him.

'The jury had seen the Brazilian?' I ask him. 'How did the prosecution let those in?'

'They didn't,' he says smugly. 'They objected to it. I needed the photo of that in to show the post-mortem staining on the tummy. To show that she may have been lying face-down in the car.'

'And it also showed her *pubis*?'

Dunn adopts a look of choirboy innocence. I tell him it doesn't quite come off. Laughter rumbles from deep inside him. 'No, we had to get them for the front, the front of the tummy,' he insists, his eyes full of mischief.

'So you think it means she was a fast woman?'

He tries for innocence again. 'Oh, you tell me what a Brazilian means. I've got no idea.'

I say it might simply mean Julie was a swimmer, to bring it down to practicalities. She'd done master classes, the Pier to Pub swim at Lorne . . .

He says in a wicked growl, 'I don't think so!' And laughs again.

There are waxing parlours in so many suburban shopping strips. Australia must be full of women who can't afford to find themselves in a shallow grave.

LECKIE MADE a mistake with his 'little flight of fantasy' into the rope, premeditated murder and possible sexual assault, Dunn says. 'It was like over-egging the pudding. And therefore, if I could disprove that, I'm undermining his credibility with the jury.'

I tell him there are still people who believe in the rope. They're just clinging to it, he says dismissively. The explanation for the rope is simple. Due to the renovations there was temporary fencing at the side of the house. The piece of rope was cut off and tied around the fencing by one of the tradesmen. Then the rope somehow ended up looped around the handle of the spade. 'So when he picked up the spade and threw it in the boot, the rope went with it. He pitched everything from that boot into the hole.'

SOME OF the therapists in this case were not happy with the way the law conducted itself. Dunn has his own criticisms of the way they operate. He believes their professional neutrality helped drive Jamie Ramage over the edge: 'Someone like James Ramage was desperate for one of the therapists to make a judgement call. One of the therapists could have said to James Ramage, rather than being so goddamned neutral and not interfering in the process, "My dear boy, she's gone. G-O-N-E. And she ain't coming back . . ." If the next thing they said was, "Every hour on the hour you have to get up and walk around the room three times and have a cup of tea," he'd have done it. If they'd given him *anything* to do! But they're so intent on not joining the fray. Anybody in crisis would like a signpost that says' – he whistles and jerks his head – *"That way!"* And nobody would give him that.'

Jamie's background is Scottish, Dunn says. A dour Scots Presbyterian, I inquire? He nods and says that's exactly it. 'I'll tell you what he's like. The last time I saw James Ramage the first thing he asked about was his children. We talked, and he asked why didn't we lead evidence about his feelings. And I said, "We have to do it as we see it, and you have to trust us in all this." And then he said, "Well, I do, but . . ." And then he burst into tears.'

Dunn has a fine sense of theatre. He makes sure he has eye contact with me and, as he talks, mimics Jamie's actions. 'He then wiped his eyes very quickly and said –' Dunn adopts a brisk, businesslike tone – "I'm terribly sorry, I'm terribly sorry." Apologising for being emotional. That's happened before. He gets that way. He then – you could see him literally . . .' and Dunn draws himself up into a rigid stance, head high and shoulders back. 'As if to say, "Shit, I've done the wrong thing here. I'm terribly sorry. I'm quite all right."' Dunn begins to laugh, struck by the brutal Pythonesque humour of it. '"It's only a leg that's been cut off. And my testicle. And my right arm. But I'm quite all right, thank you very much!"'

His voice softens. The jury man gives me his avuncular look, the one that creates a sense of mutual understanding, the one that says he is kind and knowing and that you will see the sense of what he is saying. 'And that's *not his fault*. That's how his mother and father brought him up.'

DUNN CATCHES the eye of a waitress. 'Young lady, could I have a delicious cup of tea? Please?' She nods assent and glides off to fetch it.

He thinks the Ramage case has been hijacked for a cause it does not fit. 'Ramage got up for provocation *not* because the jury said the wife deserved it. That's got nothing to do with it. No jury in Victoria has ever said that. Ramage got home because you had five therapists who said, "We understand how the mind works, and this bloke was over the edge." Take that fact out of the Ramage case, and you know what you got? What the Jews call *gornisht*. Nothing. If you take out the five therapists, you ain't got no provocation defence in this case.'

Pressed, he agrees that provocation does blame the victim. But he begins to state his case with vigour, punctuating each claim with a punchy interrogative like a series of small explosions. 'But it blames the victim because the victim has to have some provocative comment, some provocative behaviour. There's a separate thing about shooting the golden angel, right? That's a separate thing for any murder trial. The dead person's good, right? And if the dead person isn't quite the figure of sympathy, then that makes your journey home a little bit easier. Any barrister worth his salt is going to investigate that. Right?

'I mean, the fact is, Julie Ramage is what she was. Julie Ramage did have a Brazilian cut, Julie Ramage did leave in Year 12, Julie Ramage did have affairs while she was married, Julie Ramage had two affairs with married men. All these things mean that the jury then said, "Well, here's a woman as she was." And is it such a great crime, seeing it as it was? Or is it all part and parcel of it?'

I DO not know how deeply Philip Dunn holds to what he has been telling me. Much of it would fit comfortably with him; he is a product of his age (60), his sex, and his calling. As am I. And he tells me that he rarely wins a case he does not believe in. Much as he would like to believe in skill alone, he has to admit that sincerity counts for something.

But as he defends the law of provocation, he argues that he could even more easily have used it to get Julie Ramage off if she had been the one to kill Jamie. 'I've acted for plenty of women charged with murder, as well as men. If the roles were reversed, I reckon I'd have got Julie Ramage an acquittal of manslaughter *and* murder. We could have run hard and strong on years of violence and apprehended violence.'

He seems to see no contradiction here, despite the way he had argued in court that any violence in the Ramage marriage was minimal and rare. What does a barrister with a brief do with cognitive dissonance? How does a barrister hold fast to who he is when one day he is paid to argue that black is white, and the next he argues the opposite? Maybe there is an underlying principle that holds it all together, such as a commitment to the accused's right to a fair trial or a devotion to the cause of the underdog. Because to the criminal barrister, the underdog in a trial is not the victim. It is the person alone in the dock with the forces of the State arrayed against him. And from the way Dunn talks about his clients, it is clear that he feels deeply protective towards many of those he has taken under his shield. He also likes to win.

It is not Dunn's job to judge his clients or their cases. As senior British QC Richard Du Cann pointed out in his classic book, *The Art of the Advocate*, if a lawyer refuses to defend someone because of his views of the offence or of the accused, he assumes the role of judge and undermines the whole system.

Du Cann also said there is a painful prejudice against those who, like lawyers, appear to live on the misfortunes of others. But whereas others in this group, such as doctors and undertakers, try to please everyone, the lawyer does not. Thinking about this, I realise there is another difference. The lawyer is not constrained by the doctor's promise to 'First, do no harm . . .'

Though Dunn did decline to use the evidence of Julie's other affairs. He says he just needed 'Adam' to prove her duplicity. He kept his knowledge of the others as 'ammo in reserve'.

THE BACKGROUND hubbub in the restaurant has died down. We are alone but for the staff. They are too courteous to move us on and leave us to the dregs of our wine.

Dunn says again that he hates using provocation. It's like trying to force Cinderella's slipper on to one of the ugly sisters. It often doesn't fit, but lawyers must try to wrestle it into shape because, in Victoria, there is no defence of diminished responsibility. Anybody could have lost their temper like Jamie, he says. He shakes his head slowly. 'You and I are James Ramage. There has to be a space for people like you or me, or James Ramage, who a jury of twelve people can be satisfied "lost it". Whether they're good people or bad people, whether they love their wives or don't love their wives. There has to be a space there because, at the end of the day, don't you punish people for what they *knowingly* do wrong?'

A MOBILE phone call reminds him he is due at a meeting. We make small-talk in the weak sunshine on the way back to his chambers building. He farewells me with his usual good cheer and starts quickly up the bluestone steps. Back to work. Back to the adversarial system of law that he embodies.

Part Eight

AFTERMATHS

NO PLACE LIKE HOME

Saturday 4 December 2004

AT 11 am on the morning the Ramage family home is to be sold, Julie's old car is parked in Marock Place, as it must have been so many times before. The small silver Mini is now Matthew's and wears his P-plate. Even more disconcertingly, for those who would recognise it, Jamie's Jaguar is sitting in the garage. Its pistachio-green rear end is visible from the street. The car in which Jamie had transported his wife to her bush grave looks pristine. No doubt the forensic team cleaned up even the tiniest particles. Its continued presence in the family's life seems strange, verging on creepy. But how does a family clean up after the uncleanable? How do you manage the logistics of everything that has been stained by this? Perhaps the police have only just released the Jaguar and there has been no time to sell it. Or perhaps, as Lindy Chamberlain once said of the clothes and camping gear from which she washed bloodstains after baby Azaria's death, it's just that 'You can't get rid of everything'. Even if you could, it wouldn't erase what happened. You carry the experience with you whether or not you are sleeping in the sleeping bag or driving the car. But still – what must the neighbours be thinking? Is the Wisteria Lane normality of it all giving them the shudders?

Because it is a gentle suburban scene. The white shutters are open against the red brick. Jamie's elderly mother is sweeping outside. One of his brothers is mowing the lawn. Matthew is helping too, in and out of the front door. It is early summer and roses in the front yard are blooming lush and red. In the park around the corner people are playing cricket. It's all so sunny and routine. You'd never know.

By 1.45 people have begun to gather for the 2 pm auction in this 'quiet court location'. As they wander down the street the sky is overcast but the sun is struggling to break through again. In the entrance hall, the first thing I notice is the low ceilings. For a house owned by rich people in a good suburb, it has rather a claustrophobic feel. It turns out that, for all its old-English style, the house was actually built in 1970 and has the boxy proportions of that era. The house, like the Ramages, had pretensions to something it was not.

Several of the rooms have small crystal chandeliers. The walls are white and the carpet is a soft indeterminate shade, somewhere in between blue and green and grey. I go with the flow of people to the formal lounge room on the right. The house is no longer being lived in. The lounge that was so full of clutter on the night of the killing is empty but for a lonely vase of blooms on the mantelpiece: pink carnations, an old lady's flower. But left behind are two painted portraits of the children when they were much younger, framed and hanging on the wall. The wistfulness of the images stops me in my tracks, and the talkative stream of people going through the house parts around me as around a rock in a river. The portraits were painted by Sir William Dargie, Australia's official war artist during World War Two. Matthew has short hair and is looking straight ahead with that hazy sort of gaze he wore so often in court. Samantha looks to be about seven and is smiling. Her dark hair is loose over her shoulders except for the part gathered on top of her head and tied with a blue satin bow. They seem such sad pictures now, radiating innocence-lost like a soft light. They are not those children now. The past is another country.

The other people in the house chat as if they have no idea of its history or else discount it entirely. One woman demands to know whether her companion thinks the floorboards on the stairs are creaky. 'Really,' says another, 'the only problem is that there's no land. Look at the backyard.'

To get to the backyard you have to go through the kitchen and family room. Red-brown parquetry has gone down on top of the floorboards that were stained with Julie's blood. As for that wretched bench-top – the cloudy-grey granite in now in place. With sunlight streaming through the new French doors, and the matter-of-fact ordinariness of the crowd milling about, it is hard to hold on to any sense of this as a room with a sinister history. I can hear in my head the line people utter so often at funerals: 'Life goes on.'

In the small ground-floor study that was Jamie's there is a black umbrella, an industrial-sized tin of lollipops from his Jazzies days and a box crammed with belongings – the top one a compact disc of *Les Miserables*. Upstairs, the children's rooms are bare but for bed-frames. In the 'master' bedroom – unfortunate term, given the resonances – the pink curtains with frilled ties remain. But the white bed that was immortalised in the police video, the romantic princessy bed in which Julie claimed to have suffered so, has gone. In its place is a big empty bed-frame of dark carved wood. Some of Jamie's ties are still hanging in the walk-in wardrobe, gathering dust.

In the little upstairs hallway the walls are hung with several children's paintings that have been glazed and framed. Julie or Jamie – or maybe Julie *and* Jamie – must have been proud of the child or children's work. One is a confident painting by a very young hand of a woman with an orange face and black hair and a big red grin. In the background behind her is a dark, childishly shaped creature with big ears – a bunny or a puppy or a boogieman, it's impossible to know. A second painting is of a recognisable black-and-white whale frolicking in waves, and a third looks like a family holiday moment recaptured: the Ramages' black poodle is on a beach of mustard-coloured sand with its head down, warily sniffing a crab.

You can tell that this household no longer has a mother. The paintings, like the portraits in the lounge, are the kind of childhood treasures a mother would never leave behind when all else had gone.

OUTSIDE, I stand in the sun near two white-haired old ladies and we begin to chat. They live nearby and had known Julie. 'A beautiful girl, inside and out,' says one companionably, clucking her tongue against the roof of her mouth. They couldn't bear to go through the house. Too sad. But they are curious to see how the auction goes. There are almost 60 stickybeaks gathered with the same aim; only two people bid for what the auctioneer, in fine Freudian fashion, calls 'this most attractive two-storey *English-inspired* home' in 'a great value *dead-end* street in Balwyn'. The old ladies and I exchange eye-rolling glances. Later, as if some part of his mind has recognised his gaffe, the auctioneer modifies his description. He lays it on thick: the street becomes 'this lovely, *quiet and safe, peaceful cul de sac*'. As he patters on, the old ladies mutter about whether the bidders know what they are buying, and about how no one knows what goes on behind closed doors. The crowd drifts away, disappointed, when the house is passed in at $925,000. According to a newspaper listing next day, it later sold for $940,000.

The house that was the family nest, the house that was the outward symbol of so much that Jamie and Julie strove for, is gone. The remaining Ramages have shut the door on the middle-class dream that cost too much. It would not be so easy to close the door on the emotional after-shocks of the Jamie and Julie Ramage story. Her killing was a stone into the pond of their friendship circle, and the ripples are still widening.

THE LOVER

LAURENCE WEBB is living in a romantic novel. Julie is the great love of his life, his perfect woman; he still waxes lyrical about the sun shining through her hair, and he wrote a poem about their last horse-ride together, *A Perfect Day*. He sends me a copy of it. 'Eyes locked like spent lovers in rapturous wonder', reads one line. The poem calls Julie 'Our Toorak Princess in Drizabone'.

For some time after the killing, Laurence did not see his children because relatives feared a hit-man might be sent after him, and he did not want to endanger them. It's a fear that sounds a little melodramatic as we sit here in this plush office tower, a long way from those events. But then, there was a time when the thought that Jamie might kill Julie would have seemed melodramatic. When the unthinkable happens, it makes anything seem possible.

For the first year after her death, Laurence did everything he and Julie had planned to do together, including the holiday at Noosa. It was his year of mourning, firstly for her life and then for the life he might have had with her. According to Gilda, he sought out people who had known Julie so that he could learn more about her: 'He was really desperately looking for anybody who could give him a bit more of Julie. He didn't have enough. She just left too soon.' He has also missed out on job opportunities, stepped out of the fast track after starting with Telstra, and had counselling for post-traumatic stress syndrome. Not for guilt, he says, despite the defence's insinuations that Julie would be alive today if only her relationship with Laurence had not started so soon. 'I went through every second of our time together; every conversation, everything. Could anything different have occurred? And no, I don't believe it could have. He'd been pestering her to go and see those renovations for a long time. He knew all about me on the Saturday; he'd had all the Sunday to brood on that. And then he saw her. Regardless of me, he was going to try and re-establish his control. And she was strong enough to say no.'

LAURENCE WEBB saw his father hitting his mother when he was thirteen years old. He walked into the kitchen at just the wrong – or the right – moment. 'Thank goodness for my own good health, I said "Stop!", and refused to go away when he told me to get out.' He chuckles. 'I was old enough and big enough to make a nuisance of myself so then he chased me, turned his anger on me. Then I found out I could outrun him.'

It was then, he says, that he realised that he, too, would be able to hit a woman. Being aware that his own father could lose his temper this way made him fear the same potential in himself, 'like a devil inside you'. It is this awareness that saved him once when he was pushed to the edge: 'I had a partner who taunted me to the point of wanting to hit her. And I hit the wall and put a hole in it and then walked out. She egged and egged and egged me to the point where I did lose it, but I knew enough not to hit her. I'm very solidly built. I stopped boxing after I had a fight and broke a bigger person's jaw in many places. So I knew I could damage her.'

So, what's the difference between the man who loses it and punches the wall, and the man who loses it and punches the wife?

'You get to live the rest of your life as a balanced human being. If I'd have hit that woman twenty years ago, I would have suffered too, because you can't resolve the fact of being strong and powerful and having hit somebody weak. It's bad for you. Of course, it's also bad for the relationship, and it's a lot worse for the person you're hitting. But from the man's point of view, it's a terrible thing to happen.'

WHILE HE continues to burnish the memories, Laurence has moved on. He has a new partner now. He met her at a memorial show-jumping day held at Hurstbridge in Julie's honour. She's had to have counselling over Laurence's loss of Julie too. It's not easy to follow in the footsteps of the perfect woman.

THE FRIENDS

ROB MOODIE is not a close friend of Jamie Ramage's. Jamie's best friend lives in England. Despite the physical distance between them, Jamie and his English friend used to meet every year or two to draw up goals for their lives and mark themselves on how well they had achieved the goals set last time. It is a process Jamie applied to other areas of his life too. After Julie's death, Jamie asked his children to rate him as a father, to sum up the complexities of their relationship with a number and mark him out of ten. He wanted to pin down whether he had failed there, too.

But Rob Moodie, who knew him as a dinner-party companion and as a player in touch rugby, has been his most steadfast friend since Jamie has been in prison. He sees the Ramage children and visits Jamie with books and meditation tapes. Why does he still see him when so many others have turned their backs? Rob cocks an eyebrow. 'You mean, why don't I hate him? Because I have a fundamental belief in everybody's capacity to reform themselves. That everybody has the possibility of salvation, if you like. I would hope that Jamie can develop the insight to do that.'

The Ramage case has seen the personal and professional collide for Rob. As chief executive officer for VicHealth, the State's health-promotion organisation, he was overseeing a research project on domestic violence when the Ramage tragedy unfolded. He brings to our first interview the resulting report, which found that domestic violence is the most important preventable risk factor for illness and injury in women aged from 15 to 44. 'What's most staggering about this stuff is that there is an increase of partner violence when women are pregnant because they're seen as more controllable then. It seems to be to do with women being even more dependent and men taking advantage of it, when you think it would be the reverse; they've got a joint stake in the baby and the bearer of the baby, you would think. That was pretty shocking to me.'

Rob and I meet twice, once before the trial and once after it, each time at his favourite Italian restaurant in Lygon Street, Carlton, around the corner from his office. It was considered a coup when the State Government snaffled him back from the World Health Organisation. I have heard from other reporters that he is witty and engaging, but in our encounters he is subdued and barely raises a smile. Talking about Julie and Jamie, the smooth professional man who is so accustomed to public speaking struggles to find words, and there are silences while he tries to gather his thoughts. The Ramage affair has shaken his faith in his own judgement. He had not seen Jamie as controlling. Julie was so much more socially adept than Jamie that Rob had assumed she was probably the one pulling the marital strings. And the Ramages had always put up such a polished performance as a united couple that Rob was surprised when they separated. 'Of all the couples I knew . . .' he says, shaking his head in disbelief. He knew Jamie was 'a bit of a smart-arse, rather cocky' but he had never seen unpleasantness between them, much less violence. And he was deeply upset that he had seen Jamie the day before the killing and not realised he was in such a dangerous state. 'You feel guilt for, "Why didn't I see this coming? How wrong was I?" I was counselling him as a friend. I feel now like I can't give anyone armchair advice.'

Rob Moodie was the first and possibly only person to point out to Jamie that this was not a crime of passion but a crime of possession. He still holds to that. 'There's something far more deep about this than it just being a crime of passion, a one-off thing. That's the excuse that's been given to it for thousands of years. "Oh,"' he puts on a gravelly French accent and waves his fork about with Gallic exaggeration, '"Oh, I waz in lerv wiz 'er, and she waz mine, and I 'ad to kill 'er." All this sort of stuff,' he says with contempt. 'It's a complete abrogation of personal responsibility. The trouble with crimes of passion or the other names used, like honour killing, is that they completely cover over the fundamental problems underneath. If you are shamed, why is it that bad? Why is it unbearable? Why do you have disproportionate shame, where the shame about the loss of face is far greater at some point than [the shame of killing your wife]?'

What does he think went wrong for James Ramage? 'I think his issue is, if you build an image – and he's not the only one who's done that – of what your family is, and invest in the material things around, and have your kids at the right schools, and your partner, and that all fits into a preformed notion of what an ideal family is, and Julie walks away from all that – then it all comes crashing down. I think he drew a lot of how he saw himself from how other people would see him. And again, he's not the only one doing it. It's coming back to the fundamental problem of the poor mental health of men, in the sense of not being comfortable in their identity.'

Rob Moodie sees Jamie Ramage as flawed in himself, but also as a product of the society he lived in. He was trying to be a success in order to be accepted, and that is not uncommon in a world dominated by what Rob calls 'emotional materialism' – the attitude that friends and family are possessions or pawns, part of the formula required for social approval rather than sources of mutual love and support. 'There are plenty of people who prioritise their possessions over everything else, and that's what society is telling us to do: "Be wealthy, buy a Mercedes, that's what status is and that's what's important." If it isn't followed by murdering your wife, his behaviour is *normal*.'

Rob Moodie began thinking and speaking publicly about men and their mental health some years ago when a male friend suicided. Other men who knew the man who had died talked about it and decided they had better start getting together and offering each other a deeper kind of friendship. Rob also took up regular meditation. The Ramage tragedy, he says, has seen a similar emotional stocktake, with many men who knew the couple shocked into scrutinising the health of their own marriages.

But, for all his efforts to process what happened with Jamie and Julie, there are still moments when Rob Moodie feels utterly bowled over by his memories. 'I often drive up Mont Albert Road, and one day I saw Julie and Gilda there, and I hubba-hubba'd them. And every time I go past that spot, I think, "Shit! Why shouldn't she still be there? And Jamie could have a new life . . . "'

WHEN IT comes to divorce, the friends of a couple, like the house and the car, usually go with one partner or the other. This did not happen with Kate Clark. During the war of the Ramages she was their Switzerland, a neutral party who stayed close to both of them after the split. She thought she could use her position as an adviser Jamie trusted to make the adjustment easier for him and, therefore, the escape easier for Julie: win–win. But Kate Clark ended up feeling badly burned by her efforts to be kind.

Clark is the anaesthetist who first met the Ramages because she had a neighbouring house down at Eastern View. Julie dropped in one day and asked her to afternoon tea. It was later that they realised they also had sons in the same year at Scotch College. Her manner in this interview is quiet and self-contained; she chooses her words carefully and often qualifies her comments in the interests of fairness. But there is a burning intensity to the way she talks about the Ramages and about the effect they have had on her life. Every now and then – sometimes it is when she talks about Julie's happiness after leaving Jamie – a solitary tear slides down her cheek.

After the Ramages separated, Clark found it no hardship to continue the friendship with Julie, who had always been cheerful but now was the happiest Clark had ever seen her. 'Everyone would always have described her as having a cheerful disposition. It wasn't like this miserable person suddenly became happy,' she says. 'It was more like when you see somebody who's pregnant and you think, "God, doesn't she look lovely, she's just blossomed!" It wasn't that she smiled more often; it was just her sense of *liberation*.'

Clark believes that Jamie kept in touch with her because he did not see her as an enemy. He knew that she and Julie were not soul sisters; they were close but not intimate, and Clark knew nothing of any violence or abuse. She did know that Jamie 'oppressed' Julie. It's such a seventies word, 'oppressed': it smacks of blue-stockinged feminism or rantings about the proletariat. But when Clark describes what she saw, 'oppressed' – defined in one dictionary as 'weighed down, kept in subservience, governed harshly or with cruel injustice' – seems a judicious choice. Clark says that Jamie dictated every small detail of dinner parties, for which Julie did all the cooking and he merely served the wine. 'Nearly everything she did was not right. It was always small things. I remember her serving something at dinner before he had given the signal that she could serve it. I guess she would have a moment of recklessness where she thought she could decide something simple like it was all right to put the soup on the table now. The transgression was always so minor. It was never a mortal sin. He would say something that was mild in the words that were used' – she drops her voice to an undertone – '"I *told* you not to do that until we'd had the Riesling!" It was just a bit of a reprimand. But it was *all the time*.

'In conversation Julie would always defer to Jamie. She would always say, regarding her own statement of how something happened, "Is that how it happened, Jamie?" or "Do you think we should?" or "Did you say we would be going before or after?"' Julie did have a streak of steely resolve, Clark believes, but she used to say she used up all the strength she had to defy Jamie over her horse-riding. 'She wouldn't go out on a limb except for something like that.'

WHEN JULIE left him, Jamie barraged Kate Clark with phone calls. Clark was dealing with the aftermath of her own marriage ending and his relentless pursuit wore her down. 'One day, speaking to him, I started to cry. I think he probably said to me, "Are you all right?"' She grins for the first time in our interview. 'Now I was grateful for that brief bit of interest that he showed . . .' And then she begins to laugh, her shoulders shaking with the awful ridiculousness of it. 'But he managed to regroup and then we got back on to him!'

The day after Julie's death, an unknowing Kate Clark rang Jamie's mobile phone and left a message asking him whether he was all right. She had only just rung off when another Scotch College mother rang to tell her that Julie was dead. How did she die? The friend didn't know. Clark's voice is even quieter now and it trembles as she recalls her shock; her brown eyes fill with tears. She was about to leave work and had received the call in a hospital car park. She sat in her car going over the possibilities in her mind. 'And I thought, "It can't be." She wasn't sick. There's no way she killed herself because she was too happy. And it was *deep* happiness. It wasn't about the fellow Laurence, it was about her freedom. I thought, "If she'd been killed in a car accident, people would have said so. He must have done it."

'But then you just think, as I still do, that it's not possible. The horror that I feel at the idea – at the knowledge that someone with whom one was so intimate could kill another person is unimaginable. I cannot bear the thought that anyone could do that simply because he was that angry.' Now she is losing the battle with her tears. Clark says she feels like she has been violated because this happened in her private life, the place others enter by invitation only, the place that should be her 'zone of protection and comfort and happiness'. She feels betrayed and as if Jamie Ramage has robbed her and others of a kind of innocence, 'of the belief that it can't happen in our lives. And I really do mean us, I don't just mean me: her family and the school environment and the boys. Why should my sons have to have this knowledge? It's the greatest wrong, and it's stained everybody. It's a kind of hurt.' You can accept a death, she says. But evil should never have erupted *here*, with someone she has laughed and drunk and driven with; evil should be somewhere else. 'And is evil just the absence of what makes the rest of us sometimes good, sometimes bad, and feeling guilty about not having been good?'

She looks over at me questioningly. We've already discovered that we were both Catholic schoolgirls; we talk about the nuns and how they trained us to examine our consciences every night. Yes, the nuns overburdened us with guilt. Yes, they taught us to worry too much about kindness to others and not enough about kindness to ourselves; they emphasised a form of self-abnegation and humility that if taken literally would be crushing. But yes, we conclude, it's much better to have too much guilt than too little.

Julie Ramage might not agree. Her sense of responsibility towards Jamie and her children cost her dearly.

CLARK WAS once at a dinner party where a male friend who was a psychologist began speculating about what might have happened in Jamie's childhood to make him overly sensitive to being 'excluded' and therefore 'provoked' by Julie. Clark told him tersely that this was simply a case of a man who lost his temper after being given some bad news by his wife. Her friend protested that it was more than bad news. Clark retorted, 'Okay, it was *very* bad news!'

Clark's voice is tight with anger as she tells the story.

'His argument was that the male ego in some way makes the provocation enormous enough to lose it because of Jamie's background of having had a contaminated childhood, of not having those building blocks of conscience and values. I'm absolutely certain my friend wouldn't have seen the reverse [a woman killing a man who rejected her] as being acceptable. It seems to me that a lot of people believe that men do have this entitlement to not receive information that they don't like about being rejected. My friend the psychologist was saying that there was value-added in the male being rejected because our society sets up the male in our community to be more sensitive to it. I don't accept that there is a greater hurt for them. We are all hurt by rejection.

'If rejection does constitute greater provocation for men than for women, it is something in our society that is not desirable. We have got to teach our boys, and our boys have got to learn; and our women and our girls, our daughters, have got to learn the value of their own lives, of their own persons.'

IT TAKES nearly two hours to cross town and wind my way up to where Annette Luckman lives in Hurstbridge, where Julie rode her horse. She is out past Warrandyte, the outer eastern edge of town for most Melburnians. This is a place of winding roads and bellbirds and rosellas, of people who like to make earthenware pottery and blown glass and who are earnest about their recycling. Annette's house is turned away from the road to make the most of the views. It is on a hill that slopes down, with stands of eucalypts on either side, to a green valley of paddocks that blend into rolling hills. It is one of those tranquil outlooks that makes the city person exhale peacefully and ever so briefly wonder about a bush-change. An inconsequential remark from me about the beauty of the view from the window over her kitchen sink leaves her momentarily lost for words. Then she says in a small voice, 'We used to ride around the hills there. He buried her there.' Every time she looks out that window now, the view is stained by memories of Julie's bush grave. Jamie Ramage destroyed so many beautiful things.

In this interview Annette Luckman is often close to crying. Her voice frequently fades and her sentences go unfinished; she leaves thoughts hanging in the air, worried about what happened to Julie and about her part in it. She still agonises over whether she could have said anything to the police or to the court that would have made a difference. She did not see any of the rest of the trial so her field of view is filled by her own small role, and its potential failings loom painfully large for her. She tortures herself about how frustratingly vague her memories have been about Julie's black eye before Christmas, and the way she talked about getting an intervention order. Annette has no memory of thinking again about the black eye after Julie dismissed it as the result of having walked into a door. 'I really didn't want to know. I thought I'd upset her. I thought I'd be prying, especially seeing as she was embarrassed.' She keeps coming back to her inattention, circling it, trying to view it from every angle to understand why she hadn't worried more about Julie at the time. More than an hour into the interview, an explanation finally comes to her. She had had this happen before; she has seen unexplained injuries on two women who were close to her. Both women had made it cuttingly clear that she was not to inquire further. 'They didn't want me to ask about it. It's personal stuff, private. Behind closed doors stuff. And you've got no business being there.' Twice bitten, she was thrice shy; she didn't even try to breach Julie Ramage's defences.

Annette had long known that Julie was unhappy in her life outside horse-riding. Julie even phoned her one morning, speaking in urgent whispers, and said that she was leaving Jamie. Then she phoned back that night saying that she couldn't go; there was Matt, there was Samantha, there were too many things. She sounded, says Annette, utterly heartbroken. The next time she saw Julie, she was going on a business trip to Japan with Jamie and planning to renovate the house. Annette was confused: 'I thought, "What are you doing? Are you being a bit of a drama queen?" I was worried.' But Annette felt she could do nothing about whatever misery existed in the rest of Julie's life; she just tried to counterbalance it by helping make her horse-riding time happy.

Annette has a video with a fragment of filming about Julie that she brings out to show me. It was taken on a rare weekend when Julie had horse-riding friends down at the beach house at Eastern View. Jamie later banned horses at the beach house, Luckman says, because the narrow driveway meant that horse-floats had ended up on his grass. The clip begins with a slow panning of 180 glorious degrees of deep-blue ocean and white sand, the priceless view from the front of the holiday house. Julie is standing in her kitchen near the fridge; she is laughing and running her hands through her hair, relaxed and happy after a ride. It is 16 November 2002, seven and a half months before her death.

Annette heard about the killing from another of Julie's friends. They were at the riding club. An instructor was booked for a clinic, and as each woman arrived for her appointment she was told the news. It meant wave upon wave of grief. The crying would stop and start; women would pull themselves together and then begin again as someone else heard the news for the first time. Some went to visit friends who might otherwise have heard while they were home alone. There were no 'group hugs', says Annette, but they pulled together to look after each other.

THE RIDING club friends wore their uniforms of black and jade and formed a guard of honour for Julie's wake at Montsalvat. They had worked lovingly for hours beforehand stabling Julie's horse, Harley, and their own mounts. They cleaned the equipment and washed the animals, combing their manes and cutting their tails and brushing them until they were proud and glossy. Harley, like the mount of a soldier fallen in battle, was led riderless down a guard of honour to the Great Hall at Montsalvat.

Something dawns upon Annette as she tells of grooming Harley, and the reverent hush in which it was done. She realises that what they did connected with the old, old customs of women; females are traditionally the ones who deal with the tender intimacies of birth and death. 'I just had the thought then – there was so much care; it was like a holy thing to do. It was sort of our way – it was as if we had Julie's body and we were laying her out.'

JULIE'S BEST FRIEND

GILDA PEKIN is the last of Julie's friends to be interviewed. She should have been the first: the best friend is the holder of a woman's secrets and loves her like a sister. But I knew from others that Gilda had spent much of the trial and beyond distraught. My last glimpse of her had been as she was crying in the street after the sentencing. She knew I was keen to talk if she wanted to but I did not want to press it. There had been enough damage done by all this already. Several months after the trial, she contacted me. She was willing to be interviewed after all, she said curtly, in the tone of one agreeing to have a wisdom tooth pulled. Pressed about why, she said her husband had met someone on an international flight who had once worked with me and spoke highly of me. Another one of those strange chance intersections: synchronicity, or maybe just 'the village'.

Gilda lives in a brick house two streets up from where Julie and Jamie lived when they first moved to Balwyn. She opens the front door with her face bare, her wavy hair tousled, and dressed in her customary black pants, top and vest. Later she would tell me: 'Put on 12 kilos since she died. That's my Dunn protective coating.' She takes me through to her front room. Thinking to keep us together for the sake of my tape-machine, I sit down in the corner of a couch that abuts hers so that we are at close right angles to each other. 'That's exactly where Julie used to sit,' she says. 'We'd sit here with a glass of wine and just talk.' Perhaps that familiar positioning eases the way; it is also a bit like the angle of the two parties in a confessional, in which the listener can look away as the speaker exposes her sensitivities. Whatever the reason, Pekin begins to talk, and she continues long after both my tapes have finished. She is by turns funny, self-mocking, furious, guilt-ridden and sad.

Gilda is still struggling to make sense of Julie's death. Like anyone in the first couple of years after a loss she keeps finding, around each bend in the road, something new that must be grieved over. Most recently it was her birthday, about which Julie had always made a fuss. But there are ways in which this is not like any other loss. This was bizarre; this was a *killing*. She says with bewilderment, 'I look back over the whole thing now and say to myself, "How did I get in on the sideline of this? How did I get swept up at all? How has that happened to somebody who thinks they've got a normal life?"'

WHEN GILDA spent six sleepless months nursing her dying father, it was Julie who would drop around every week with casseroles and whip Gilda's toddlers off for plays, bringing them home happy and exhausted enough for sleep. The two women played sport and went shopping together and looked after each other's children to the point where, early on, Gilda began feeling irritated with Julie. 'She was always there, she was always asking me to come over, always wanting to go out together. It was like she couldn't do anything without me. It wasn't until I realised she was a twin that I thought, "I understand that." She had to be very close. She had to be *amazingly* close.

'Julie was like my sister. We discussed all sorts of things, but there was this one part where we wouldn't go, which was the state of her marriage. We would talk about sex, we would talk about episiotomies, we'd talk about kids in nappies and every manner of thing about their development, but there was a bit there that you just didn't quite go to. And it was about the emotional content of the relationship with Jamie.'

Gilda only began to glimpse the truth of that in 1997, the year she discovered Julie was having a relationship with a father at the primary school. 'The affair was about being appreciated, and comfort, security. He was attractive and very wealthy, and attractive in a non-physical sense because he was English.' Julie was deeply attached to the man but always thought that he would not want her because he was professionally very successful and she felt she wasn't able to 'cut it' in his environment. Julie also wasn't ready to leave Jamie. At this stage they used to row a lot but never in public.

Later, there was another man Julie met while out with Jane. She told Gilda only that she had coffee with him a few times. After him came another local man who was married. 'They had a good relationship [afterwards]. He has a good marriage and would never leave his wife and she knew that and so she broke it off with him. He was very nice. He went to the funeral. He cried.'

Julie had been seeing 'Adam' for several months before she told Gilda about him. 'I suppose she got the impression that I didn't think that what she was doing was a fair thing, to herself or to Jamie. And it certainly wasn't fair to the kids. Look, I understood why she was doing it, but I didn't like it.' Gilda never told her to leave Jamie, but she told her often that she should make a decision about whether to stay in or leave her marriage. 'I told Julie that she was dancing with the devil many times, and we both knew what that really meant given Jamie's history of violence.' Gilda knew that the affairs were partly about Julie's anger: 'It was like a war, and Jamie had to be punished for treating her the way he did. So she would look for someone to pamper her.' When Gilda remonstrated with her, Julie would say, 'I know I'm playing with fire but he's not going to control every little thing that I do.'

Gilda was torn because she also understood why Julie didn't leave. She believes Julie wanted to reassure herself that there would be someone else out there for her; it was as if she doubted her own attractiveness. Julie was also terrified of Jamie's reaction. 'She was always very fearful about leaving.' Gilda's face closes and her voice becomes earnest. She can't impress this upon me enough. 'She would say, "*If he catches me, he will kill me*"; before, during, after leaving. She told me that as early as '97. She meant it. I can tell you categorically that *she meant it*. She would say, about her injuries, "I don't know how I did this", or "I slipped taking the washing basket out" or "I walked into a cupboard", and you'd think, "There's no sincerity there; I can't believe that." But she had an *absolute belief* that when she left he would kill her if he found out that she had been with another man.'

I think of Dunn's claims that no one had seen or heard of violence from Jamie towards Julie for years; of his argument that Julie exaggerated the situation in order to justify her own infidelities. I ask Gilda, 'Do you think Julie ever embroidered stories?'

'I think she was selective about what she owned up to, to various people. I don't think she embroidered at all.'

Gilda Pekin does not believe there is a snowflake's chance in hell that Julie wound Jamie up on that last day. Firstly, she says, the tone of the conversation itself does not ring true to her. In all her years of intimacy with Julie, in all their hours of girl talk, she never heard her use the word 'wanker'. Julie never used vulgar language at all, and Gilda cannot imagine her going even further to make the claimed 'wank-wank' gesture. 'She was a *lady*!' And she was always so careful what she said to Jamie. 'After I told her that I'd told Jamie that she'd met Laurence, she was furious. "Gilda, don't you tell him anything! It's none of his business!" Oh God, she was so worried. I said, "I'm so sorry, Julie."'

And here is the essence of the Ramage tragedy for those who were swept up in it like Dorothy in the tornado: while Gilda feels guilty for having said too much, she also feels guilty for having not said enough. The possibilities for self-flagellation offered by the 'if onlys' of this maelstrom of a marriage are endless. It's like the random complexity of chaos theory: the action or inaction of so many people at so many moments might have changed the course of events. Or – given the one brooding constant of Jamie's obsessiveness – they might not.

JAMIE CAME to see Gilda a week before Julie died. Gilda was ill with bronchitis. She had been unable to take time off work and come Saturday morning was dropping the kids off at sport and trying to get herself to medical appointments. 'And he kept ringing me. He must have rung me twenty times. Now, I keep the phone on no matter what I'm doing because of the kids, so I kept hanging up on him. Dunn got shitty with me in the committal hearing over that; "You hung up on him, didn't you?" Well, yes, "I'm trying to go to the doctor, I'm trying to get an X-ray, will you *go away* . . . !"' Gilda promised to have coffee with him some time but they made no specific arrangement.

Then Jamie arrived unannounced at Gilda's house at 8.30 the following night. Gilda felt like death and was reluctant to see him. 'What had he ever done for me but be perfectly obnoxious?' Jamie sat in the centre seat of her kitchen bench and leaned over Gilda to fire off his questions: What would get Julie back? Was there anyone else? Had there ever been anyone else? 'He was aggressively, intimidatingly insistent. It was horrible, and I was terrified of him. I got up and moved around to the other side of the bench. He was frustrated to the point of immense anger. She was not behaving as he expected her to. He couldn't control what she did. And it was just something he couldn't deal with. He was right on the edge.

'And he bullied me until I said, "Look, Jamie, if there'd ever been anybody I would know." That's all I said.' She chuckles, the mouse whose cleverness got her out from under the foot of the elephant. 'What could I do? If I knew, obviously I'd helped her and he'd punch my eyes out. So I wouldn't tell him about anybody else. And what difference would it make anyway?'

But her amusement at his expense doesn't last long. It doesn't survive my putting to her that others have wondered whether it might have been better just to tell Jamie that it was all over because he was so desperate to turn his anxiety into action. She sags a little in the couch.

'That's one of the things that I regret entirely, as a personal failure, that I didn't sit there in a calm, controlled manner and tell him. Because I knew she wasn't going back.'

'Do you think it would have made a difference?'

She looks back at me grimly. 'He wouldn't have killed her right then and there on the spot, would he?'

It's not the only 'failure' she tortures herself with. 'Oh God, I sat here the day she was killed and I looked at my computer and my emails and I tried to ring her several times. I knew that she was going to have lunch with him, and I just should have done something. I should have warned her more. I told her never to see him alone.'

AS A lawyer, Pekin knew about the defence of provocation and how it played out in domestic killings. 'Every bitch who leaves deserves it, don't they?' She laughs bleakly. 'If you're a defence lawyer who wants to portray the poor fellow as a victim, that's what you have to honestly believe. I've seen them. And that means you must annihilate the real victim by saying that she and her friends are all tarred with the same brush. And the women are bullied until they give in.'

Gilda Pekin doesn't believe in therapy. She says she's the kind of person who would never have given a cent to a psychiatrist. But she has now been told she has a textbook case of post-traumatic stress syndrome. She has panic attacks over everyday experiences, such as the speed and motion of a bus ride. She bursts into tears over little things. And she often wakes at three or four in the morning with bad dreams.

Sometimes her dreams are happy ones of Julie: they laugh together over inane little jokes the way they used to. But she also dreams of Jamie. In one nightmare he is incredibly thin and walking along a narrow, winding corridor inside a prison. 'He is wearing shorts and just an ordinary T-shirt. And you can see his spindly legs and all of a sudden he just falls flat on his face. And then I wake up. I pity him. I feel sorry for such a forlorn, miserable individual. There's something wrong with the chemistry of his brain. He is so cold, so unable to appreciate what he has done, so lacking as a person.'

While this dream vanquishes her nemesis, another tells her that she is still struggling to defeat it. 'I'm swimming around this whale to get to a boat. I keep swimming and swimming and swimming. And I know that any second the whale's mouth is going to rise up and get me, and it does.'

She laughs again. It seems a strange moment for a laugh, unless you take Freud's view that we laugh at that which we fear. She says quietly, 'I never make it to the safe place.'

TEN MONTHS after that interview, the nightmares have nearly stopped. Gilda says she is no longer feeling so angry and so brutalised. 'You can't carry it forever. It's destructive and it changes nothing.' She has lost half of her Dunn protective coating and says she is looking forward to the future. And to opportunities to making a difference to the legal system.

JULIE'S SISTER

WHEN I first meet Jane Ashton, I find it eerie looking into her blue-green eyes and listening to her voice. What she is saying washes over me because I am so distracted by the possibility of seeing Julie in her. Is this what Julie looked like? Sounded like? Laughed at? Said? I can see in the back of her eyes that she is wondering what is happening in the back of mine, and I try to shake it off. I remind myself that they each had a separate consciousness, and of the ways their friends had described them as different: Julie was softer, more refined; Jane blunter and more 'out there'. It must be the lifelong struggle of the identical twin, balancing the urge to merge with the need for a separate identity. That struggle is over now for Jane. She faces a different task: learning to live as a twinless twin.

I meet Jane first at Christine Howgate's home. The three of us sit in a book-lined study overlooking a kidney-shaped pool. Ashton's trim figure is wrapped in a soft brown jacket, trousers and boots. Christine has made us a lunch of chicken and mayonnaise sandwiches and large glasses of chardonnay. Ashton could do with the fortifying. Her voice is flat and low, and she often pauses for little sighs or intakes of breath as if she's slogging up a hard slope. Although she finds it hard to talk about Julie's death and Jamie's trial, she persists with it. She will ring me several times during and after the court case, and we meet again for a quick lunch the day the jury goes out. Though forthright in some ways, in others she keeps her personal shields up; she rarely touches on the devastation this has wreaked on her inner world. But from early on it is clear that Ashton has a sharp mind, a black sense of humour with a matching wicked-witch cackle – and a long-standing hatred of Jamie Ramage, the man she feels took her sister from her long before he killed her. 'I'm so angry that he had her for such a long time and she had only six weeks of freedom.'

Jane believes that Julie truly loved Jamie up until ten years before her death. 'I think she stopped loving him when he broke her nose.' Julie left when she realised he was never going to follow through on his promises to change. 'It wasn't a shock to him when she left. She had tried to leave numerous times before. He knew his behaviour had contributed to that.' Jane believes Jamie sought everyone's advice during the separation not because he truly wanted to work on himself but as a manipulative strategy to win others to his cause. 'Every time someone that he thought was important suggested something to him, whether it was Kate Clark or Dr Moodie, he went off and did it. He didn't go off and do it because it would make him a better person. He thought that if he could impress other people, they would intercede on his behalf and tell Julie. She knew he was never going to change. He'd promised to change in the past. And she'd given it her best shot, 23 years.'

For all the distance created by the seesawing relationship with Julie, Jane must have loved her dearly. She always took her in. When Julie finally left, it was Jane and the Garretts who helped her pack her belongings and set up her new home. It was Jane who was targeted most fiercely by Dunn, who insinuated at the trial that her introduction of Laurence to Julie had set the dominoes falling.

Jane will have none of it. The trial had made so many people feel guilty because Dunn 'continually blamed myself, Gilda Pekin, Laurence Webb, anyone who didn't tell this man the truth, as if we were in some sort of Machiavellian conspiracy, and put the blame for her death on to us. People came away feeling really bad – and yet, you have to remember that it's no one's fault but Jamie's. He did this to her. He was always going to get her.'

She is convinced that Jamie would never have let Julie go. 'If I'd have said, "She's not coming back, she hates your guts and she finds sex with you repulsive" – which she did – he'd have left the house and gone straight round to her and had a big argument. It wouldn't have mattered what anybody would have done. This man wanted her back in the marriage. In the end the only way he could control her was physically. He'd been through all his usual tactics and she wasn't coming back.'

But Jane does have regrets. 'For me and for some of her friends, there are huge questions about "Could I have done anything? Could I have stopped it?" My father was terribly distraught because his whole life he has protected us girls. He's a very masculine man. I should have known – people should be aware, Julie wasn't aware – that leaving was the most dangerous time. All I needed to do was go to the Web, look up "domestic violence" and look up "leaving", and we'd have been aware in about 30 seconds how dangerous it was.' Jane has done plenty of Web research since. She talks about an American helpline that has led her to believe that letting Jamie down gently was the wrong approach: 'What she should have said to all of us was, "Don't converse with him." She should have had a restraining order to stop him talking to her friends and to her because, really, what he was doing was stalking us too.'

Jane is still furious at the way the family and friends were treated by the court system, particularly at the committal, where witnesses felt they were not prepared for the ordeal and felt like cannon fodder. Their grief and rage and helplessness turned in on themselves: Jane Ashton developed stomach trouble, her father got gallstones and her mother had a nervous collapse. Even now, says Jane, 'I don't talk to my mum about it. She's too fragile.'

Jane Ashton is holding the banner high. She is speaking at rotary clubs and schools about how men and women can respect each other. That is the outward Jane.

The inward Jane is still trying to imagine life without the sister with whom she was conceived. It has practical implications: 'Suddenly, I'm an only child, and there's pressure not to fall off my horse or get run over or die of lung cancer. I'm now "it" with Mum and Dad. When they're sick I'll look after them; I'm going to have to be there for them. And in the past Julie and I have always shared that responsibility.' She had to ring up the medical researchers doing a twin study and ask to have herself and Julie taken off the database. She's been in touch with a group for twins who have lost their other half. 'Being a twin, you always expect that you'll grow into two little old ladies, that you're not going to be on your own but pottering around together. It's been really strange. I just want to ring and talk to her, call her.'

WEEKS LATER, as I am about to file my feature on the trial for *The Age*, Jane and I talk on the phone to check some details for photo captions. The images from the family album start her on a trail of memories. 'We had pony club. Went on holidays to France. Loved to sail together. She was five minutes older than me; she was always confident. The first day of school, she was the one looking after me. She always knew what to do. Julie was really cool and calm. It's hard on my own.'

Her favourite photograph, she says wistfully, is of the two of them as little girls standing in a park, Julie's small arms wrapped around Jane. 'I still want her back. When I dream of her, she won't age, and I will.'

JAIL

HER MAJESTY'S Prison Barwon, where Jamie Ramage now lives, is Victoria's only maximum-security facility. It is a country jail and to get there from town you must take the Geelong Freeway. The first hour of the trip is a run that Jamie and Julie would have made often in a car loaded with children and holiday clobber on their way to the beach house. The freeway unrolls through drearily flat country on the now-gentrifying western side of town, where Melbourne used to dump its poor and its poisons. The signs to Barwon start at the highway itself and appear at every turn of an obscure country road for 15 minutes, nudging the uncertain newcomer past the clumps of unexpectedly large new houses surrounded by paddocks; past the wildlife sanctuary where flocks of grey wallabies graze in peace, indifferent to the passing traffic; and past the last lone house, 2 kilometres from the prison, which offers bags of manure for sale.

The first impression of Barwon is of blankness: large, dominating blankness. The 38-acre prison compound sits back from the road at the top of a low hill. Pale green roofs can be glimpsed above its all-encompassing cream walls, which rise 8 metres above the ground and run for 5 metres below it. Tall spikes soar into the sky at regular intervals around the perimeter. Their floodlights stay on all night and can be seen from as far away as the nearest regional city, Geelong. The entrance to the driveway is flanked by multilingual signs warning that no drugs, alcohol or weapons are permitted, and the brisk guards who greet visitors do their best to ensure the rules are obeyed. Visitors must be approved by Corrections Victoria, and on arrival submit to security scans of themselves and their belongings. Pockets must be turned out and trouser legs raised above the socks. Mobile phones and keys must be put in lockers. Signs warn that scantily clad women will not be admitted – a concession to the feelings of men who are locked away for years without the pleasures of close feminine contact. A poster on the wall at reception is headlined 'Personal Distress' and asks visitors to contact staff if they think a prisoner is deeply upset. Other signs warn that only $145 in total can be left for each prisoner each month and specify the visiting hours – contact and non-contact – for prisoners in different units. Like school life, jail life is a tightly spun web of rules. Here, though, a note from mother carries no sway. There is no 'out' – at least, no desirable out. Barwon has had more than one murder in its 15 years of existence, but no one has ever escaped from it. The best a prisoner can hope for is that good behaviour will earn him a move to a medium-security jail followed eventually by a low-security jail.

A new prisoner arrives on a Tuesday or a Thursday, Barwon's 'reception' days. He will be met by a prisoner who is part of the jail's peer-education network and given a cup of coffee and a rundown on how the place works. Barwon holds 460 serious offenders and was the first Victorian prison to be designed for 'unit management', where prisoners are managed in smaller groups in environments that are more similar to the world outside. It's safer for both inmates and staff, who know the prisoners better and so find it easier to detect problems and defuse situations as they arise. Acacia has the gangland killers, Grevillea and Hoya the sexual offenders and prisoners who need protection for other reasons, and Eucalypt is the 'honour unit' for men at the heavy end of the criminal market

– murderers, rapists, armed robbers – who have been free of any violence or drugs since they have been in prison. Banksia is the jail within the jail, for prisoners who have lost privileges for offences such as assault or drug use. Cassia is one of several mainstream units and it acts as the reception unit for all newcomers. Those who visit inmates from the outside world may come no further into the jail than the visitors centre outside the perimeter wall, where prisoners and their families can sit together for a sterile hour or two at Laminex tables with plastic chairs. They may hug and kiss briefly, and fathers are permitted to hold children on their knees, but time is limited and there is no privacy.

To the stranger walking into the compound itself for the first time, Barwon does not look like a prison. It seems more like an industrial complex of buildings separated by cyclone fencing. Razor wire has been kept to a minimum. The three mainstream units open on to a wide grassed area where the men of those units can mingle with each other (but they may not enter any unit except their own). This garden seems curiously shadeless and bare of trees, but perhaps in a prison even the garden must be free of hanging points. Elsewhere prisoners must carry their identity cards and a permission slip to be allowed through guards' security-latticed checkpoints, but in this area they can walk about freely in their bottle-green tracksuits. It could just as easily be a workplace as a jail.

That impression shatters at the entrance to any residential unit. First comes the smell: close, stuffy, a mild but undeniable male locker-room blend of sweat and dunnies. A glassed-in guards' station staffed by men and women in navy uniforms is at the front door. To their right is the breakfast area, a bare space with a few tables and chairs and a stainless-steel kitchenette along one wall. Directly in front of the guards' station is what can only be called a cell-block: one set of stairs with metal railings goes up and another goes down, and each leads to a small corridor closely lined with cell doors. And they are cells, not rooms, the length of three steps in one direction and four steps in another. A small white toilet and hand-basin sit just inside each cell door, alongside a cramped shower space barely wide enough for a person to stand in. A tall man would be able to touch the ceiling with his hands. A single bed is against one wall, a curved ledge along another, and a small cupboard with four open shelves holds the prisoner's uniform. The minimal storage spaces are designed to make the guards' regular searches of prisoners' belongings easier. A man is locked in here at 5 pm every night for fifteen hours. If he has lost privileges for committing an offence in prison, he will be locked up earlier, without a TV. Grim as that prospect might sound, some of the old hands actually want to be in their cells after dinner. They will ask the guards to 'Lock me up, boss.' For them, the clanging of the door means another day over and another day closer to release. For others, it is a bitter reminder of their loss of liberty; when the door closes, a prisoner is by himself, and his family is far away on the other side of the wall.

A prisoner must work: in the garden, in one of the three metalwork or woodwork factories, in the kitchen or the laundry. He is paid between $6.05 and $8.25 a day but he is not permitted to be reckless with his income: 20 per cent of it must be saved on his behalf. His day formally begins at 7.45 am when the trap window on the locked door of his cell is flipped open and a guard peers in to ensure he is present and that he has not hanged or slashed himself. Once the 'trap muster' is pronounced correct, he will be released to make his own breakfast of cereal and toast in the unit's mini-kitchen. Prison life is a long series of great and small variations from normality; there is no Vegemite in the kitchenette because it contains active yeast and can be turned into home brew. Between 8.30 and 9 am he will go to work or to any program he is attending, such as anger management, alternatives to violence or parenting skills. Lunch is sent around to the units at 11.30 am from the prison's central kitchen. It will be hot food one day – pie and chips, perhaps – and cold sandwiches the next. Dinner is at the institutional hour of 4 pm. Dishes include macaroni cheese, stuffed zucchini or vegie burgers, with desserts such as peppermint slice and rice custard. There is a roast every week and steak once a month. Prisoners are fed on $5 a day. That's one of the reasons Barwon converted to longlife milk, despite the inmates' grumbles; it's cheaper. Jail is no place for the gourmand.

There is a little room to move at Barwon: footy and soccer on the oval at weekends, a cement path for walking or running, and small swimming pools that double as emergency water supplies in this high-fire-risk area. There is snooker and billiards, and each unit has a tiny room with weights and a punching bag rather vaingloriously known as a 'gym'. The smell of sweat suggests it is well-used. But a prisoner is never allowed to forget that he is not free. Before and after every contact visit from friends or family, he is strip-searched for drugs. He is taken into a cubicle where he must remove all his clothes so that a guard can run his hands over them. He must stand while one guard watches and another guard runs fingers through his hair, peers into his open mouth and checks under his armpits. He must wiggle his toes to prove there is nothing held between them. He must lift up his now-misnamed 'privates' for inspection. Then he must turn, bend over, and part the cheeks of his buttocks.

There are people who believe that prison life is not punitive enough. They suffer from a failure of imagination.

FOR THE vengefully minded, there would be a sweet aptness to Jamie Ramage's current fate. So much of his life now is controlled the way he tried to control Julie. He must bow to a routine that is imposed upon him; he must jump to other people's orders. With strip-searches, he has lost sovereignty over his body – to a smaller degree than she had, but in a way that nevertheless must be experienced as a ritual humiliation. Will it lead to a new Jamie? Or will it just reinforce his existing world view, in which one is either controlled by someone else, or is the person doing the controlling?

Since his arrest he has told many people that he is remorseful, and some of them believe him. Kate Clark is not one of them. She received a letter from him in which he talked about conditions in prison and his regret for what he had done. She thought he sounded apologetic over something inconsequential, like scratching the Jag or dropping a piece of Dresden china. She sent him a postcard in return. 'It didn't have the intimacy of a letter; more like "We acknowledge receipt of your deposit" or something. And I just said, "In the circumstances I can't possibly write to you. But be assured I will do anything, anything at all, for Matt and Samantha."'

It doesn't sound like Jamie confided in family about his feelings. One of his brothers told police that in the period after his arrest, Jamie did not speak to him of what he had done but rang him nearly every day to talk about Matthew, business arrangements, paying bills and Julie's will. Jane Ashton does not believe he can change and is contemptuous of what she has heard about his plans for prison life. 'I think the best thing people can do is totally ostracise him. I think that's the only time he will even consider what he's done is wrong. He's boasting about being promoted and working within the prison system and mentoring young offenders and he's going to be a model prisoner. He's clever.'

But his solicitor, Steve Pica, still maintains that Jamie does have genuine regret over Julie. 'What a lot of people do not appreciate about James Ramage is that he is truly remorseful for having taken away the life of the woman he loved. On numerous occasions, from beginning to end, he displayed what I would describe as true remorse for having killed his wife. He did not bathe in self-pity and was more preoccupied with the harm that he had caused to his children, Julie's family and friends. During the course of the months leading up to his trial, he continually told me, ". . . If what I have done is murder, then I will plead guilty to murder."'

Pica declined to release the psychological assessments of Jamie that were tendered at the plea hearing, but he did send me a bundle of testimonials by people who had dealt with Jamie in prison. Most came from people who had spoken to him at the first jail he was assigned to, the Melbourne Assessment Prison. Philip Newman, the Anglican archdeacon who officiated at Julie's funeral, visited Jamie a dozen or so times. Newman wrote, 'He talked about how he could not understand how he could have done it (emotionally and intellectually, not physically). He was frightened of himself, saying that it had felt as if it was someone else killing Julie, and he was almost an observer. He latched on to a remark from Matt that he had to use the time in jail to change, and he talked about what that might mean, and how he might do that . . .'

But his preoccupation with his crime began to fade, according to Newman: 'Over the weeks and months he spoke less about his wife and what he had done and more about ways he could cope and of his family, and how he might relate to them and support them – and of how proud he was of them, especially, of course, Matt following his VCE results . . . Realising his tendency to control, which he frequently referred to, he talked of how he might relate to his children in a way that was encouraging and affirming of them and not controlling.'

Major Stanley Caple, formerly the Salvation Army chaplain at the Melbourne Assessment Prison, wrote that Jamie was often tearful in the early days after his arrest. 'In the privacy of his protection unit cell, he began to see himself in a new light, as it were. No business pressures to intrude upon his reflections. No external demands to impose time-frames for business commitments. He was alone with his "naked self". I saw a man who had felt the full waves of intense remorse as the enormity of his act of irrational passion bore full weight upon his conscious mind. Nowhere to hide.' John Cronin, family relationships counsellor at the prison, also often saw Jamie distraught: 'On a regular basis counselling sessions have stopped due to James' difficulty in dealing with emotions, crying openly and talking about his overwhelming loss and regret for what happened. James was also seeking support to help him sleep and to try to repress the memory of the incident.'

Jamie shortly after the killing sounds the same as Jamie shortly before it: tearful, sleepless, clutching for any help available and still clinging to the fantasy that he and Julie could have saved their marriage. Sister Mary O'Shannassy, the Catholic chaplain who saw Jamie at both the Melbourne Assessment Prison and his next home before Barwon, Port Phillip Prison, wrote that Jamie was still confused about his relationship with Julie and what he believed a future together for them might have been. While he had found the committal hearing painful, other people's evidence helped him to understand more about Julie's need to separate. He also told O'Shannassy that his training as a prisoner listener at Port Phillip Prison had helped him gain a better understanding of himself and others.

And this leads to the strangest of the testimonials about Jamie Ramage's life in prison that were handed up to Justice Osborn. It comes from an inmate. It is addressed to Steve Pica and signed 'warm regards' by the prisoner, who must remain anonymous here. He said that Jamie, as a prison 'listener', had given him many hours of time 'to help me in not only adjusting to prison life but also coming to terms with the core issues behind my own incarnation. He has done this for many inmates and has become one of the most respected prison listeners in the program'.

The prisoner told of hitting rock bottom when he received a much higher sentence than his lawyer had led him to expect. 'Things just became very confusing, and my field of possibilities seemed very narrow. James had noticed my behaviour and stayed in touch daily. However, I reached a point where I stopped seeing options clearly and I tried to commit suicide by hanging myself. As the English poet Sylvia Plath wrote before committing suicide, "the only way out of the box is out". I wanted to try a dry run first, which I did, and James unexpectedly came into my cell just as I was writing my suicide farewell note for the real thing.

'He immediately noticed I was in a very detached state and asked what was going on. Had it been anyone else I would have said "nothing", but since I knew how sincere a person he is, I confided in him what was about to happen and the reasons why. James spent the next one hour talking with me about all the options I forgot to consider, and how many loved ones would be severally [sic] affected. After a short time I saw how limited and narrow my field of vision had become and that there were many options available, such as appeals. James then helped me relate my inner pain back to my unique journey of healing. He helped me see the big picture in clear terms of this prison experience being one of the many chapters of my life experience and certainly not the last one.

'After our discussion I went to the hospital and was there for three days under observation. During that time James visited me several times and recommended that I be returned to my unit as being with friends was the best thing for me at that time. I can sincerely say that if it wasn't for James's deep interest and real concern for me there is a very strong chance I would not be alive writing this letter today.'

What is to be made of this? It might be something the inmate and Jamie cooked up together. 'My unique journey of healing', 'the core issues of my own incarnation' – are these phrases piss-takes, or an ardent mimicking of psychobabble? Either way, it sounds as if Jamie Ramage can now talk the talk. Maybe he has sniffed the wind, recognised which way it is blowing in his new world and set himself on a new career trajectory, a new social ladder to climb.

Or maybe he has taken seriously Rob Moodie's advice to look to his spiritual side and to see how he can give back to the community. Maybe the tale is utterly true in every detail, and both Jamie's and the prisoner's responses are heartfelt and sincere.

If that is so, in the great karmic balance, would the saving of this life compensate for the life that he took?

VICTORIA FORBIDS Jamie Stuart Ramage to be interviewed by the media, even if he wanted to be. The only words that come directly from him on his new life are in a letter he wrote to his old friends, Nick and Jeanette Farley, about six weeks after Julie's death. His letter is written in a neat schoolboy hand.

Dear Nick and Jeanette,

Matt passed on that you wanted to get in contact by letter. Thank you for your concern for my well-being.
    I make no excuses. I regret what I have done and I wish I could turn back the clock. Considering everything I am amazed how

kind and thoughtful people have been. I do not deserve it. I have hurt so many people.

I also appreciate what everyone has done for Matt and Sam. I am very proud of them both and know they will be strong. I really want them to stick together.

Well life has changed a great deal for me. Apart from dealing with what I have done I also have to deal with living in here. The violence etc I think is a little exaggerated. As long as you stay away from the troublemakers it seems to be OK. A little like the playground. There's actually some quite interesting characters in here. Apart from a job in the office I'm also talking to some of the young guys, helping where I can. Nick and Jeanette as good friends I'm sorry I've let you down. I fully understand if you don't want to write back. In here (and I don't meant to trivialise it) little things became so important and very quickly you learn what is important in life. Good friends is one of those things. I will miss our friendship.

I will finish now as at the moment things also get me down easily. I'll write more another time.

He signed his name with a vigorous old-fashioned capital J; the descending loop on it was as long as the rest of his signature was wide. And he signed using his childhood name, the one Julie and his family knew him by, not the more adult name he adopted for himself in mid-life.

'Love to all,
Jamie.'

EPITAPHS

JAMIE RAMAGE has a lot of time to meditate upon his sins. There will be more dark nights of the soul in prison, hemmed in by four small walls and his own melancholy thoughts. The passing of time itself might do something to soften him. But when his crime was fresh and the hurt to others still raw, it looked as if what Jamie Ramage clung to for comfort was the tattered remnants of his family's formerly perfect public face.

The modern funeral is silent about death. It focuses on life. 'A celebration of the life of Julie Anne Ramage' was held at St John the Evangelist Anglican Church in Clendon Road, Toorak on Thursday 31 July 2003. St John's – Jamie's choice – is a sweet little church that was created with much love and not a little money. It was built by Toorak's wealthy establishment families because they did not want to travel down the road to the nearby Christ Church South Yarra. St John's is like a mini cathedral, its interior space at once majestic and intimate. The walls are bluestone, and it has a high-ceilinged central nave with ceiling joists crisscrossed like the keel of a ship, symbolising the ark. But it is in the lovingly detailed ornamental work of long-ago artisans that its real beauty lies. The oak pews are carved with Australian flora and fauna – gumnuts, bottlebrushes, owls and kingfishers. The side walls are lined with hand-painted tiles telling stories of the spread of Christianity: Joseph of Arimathea converting the Britons; the first church in Australia, humble and wooden, surrounded by a crowd of bonneted women.

St John's greatest pride is its stained-glass windows. Over the altar, four panels depicting Christ's nativity, his baptism by St John, his crucifixion and resurrection are a glory of rich blues and golds and magentas. On the walk back down the aisle you see sunlight radiating through an equally breathtaking rose window over the front entrance. St John's charm and position make it a favoured venue for society weddings. With its mix of Englishness and Australianisms, it is a nicely symbolic church for the funeral of an English migrant who had made her life here. But perhaps it was other associations that made it Jamie's choice: St John's has long had links with Melbourne's richest families, such as the Coles and the Baillieus, and many of the faces of characters in its tile-paintings are establishment notables of their times – bishops, mayors and wealthy benefactors. The day of Julie's funeral it was filled with establishment colours: rows of private schoolchildren in their blazers. To the very end, Julie Ramage's life in Australia was interwoven with social ambitions. To the very end, Jamie Ramage kept up appearances.

Jamie did not attend the funeral – 'He would have been lynched,' says Jane Ashton tightly – but his mother and his brothers came. Matthew laid a single red rose on the coffin on behalf of his father.

Julie's horse-riding friend from Hurstbridge, Annette Luckman, felt bewildered by the setting. She was 'off with the fairies' the day of the funeral, lost in her sadness and shock, but one thing she does recall is her surprise. 'The fact that it was in Toorak; I don't know why we were there. And that wasn't the Julie I knew. She told me she wasn't religious. I have a very clear recollection of her saying you're only here for a short time so make it a good time. "You've got to make the most of your life while you're here because there's nothing afterwards."'

The funeral was the first time that all the different people in Julie's compartmentalised life connected with each other. Her family finally met her friends from Balwyn; her friends from Balwyn met her horse-riding mates. There were several eulogies during the service. Jane spoke about how she and Julie had done everything as a pair when they were girls, including vowing that they would never again do cross-country racing. Gilda Pekin had been phoned the night before and asked to speak. She was up until 2 am struggling to work out what to say – and what not to say. 'I didn't know what to say about Jamie so I ignored him entirely. I couldn't talk about Julie as a wife and a partner, so I talked about her as a friend and a mum.'

The Julie whom Gilda remembered bore no resemblance to the portrait of Julie Ramage that would later be painted in court. Pekin, sad and determined, stood in the white stone pulpit and told the sea of faces about her friend. 'She was always there. Julie was there when I needed help nursing my dad. She took all four children to the park regularly so I could rest. Call it Julie's caring recipe. Remember fruit duty, the Easter Bonnet parades? Julie was always there with style and a smile. Remember the Deepdene Primary fete? Jules was there, capable and a team player with sweets, or running the hot food . . . Remember VicKick and the basketball at Kew High School? Julie was there with the same style and smile, proud of her kids. Julie was inclusive and generous.'

Most of the funeral music was classically subdued: Bach and Mozart, hymns such as *Jerusalem*. It was Julie's favourite music that was the most poignant. As her casket was wheeled out of the church, the air filled with the funky Motown beat of Diana Ross's *You Can't Hurry Love*. Her children chose it because it had been one of Julie's favourite songs.

That is not what people remember most clearly about this funeral. When talking to her friends, what comes up time after time is the eulogy delivered by Julie's son, Matthew.

The grieving boy told the congregation that his mother was 'an awesome lady'. So many people loved her and loved her company, and she was always happy, always laughing and smiling. She loved her children very much and was proud of everything they did. He said she was a great mother and wife to a great family – a family he would not swap for anything.

Matthew said there was a song his mother used to sing to him and Samantha. The song itself, *Summertime* from Porgy and Bess, was played later in the service when candles were lit in Julie's memory. But during his eulogy Matthew read two verses to the people who had come to mourn for this woman killed by her husband; for this woman who died trying to escape the prison of her marriage.

Summertime, and the livin' is easy
Fish are jumpin' and the cotton is high
Your Daddy's rich and your Momma's good looking
So hush little baby, don't you cry

One of these mornings you're gonna rise up singing
You'll spread your wings and you'll take to the sky
But till that morning, there ain't nothing can harm you
With Daddy and Mommy standing by

If only.

POSTSCRIPT

WHEN I talk to readers of this book, there are two questions they always ask. How are the Ramage children now? And how is Jamie Ramage coping with jail?

Matthew and Samantha have got on with their lives. The year after their mother's death was very difficult and their initial attempts to live together independently did not work out. It was hard to manage because Matthew was too young to drive. Matthew became a boarder at school while he finished Year 12 and Samantha moved in with a family from her school. Both finished Year 12 successfully and got into university courses. They bought a small house and moved in together.

That is as much as I am willing to say about what happened to the children after their public role in their father's trial ended. They have done nothing wrong, and should be allowed to live the rest of their lives shielded by the normal privacy the rest of us take for granted.

As for Jamie Ramage; after his conviction, Jane Ashton had predicted he would ingratiate himself with the authorities and work his way into the jail's most prestigious job. According to a former prisoner who did time with him, that is exactly what has happened. In one of those quirks of coincidence, I came to know the ex-prisoner through a colleague – the former inmate has a friend who is a journalist with me at *The Age* newspaper.

The man does not wish to be named, but is happy to be quoted. He was convicted of non-violent offences, and recently released from medium-security Loddon prison near the rural Victorian town of Castlemaine.

Here is an edited version of the man's account:

I first met James Ramage at Port Phillip jail in 2004. We were both on remand together. We both went to court at the same time. I spent a fair bit of time with him. Everybody was under pressure then, and he was not feeling very happy about things on account of *The Age* coverage of his case. He did some time at Barwon in maximum security. In 2006 he came to Loddon.

A whole lot of wife-killers were brought from Barwon at the same time, about 10 of them. There was a unit of 70 people and 12 or 14 were wife-killers. They're not very well-liked in jail. People think it's cowardly. And it's a very avoidable thing. You can always walk away; you can turn on your heel and leave the room. Wife-killers are almost regarded with the same odium as sex offenders; not quite, but almost. There's this hierarchy of offenders and if you've knocked your missus, you're a low-life.

Loddon is a medium-security jail. It's open within the walls and has about 300 prisoners. It was built for about 250, so they're packed in. About half are in shared rooms but longer-term prisoners and violent prisoners get a single cell. James was always in a single cell. He was given priority because he had already done time at Barwon.

I was doing art work for the screen-printing business and he was put in to work with me. I didn't want that to happen, because I wasn't terribly keen on him. The first day he was there, I heard him say twice to people that he thought he had been hard done by in his sentencing and it was too long a sentence for what he had done.

He's a very English guy. He's got control issues. He didn't want to work in screen-printing because it would be work-work: 'I am a businessman and I am used to running my own business'. Doing work and having to do regular hours was beneath his dignity. He has a private-school kind of sense of entitlement – he went to a school where they played rugby, so I think he thought he was upper class. He does mix a bit, but I found his manner highly off-putting.

His mum used to bring him out books and encouraged him to read fiction. He used to read *The Financial Review* and business papers. He was in a cell two doors away from me. That's how we came to exchange books and stuff.

Nobody reads there; if they do, they read true crime, the *Underbelly* books. There were a couple of people who would read potboilers, like Bryce Courtenay books, but they were the disgraced accountants. That prison was full bogans and hill-billies: moccasin-wearing, broken-toothed, tattooed half-wits. It's not an intellectually enlightening environment. James found relief in reading fiction.

His mother brought him in *On Chesil Beach* by Ian McEwan. He was amazed that he enjoyed it so much and he offered to lend it to me. Then I loaned him *Atonement*. It was a bit of an epiphany. He was all excited. He came and said, 'This is wonderful!' I think the Englishness appealed to him. He was very fond of England and all things English. Then I gave him Alan Hollinghurst's *The Line of Beauty*. And because it was a book about a Henry James scholar, he asked me about Henry James. I said, 'I think you will really love Henry James; you should give it a try.'

But after that I didn't really speak to him much about things, and our conversation was mostly related to the art program Loddon started up. James is working for the recreation officers; he is secretary and right-hand man/girl Friday to the recreation officer. The sports and recreation jobs are the most sought after in jail because they don't involve any hard work. You hand out footballs. He also has meteorological duties. Loddon prison is the weather station for

Castlemaine. He does the weather at about 3 o'clock every day, checks the rain gauges.

He's been very good for helping get the art program up and running in a way that's going to benefit the prisoners rather than simply the jail. James got money from a private foundation for this program, and he did all the paperwork for that; submissions and writing reports. He does an awful lot of the work for the jail where it interfaces with the outside world. There's a food-fair day once a year, and ethnic communities set up food stalls on the recreation oval. James has put a lot of time into trying to improve it. James was outstanding in that respect. But he did get up my nose with his poncy English ways.

I deplore what he did, but I am also amused by the fact that the wife said, 'You're not as good in bed as the new bloke'. A lot of people think he's a pussy 'cos he snapped and killed his wife. But on the whole he's a charming, plausible type; very much an eastern suburbs 'wanker-banker' type. But he also had a caved-in sort of look; he was like a broken man, a whipped man. He had a hunched-over, busted-up, feeling-sorry-for-himself kind of look about him.

Jamie Ramage was given a maximum sentence of 11 years and a minimum sentence of eight years. He will be released some time between 2012 and 2015.

Karen Kissane
November, 2008

ACKNOWLEDGMENTS

LIKE BLANCHE DUBOIS, the journalist always relies on the kindness of strangers. I thank most sincerely all the people associated with the Julie and Jamie Ramage story who agreed to be interviewed for this book and who gave so generously of their time, their thoughts and their feelings, even when, as was so often the case, it was painful for them to do so.

Among my colleagues, Jo Chandler gave me the initial brief for the Ramage feature for *The Age*, even though she badly wanted to cover it herself, and has been unflagging with her friendship and with her cheerful belief in both me and this book. Kate Cole-Adams provided kindness and clarity at key moments. Peter Gregory unstintingly shared his professional turf and taught me how the Supreme Court operates. David Elias brought a hard-news man's rigour and his mental library of background facts to the manuscript, Julie Szego cast a writerly eye and lawyerly mind over it, and Denis Muller wrote an insightful, imaginative and meticulous critique. Alice Freyne employed her clear thinking and strong sense of ethics – and fought to overcome the handicap of our many years of friendship – in order to review the manuscript objectively as a nonjournalistic 'ordinary reader'. David Poulton helped with the analysis of early legal questions, and the inside of his head was, as always, a thought-provoking place to visit. At Hachette Australia, I would like to thank publisher Matthew Kelly for his vision, his habit of making extremely good calls and his deft touch on the reins, and editor Vanessa Radnidge for her intuitive understanding, her forensic eye for detail, and the title and cover-line.

Troy Butler and Peter Buckingham of Spectrum Analysis Australia Pty Ltd kindly provided the demographic information about Balwyn from Census 2001 that has been used in this book.